ZIMBABWE TAKES BACK ITS LAND

ZIMBABWE TAKES BACK ITS LAND

JOSEPH HANLON, JEANETTE MANJENGWA,
AND TERESA SMART

Kumarian Press
An Imprint of Stylus Publishing
Sterling, Virginia

Published by Stylus Publishing, LLC
22883 Quicksilver Drive
Sterling, Virginia 20166-2102

Design by Pro Production Graphic Services
Copyedit by Jean Bernard
Proofread by Holly Fairbank
Index by Robert Swanson
The text of this book is set in 11/13 Adobe Garamond

Unless noted, photos are by Joseph Hanlon.

Library of Congress Cataloging-in-Publication Data
Hanlon, Joseph.
  Zimbabwe takes back its land / Joseph Hanlon, Jeanette Manjengwa and
Teresa Smart. — 1st ed.
    p. cm.
  Includes bibliographical references and index.
  ISBN 978-1-56549-519-7 (cloth : alk. paper) — ISBN 978-1-56549-520-3
  (pbk. : alk. paper) — ISBN 978-1-56549-521-0 (library networkable e-edition) —
  ISBN 978-1-56549-522-7 (consumer e-edition)
  1. Land reform beneficiaries—Zimbabwe. 2. Farm ownership—Zimbabwe.
3. Land use—Zimbabwe. 4. Agriculture and state—Zimbabwe. I. Manjengwa, J. M.
II. Smart, Teresa. III. Title.
  HD1333.Z55H36 2012
  333.316891—dc23
                                                                   2012014825

13-digit ISBN: 978-1-56549-519-7 (cloth)
13-digit ISBN: 978-1-56549-520-3 (paper)
13-digit ISBN: 978-1-56549-521-0 (library networkable e-edition)
13-digit ISBN: 978-1-56549-522-7 (consumer e-edition)

Printed in the United States of America

∞ All first editions printed on acid-free paper that meets the American National Standards Institute Z39-48 Standard.

Bulk Purchases

Quantity discounts are available for use in workshops and for staff development.

Call 1-800-232-0223

First Edition, 2013

   10 9 8 7 6 5 4 3 2 1

Contents

Abbreviations, Acronyms, Words, and Conventions

A1, A2	Small and large farm models in fast track land reform
ACCORD	African Centre for the Constructive Resolution of Disputes
Agritex	Agricultural, Technical and Extension Services
AIAS	African Institute for Agrarian Studies, Harare
ARDA	Agricultural Rural Development Authority
Arex	Agricultural Research and Extension
AU	African Union
bn	billion
Campfire	Communal Areas Management Programme for Indigenous Resources
chap.	chapter
Chimurenga	A fight in which everyone participates (Shona). The *First Chimurenga* (1896–97) was the fight against the British South Africa Company; the *Second Chimurenga* was the independence war (1966–79), and the 2000–1 land occupations are sometimes called the *Third Chimurenga*.
CIA	US Central Intelligence Agency
CIMMYT	International Maize and Wheat Improvement Centre
CSAE	Oxford University Centre for the Study of African Economies
CSC	Cold Storage Commission
DTZ	Development Trust of Zimbabwe
EISA	Electoral Institute for Sustainable Democracy in Africa

EMA	Environmental Management Agency
ESAP	Economic and Structural Adjustment Program
EU	European Union
FAO	UN Food and Agriculture Organization
fn	footnote
FTLR	Fast Track Land Reform
GAPWUZ	General Agricultural and Plantation Workers Union of Zimbabwe
GMB	Grain Marketing Board
GNU	Government of National Unity
GoZ	Government of Zimbabwe
GPA	Global Political Agreement
Gukurahundi	Military action to suppress South African–backed dissidents in Matebeleland in the 1980s
ha	hectare (1 ha = 2.471 acres)
IEG	Independent Evaluation Group
ILO	International Labour Organization
IMF	International Monetary Fund
IRIN	Integrated Regional Information Networks
jambanja	force or action taken in anger (Shona)—2000–1 land occupations
kg	kilogram (2.204 pounds)
km	kilometer (0.6214 miles)
MDC	Movement for Democratic Change
MDC-M	Movement for Democratic Change—Mutambara
mm	millimeter (0.3937 inch)
mn	million
MP	member of parliament
n.d.	no date
NDP	National Democratic Party
NGO	nongovernment organization
NPA	native purchase area
NR	Natural Region
NSSA	National Social Security Authority
PLAAS	Institute for Poverty, Land and Agrarian Studies
SADC	Southern African Development Community
SG	success group
t	tonne
tonne	1,000 kg, 2,204 pounds
TTL	Tribal Trust Land (later communal land)

UDI	Unilateral Declaration of Independence, on November 11, 1965, by Rhodesian government
UK	United Kingdom of Great Britain and Northern Ireland
UN	United Nations
UNAC	União Nacional de Camponeses
UNDP	United Nations Development Program
US	United States
WFLA	Women Farmers Land and Agriculture Trust
WLZ	Women and Land in Zimbabwe
WSWB	willing seller, willing buyer
Zanu	Zimbabwe African National Union
Zanu-PF	Zimbabwe African National Union–Patriotic Front
Zapu	Zimbabwe African People's Union
ZCDT	Zimbabwe Community Development Trust
ZCTU	Zimbabwe Congress of Trade Unions
Zimcord	Zimbabwe Conference on Reconstruction and Development
ZIMPREST	Zimbabwe Programme of Economic and Social Transformation
Zisco	Zimbabwe Iron & Steel Company
ZNLWVA	Zimbabwe National Liberation War Veterans Association
ZWRCN	Zimbabwe Women's Resource Centre and Network
Z$	Zimbabwe dollar
$	US dollar
¶	paragraph

1

Veterans and Land

THE WAR WAS OVER AND RETURNING VETERANS WHO WANTED TO FARM WERE GIVEN land; roads were built to the farms; seed, fertilizer, and implements were provided; and 40 ha of land were plowed for the farmers before they arrived. For those without farming experience, two years of training in farming and financial management were available. Much of the land was already occupied, so the existing farmers were forced off—often loaded into lorries and simply dumped far away, while their homes were burned. It was 1945–47 in Rhodesia, and the veterans were from the Second World War.

Some farmers resisted. Mhepo Mavakire Mashinge talked of the arrival of "the man who killed the Germans" who would ride out on horseback with his "black watchmen" to force the community's cattle off "his" land, often burning a few houses, and eventually erecting fences. The battle continued for a decade, as Mashinge's people cut fences and set fires on the "white land" while the white farmers burned houses and took young men for forced labor.[1] Eventually the local community was pushed back to the small area of Mashonaland East it occupies today.

In the decade after the Second World War, the white population and the number of white farms doubled, and black people continued to be forced off the land. The 1952 *Official Year Book of Southern Rhodesia* notes, "Natives are being moved progressively from the European Area to the Reserves and Special Native Area."[2] Joe Musavengana recounts his story: "I was only five years old, so I do not recall much. But I do remember people being forced into trucks by soldiers and policemen, and their small belongings being just thrown into the backs of the trucks. The trucks were packed full and people did not know where they were going. And I remember I could not take my little dog. Some of our houses were burned, and many people were simply dumped in the forest in Gokwe." The year was 1958.[3]

One of the new farmers was a Spitfire pilot, Ian Smith, who admitted in his memoirs that his new land had been occupied by black *squatters*[4]—the term used for black Zimbabweans who for generations had lived on land that was suddenly declared to be "white." Smith went on to rule Rhodesia, announce the Unilateral Declaration of Independence (UDI) in 1965, and then fight a brutal war to keep Rhodesia white-ruled. And 15 years after Joe Musavengana was forced off the land, he and many others joined the guerrillas, who in 1979 helped to beat the forces of Ian Smith's government. Rhodesia became Zimbabwe.

Land had been explicitly racialized in 1930 by the Land Apportionment Act, which defined that the half of the country with the best land and water was "European" and said European land could not be sold to non-whites. The rest was left for 95% of the population. There had not been enough white people to occupy all of the "white" land, so black people had been allowed to remain as "squatters," but this ended with the huge white influx after the war. As more people were pushed into the poor half of the land designated for "Africans," overcrowding became so bad that it led to land degradation. Ken Brown, a former Land Development Officer in the Native Agriculture Department, wrote in 1959, "The majority of arable areas in reserves are already so eroded and so exhausted of fertility that nothing short of a 12 to 15 year rest to grass will restore them to a state of structure and fertility which would enable economic crop production to commence."[5]

The white minority fought hard to maintain its privileges, and majority rule came in 1980 only after a 14-year liberation war. The new government moved quickly to redress inequalities, and the first decade of independence brought huge transformations. Health and education were expanded and agricultural marketing and agricultural extension services[6] were radically shifted to serve all farmers. Meanwhile, apartheid had not ended in South Africa, where the government fought for another decade to maintain white rule; a successful multi-racial Zimbabwe was a serious ideological and practical challenge, so South Africa attacked and destabilized its now independent neighbor.

Regaining the land had been central to the liberation war, but the new government had so many issues on its plate—reversing decades of white priority at home while facing a hostile white-ruled neighbor to the south—that land reform was not a priority. Even though the UDI government lost the war, white farmers mostly kept the land. Soon after independence the first land reform[7] began; 75,000 families received new land—the largest land reform in Africa,[8] but small compared to the demand. And it was a clear success; even World Bank researchers found that "settler households increased their productivity tremendously."[9] But the best land remained largely in white hands, and many white farmers continued to prosper, particularly with the expansion of export horticulture that came with the end of sanctions against Rhodesia.

Destabilization until 1990, several serious droughts, and the costs of restructuring a racially divided society took their toll and forced Zimbabwe to accept a structural adjustment program, which put pressure on the economy, as factories closed and jobs were lost. The World Bank and government donors to the newly independent country thought land reform was too expensive and the government was not enthusiastic, so such reform ground to a halt. By the mid-1990s, the economy was in trouble, as the Zanu-PF[10] government failed to manage the conflicting global and national pressures. There were strikes and protests, and a new opposition party was formed. Liberation war veterans became increasingly restless, arguing they had gained nothing from the war; the issue of land came back into prominence, although the Zanu-PF government failed to make it a priority.

Finally, in 1998, the war veterans began to take action. Using mobilizing skills learned during the liberation war, they organized landless and unemployed people and—in a pattern similar to the landless movement in Brazil—targeted farms and occupied them overnight, in a process called *jambanja* (force, or action taken in anger, in Shona[11]). At first, the Zanu-PF leadership was opposed, but the occupiers had party and government support at lower levels. Eventually, Zanu-PF reversed itself, legalized "fast track land reform," and tried to take credit for it. But the veterans knew otherwise—they were challenging their own Zanu-PF leaders.

Agnes Matsira[12] was an 18-year-old guerrilla when she lost her leg to a land mine in 1979. Two decades later she helped to organize the *jambanja* and now is a farmer with 6 ha in Goromonzi district. Her best crop most recently was 27 tonnes of maize from just 4 ha—a better yield than that of most white farmers. She now has a brick house on the farm and, since her daughter died, looks after three grandchildren.

Not far away is Mrs. Chibanda. She and her husband, who had lived on her father's land in a crowded communal area nearby, joined the *jambanja*. "Life is difficult, but it is better now because we manage to produce enough to eat," she says. They cleared their 6 ha, which was just unused bush when they arrived. They now have two small children and have built a two-room brick house as well as a traditional round Shona kitchen. But she laughs as she shows us the kitchen—it has become the tobacco-grading room, and she points to the cooking area, which is outside again. This is their first year for tobacco. They are growing 1.5 ha and have their own small tobacco-curing barn. Tobacco must be cured carefully, and this year they slept next to the barn to ensure that the fire did not go out at night. When we interviewed them in April 2011, they had already sold eight bales of tobacco for $1,100 and expected to sell another seven later in the month.

Agrarian reform is a slow process, and it takes a generation for new farmers to be fully productive. A decade after *jambanja*, Zimbabwe's agricultural production has largely returned to the 1990s level. Small-scale black farmers such as the Chibandas now produce together almost as much tobacco as the big white farmers once did.

It has been hard work, and the new farmers started out in conditions that were not always propitious. There has been political violence, particularly around elections, and greed and corruption at high levels. Post–land reform Zimbabwe has been subject to sanctions and a major cut in foreign aid, and the government managed its response badly, opting to print money, which led to hyperinflation in 2007 and 2008. In 2009, Zimbabwe abolished the local currency and switched to use the US dollar, which led to an unexpectedly rapid revival of the economy and a return to some sort of normality.

The new farmers have some advantages. Zimbabwe is built on modern agriculture with hybrid seeds, fertilizer, tractors (or at least ox plowing), and irrigation. Hyperinflation made key supplies erratic, but dollarization means these farm inputs are available. Zimbabwe has the highest literacy rate in Africa, so new farmers can make correct use of inputs and gain high yields. Two state institutions, the Agritex extension service and the Grain Marketing Board (GMB), struggled through the hyperinflation, have come back to life under dollarization, and are effective. Contract farming of cotton, tobacco, soya, and other crops is also expanding rapidly, offering an important boost for small farmers.

Colonial and Resistance History

To understand land reform, a bit of Rhodesian and Zimbabwean history helps. There are many good history books, and we do not want to cover the same ground. And Zimbabwe has a long history, including trade with the Arabs[13] on the coast of Mozambique from the eighth century and the rise of Great Zimbabwe in the fourteenth century. But a few key benchmarks in the century of colonialism and resistance are important to this book:

- In 1886, gold was discovered in South Africa, and many believed there was also gold on the Zimbabwe plateau. Cecil Rhodes's British South Africa Company was granted its royal charter in 1898 and immediately began its occupation of what it called Southern Rhodesia, now Zimbabwe. When it failed to find huge amounts of gold, it instead took land for cattle and farming. Resistance wars in 1893 and 1896–97, known as the *First Chimurenga,* were defeated by the superior firepower of the settlers.
- The colony was then ruled as a commercial company until settlers were granted self-governing dominion status in 1923. Increasing racial segregation was imposed, highlighted by the Land Apportionment Act of 1930, discussed in chapter 3.
- The post–World War II 1945–55 period saw industrialization, urbanization, the development of mining, an agricultural revolution for white farmers, a major migration of "Europeans" to Rhodesia, and the eviction of more than 100,000 Zimbabweans from European land.
- By the late 1950s, there was a move under Garfield Todd to make a few concessions to the majority, but he was removed as prime minister in 1958 for being too "pro-African." White intransigence increased with the victory of the Rhodesia Front in 1962: Ian Smith became prime minister in 1964, and on November 11, 1965, he signed Southern Rhodesia's Unilateral Declaration of Independence to try to stop the decolonization and majority-rule process that was moving south across Africa. Malawi and Zambia had both become independent in 1964.
- African resistance began first in the labor movement, with a railway strike in 1945 and a general strike in 1948. In 1960, the National Democratic Party (NDP) was formed to demand majority rule; the movement split in 1963 into the Zimbabwe African People's Union (Zapu) and Zimbabwe African National Union (Zanu).

Joshua Nkomo and Robert Mugabe, founders of NDP, were jailed by the Smith regime in 1964–74. When released, they went on to head Zapu and Zanu, respectively. In 1962, people left for Zambia and from there were sent abroad for military training—Zapu in the then–Soviet Union and Zanu in China. The first military action was in 1966, and the *Second Chimurenga* had begun; the war escalated in the early 1970s.

- In 1966 and 1968, the United Nations imposed comprehensive mandatory sanctions on UDI Rhodesia. Independence in Mozambique in 1975 meant Rhodesia lost an ally that had helped to circumvent sanctions, while Zanu was able to establish rear bases and escalate the war. South Africa reduced its own sanctions-busting support, and finally the white government capitulated.[14]

- Talks took place in Lancaster House, London, beginning in September 1979 and an agreement was signed on December 21, 1979. Elections in February gave 57 of 80 seats to Zanu and 20 to Zapu. (Twenty seats were reserved for whites; all were won by a Rhodesia Front still headed by Ian Smith, showing how little had changed in 20 years.) Robert Mugabe became prime minister and independence was declared on April 18, 1980. By the end of the war, there were up to 50,000 guerrillas, at least 40,000 people had been killed, and 20% of the African rural population was detained in "protected villages."[15]

Sources

Zimbabwe is one of the most-educated countries in Africa, and there has been substantial high-quality research and fieldwork on land reform. Five researchers in particular have followed resettlement over the long term: Sam Moyo, Bill Kinsey, Prosper Matondi, Nelson Marongwe, and Ian Scoones. Without their research, insights, and help, this book would have been impossible. Of course, we take responsibility for what we have done with their data. We have also drawn on fieldwork by PhD and MSc students and by other researchers at the University of Zimbabwe and elsewhere, including Angus Selby, Wilbert Sadomba, Easther Chigumira, Shingirai Mandizadza, Ruswa Goodhope, Wilson Paulo, Nkanyiso Sibanda, Admos Chimhowu, Blessing Karumbidza, Mette Masst, Creed Mushimbo, Asher Walter Tapfumaneyi, and Precious Zikhali. And we drew on a prescient 1968 thesis by Malcolm Rifkind.

Our own fieldwork was done in Mashonaland Central and East in 2010 and 2011. Our research team included Collen Matema, Phides Mazhawidza, Fadzai Chiware, Bella Nyamukure, and Stephen Matema. This book could not have been done without the farmers who gave us their time (and often pumpkins as well) and the excellent Agritex officers Herbert Harufaneti, Innocent Govea, and F. Kudzerema.

Note that numbers are surprisingly hard to establish. Colonial records claimed to be able to identify black and white farmers down to the last one, but in fact, they were often inaccurate, even on basics such as the number of white farmers, where numbers were not precisely known, and increasing numbers of white farmers had multiple farms. Land reform was done with old and inaccurate maps and poor records. The Utete Committee looking at land reform in 2003 cited the most commonly used figures, that "6,000 white farmers owned 15.5 million hectares." But the Committee went on to note that Ministry of Lands, Agriculture and Rural Resettlement officials said there were 8,758 white farms while the Committee's own District Data Collection Teams found 9,135.[16] There are even disagreements about the figure of 6,000 white farmers.[17] Table 1.1[18] appears to be the most complete set of figures, but it disagrees in some places with other reports, including Utete.

Two Land Reforms

Zimbabwe came to independence with 700,000 black farmers squeezed onto 53% of the farmland and about 6,000[19] white farmers on 46% of the farmland, which was also the best land. But white farmers were using less than one-third of that land—and they were not doing very well with it. At independence, one-third of white farmers were insolvent and one-third were only breaking even. The rest were profitable, and a few hundred were spectacularly successful (see chapter 3). Although a few white families could trace their ancestry back to the soldiers who were given land by the British South Africa Company in the 1890s, or to early twentieth-century settlers, by 2000, less than 5% of white farmers in Zimbabwe were the descendants of pioneers. Indeed, less than 10% were from families that had settled before World War II, according to Commercial Farmers Union records. And only a few were ancestral farms; nearly half of all white farms in 2000 had been bought and sold at least once in the 20 years after independence.[20] White farmers had created an image of themselves as pioneers who had turned a hostile land into a new Eden.

Table 1.1 Land in 1980, 2000, and 2010

	Farm households						Area (million ha)					
	1980		2000		2010		1980		2000		2010	
	No.	%	No.	%	No.	%	mn ha	%	mn ha	%	mn ha	%
Smallholders												
Communal	700,000	98	1,050,000	92	1,100,000	81	16.4	50	16.4	50	16.4	50
1980s resettlement			75,000	7	75,000	6			3.7	11	3.7	11
A1					145,800	11					5.8	18
Sub-total	700,000	98	1,125,000	99	1,321,000	98	16.4	50	20.0	61	25.8	79
Middle farms												
African purchase	8,500	1.2	8,500	0.8	8,500	0.6	1.4	4.3	1.4	4.3	1.4	4.3
Small A2					22,700	1.7					3.0	9.1
Sub-total	8,500	1.2	8,500	0.8	31,200	2.3	1.4	4.3	1.4	4.3	4.4	13
Large farms												
Large A2					217						0.5	1.6
Black large-scale			956	0.1	956	0.1			0.5	1.6	0.5	1.6
White large-scale	5,400	0.8	4,000	0.4	198	0.1	12.5	37	8.7	25	0.1	0.4
Sub-total	5,400	0.8	4,956	0.4	1,371	0.1	12.5	37	8.7	27	1.2	3.5
Agro-estates	296		296		296		2.6	7.9	2.6	7.9	1.5	4.5
Total	714,200	100	1,138,800	100	1,354,000	100	32.9	100	32.7	100	32.9	100
Total land reform			75,000	6.6	243,717	18			3.7	11	13.0	40

Source: Sam Moyo, "Three Decades of Agrarian Reform in Zimbabwe," Journal of Peasant Studies, 38, no. 3 (2011): 512, Table 4 [Moyo, "Three Decades"].

In practice, a few were world-class, but many were making poor use of some of the best farmland in Africa and were leaving large areas vacant.

There have been two land reforms, the results of which are detailed in Table 1.1. The first, in the mid-1980s, was under the Lancaster House agreement that ended the liberation war, which meant the government had to buy resettlement land on a "willing buyer, willing seller" basis. In general only the most unsuccessful farmers with the poorest land wanted to sell, but 75,000 farm families were resettled.

The "fast track land reform" that followed the *jambanja* in 2000 set out two models. The small-scale or A1 model divided former white farms into about 40 small farms, typically with 6 ha each of arable land in the areas of best land such as Mashonaland, and larger plots in cattle areas. The A2 model split white farms into four to six farms, typically with 50–70 ha arable each in the best areas. (The scenery of Zimbabwe is dramatic because of the hills and large rock outcrops, which also means that parts of most farms are not suitable for agriculture.)

A1 farms initially largely went to people who had occupied in the *jambanja,* and later to people who applied. Plots were formally marked out, and farmers have permits or letters from the government giving them the right to occupy the plot. Under the A1 scheme, 146,000 families received land. A2 farms required a much more complex process, with a formal business plan and evidence of farming skills and some capital; broadly speaking, many A2 farmers have urban links because they were able to mortgage properties such as a Harare house. Nearly 23,000 families received A2 farms. Including the first resettlement, 245,000 resettlement farm families now have 40% of the farmland.

Most farmers are still on communal lands, accounting for 50% of the farmland. The remaining 10% of the farmland is accounted for by 8,500 black farmers allowed to buy land in colonial times (4% of land); 950 large-scale black farmers[21] (2%); fewer than 400 large-scale white farmers (less than 1% of the land); and 250 large corporate or state-owned agro-industrial plantation estates and wildlife conservancies that remain mostly untouched, accounting for 4% of the land.[22]

Eddie Cross, the opposition Movement for Democratic Change (MDC) MP and policy coordinator general, said in April 2011 that white farms had been "invaded and occupied by this rag tag collection of people" who are just "squatters" and that "the majority of these farms have become largely defunct, their homesteads and farm buildings derelict and their arable lands have returned to bush."[23] This is a line also taken by many international agencies.

But we have seen something different. We visited A2 farmers who are major commercial farmers turning over more than $100,000 per year, and A1 commercial farmers with a few hectares but who are making a profit of more than $10,000 per year and who are more productive than the white farmers they replaced. To be sure, we have also seen both A1 and A2 farms that are unused or underused. Just as there was a spectrum of white farmers, some good, some bad, and most in the middle, there is also a spectrum of resettlement farmers. But, on average, in just a decade the new farmers have caught up to the white farmers' production; it is widely estimated that new farmers take a generation to reach full production, and this was the case with both the white farmers and the first land reform, so the new farmers can be expected to develop significantly in the next decade.

Furthermore, the picture is rapidly changing, in part because of the harm done by hyperinflation and the recovery post-dollarization. Any land reform will be disruptive in the short term, and the fast track land reform did hit export agriculture and food production. The hostile response of the international community meant a decrease in aid and the imposition of sanctions, which cut loans and even short-term bank credit. When faced with sanctions in the 1970s, Rhodesia responded with very tight control of foreign exchange and of the economy in general. In the early 2000s, Zimbabwe tried an opposite policy, of simply printing more and more money in the hopes of boosting the economy. The policy failed disastrously, and the result was hyperinflation. There were 55 Zimbabwe dollars to 1 US dollar in 2002, 800 in 2004, and 80,000 in 2005. After that the number spiraled up meaninglessly; commerce was increasingly by barter or in dollars or rand for those who had access to foreign currency. Agriculture, and land-reform farmers especially, were hit particularly hard; it was difficult to obtain essential inputs and pointless to try to sell produce for cash that would have lost its value the next day. In January 2008, the government issued a Z$10 million banknote, but by July it had to issue a Z$100 billion banknote. The 2007/8 season was the worst, with food production down to 37% of the 1990s average.[24] The Southern African Development Community (SADC) mediated talks that led to a September 2008 agreement for a Unity Government, which took office in early 2009. On January 29, 2009, the government legalized the use of foreign currency and in February started to pay civil servants in US dollars and do its own accounts in that currency. The Z$ was dead and the US$ kick-started the economy in a dramatic way. Recovery was rapid. The Confederation of Zimbabwe Industries reported that manufacturing sector capacity utilization, which had fallen to 10% in 2008, rose to 57% in the first half of 2011.[25]

In the 2009/10 season, the first season under dollarization, food production returned to 79% of the 1990s average (see Table 1.2). The 2010/11 season saw some variable rain in January, which caused a loss of 10% of maize;[26] nevertheless, food production was 83% of the 1990s average. Resettlement farmers, with 34% of the farmland, produced 49% of the maize; the most dramatic increase was by A1 farmers, who increased production by 20% over the previous year, despite difficulties with rain.[27] And prospects for the 2011/12 season are good. In October 2011, the *Financial Gazette* commented, "For the first time in more than a decade, inputs such as seed, chemicals, and fertilisers are in abundance."[28] (See Table 1.3.) The recovery has been so rapid that in July 2011 Finance Minister Tendai Biti reimposed import duties of 10% to 25% on foodstuffs such as maize meal and cooking oil, to protect local producers;[29] the duties had been suspended in 2003 when not enough food was being grown and local food-processing industries were not producing. Tobacco was the most profitable crop for white farmers, who always stressed that it needed high skills to produce successfully. Production is returning to former levels and 40% is grown by resettlement farmers; the number of smallholders growing tobacco has increased from a few hundred to 53,000.[30]

Table 1.2 Zimbabwe National Agricultural Production

Crop	Agricultural production (000 tonnes) 1990s average	2007/8	2009/10	2010/11	2010/11 as % of 1990s average
Food					
Maize	1,686	575	1,323	1,458	86
Wheat	284	35	42	12	4
Small grains	165	80	194	156	95
Groundnuts	86	132	186	230	267
Soya beans	93	48	70	84	90
Export					
Tobacco	198	70	123	132	66
Cotton	207	226	260	220	106
Estate					
Sugar	439	259	350	450	103
Tea	11	8	14	13	118

Source: Moyo, "Three Decades," corrected and updated.

Table 1.3 Contribution to Maize and Tobacco Production by Sector, 2011 Harvest

	Maize			Tobacco		
	2011 (000 t)		% share	2011 (1000 t)		% share
Resettlement	712		49	53		40
of which						
A1		357	24		37	28
A2		285	20		16	12
Old resettlement		70	5			na
Communal areas	627		43	22		18
Commercial	87		6	56		42
of which						
Small-scale		30	2		14	11
Large-scale		57	4		41	31
Peri-urban	32		2	0		0
Total	1,458			132		

Note: na = not available.
Source: Tendai Biti, "2011 Mid-year Review," *Financial Gazette* (November 2, 2011): 20.

We cannot give a totally up-to-date picture, but we believe that the new farmers are now using much more than the one-third of the land once worked by the white farmers, although they have not yet reached the intensity of those farmers—meaning that production is already returning to 1990s levels because of the more extensive land use.

Zimbabwe is different from the neighboring countries of South Africa and Mozambique in that the loss of land was within living memory, and Zimbabwe's independence struggle was led by people with a rural background, compared to the urban leadership in South Africa and Mozambique. The history of white commercial farming, and the recent rural history, combine to make farming seem an attractive way to provide for the family, and for elites a serious means of accumulation. We interviewed schoolteachers who had become A1 farmers and who felt they were earning a better living, and we met members of the elite who had moved away from Harare and were living and working on their farms.

Agriculture in Zimbabwe can be highly profitable, but it is also capital-intensive, and successful farmers had initial investment capital, which they actively reinvested. For both A1 and A2 farmers, having urban contacts and the ability to raise money, for example, if a family member had an urban job, helped kick-start them in farming. But the other key factor

Photo 1.1 A1 farmers taking maize to market, Goromonzi.

has been reinvestment—not building a fancy house or buying a car, but putting the initial profits back into the farm. Another key lesson is that when successful farmers sell their crop, they immediately buy the next set of inputs—seed, fertilizer, and tools. If all the revenue from sales is brought home, the conflicting demands of school fees, improvements, and other expenses often mean that not enough is left to buy essential fertilizer, thus creating a downward spiral of lower production and lower income.

This Book: Not What Might Have Been

The Global Political Agreement that now governs Zimbabwe accepts "the irreversibility of . . . land acquisitions and redistribution."[31] The World Bank in a recent study notes that "Zimbabwe's land redistribution program cannot be reversed."[32] This book agrees and sets out to present a picture of the reality on the ground in 2012. It is important to understand how Zimbabwe reached this particular land reform, and to set out the serious challenges that remain. But it is not the role of this book to analyze the rights and wrongs of colonial administration and the governance of contemporary Zimbabwe—understanding how we arrived here and how history constrains the way Zimbabwe can move forward should never be confused with a justification of misconduct.

In chapter 2, we set out just such a context of past and future action. Chapter 3 gives the colonial history, showing how the definition of *land* in racial terms, as well as other policies, set an often unfortunate model for the independence era. Chapters 4–6 look at the three decades of independence, and at the two land reforms, first in the 1980s and then the fast track beginning in 2000. They also show how land and agriculture policies were shaped by colonial precedent and attitudes, by the way structural adjustment caused such an increase in poverty, and by the hyperinflation of 2003–8. The next three chapters (7–9) look at the on-the-ground reality of land reform. In particular, this is the first book to take into account the remarkable economic recovery since the US dollar became the dominant currency in early 2009, which has given a huge boost to land-reform farmers. The next three chapters (10–12) tackle a set of problematic issues. We find women improving their position but also serious challenges relating to environment, irrigation, former farm-workers, and land tenure and security. It will be for Zimbabwe's political process to decide how to move forward, but in chapter 13 we draw some conclusions and underline priority problems that remain unresolved.

Land in Zimbabwe has been a contentious, polarizing, and highly politicized issue for a century. Sir Malcolm Rifkind, who later became British Foreign Secretary,[33] wrote his MSc thesis on land in Rhodesia. He wrote: "Today [October 1968], land is a burning issue in Rhodesia, but only for the Africans. As far as the Europeans are concerned, the problem has been resolved—in their favour. . . . However, a settlement which is opposed to the wishes of 95% of the population cannot be declared to be final and land will remain a vital problem, at least until the whole political system has changed."[34] What would have happened if government had listened to Rifkind when he was a mere student, and not yet Sir Malcolm?

There are countless such questions, and there has been endless debate over what would have happened: if Zimbabweans had not lost the *First Chimurenga* in 1897, if the Land Apportionment Act of 1930 had been different, if returning black war veterans in 1945 had been treated in the same way as white veterans, if Zimbabwe had moved faster with land reform in the 1980s, or if donor countries had accepted government proposals on land reform in 1998.

This is not a book about what might have been, could have been, or should have been. Instead, this is a book about Zimbabwe land reform in 2011 and about the new farmers on the ground—about their successes and failures, their hopes and prospects. Zimbabwe has taken back its land, and the new occupants will not allow that land reform to be reversed.

Notes

1. Recorded by his grandson, George Shere, as part of a series of interviews, February–March 1962, written down in 35 school exercise books.

2. Central African Statistical Office, *Official Year Book of Southern Rhodesia, With Statistics Mainly up to 1950–No 4-1952* (Salisbury, Southern Rhodesia: Rhodesian Printing and Publishing Company, 1952).

3. Interviewed on his farm, Mazowe, August 30, 2010. Note that all names in this book are real; no pseudonyms have been used.

4. Ian Douglas Smith, *The Great Betrayal: The Memoirs of Ian Douglas Smith* (London, UK: Blake, 1997).

5. Charles Utete, *Report of the Presidential Land Review Committee on the implementation of the fast track land reform programme, 2000–2002* (Harare, Zimbabwe, 2003) [known as the Report of the Utete Committee and cited here as the Utete Report], 12, citing Ken Brown, "Land in Southern Rhodesia" (London, UK: Africa Bureau, 1959), available at http://www.sarpn.org/documents/d0000622/P600-Utete_PLRC_00-02.pdf (accessed October 23, 2011).

6. Agricultural extension officers are trained advisors, usually government staff, who help farmers improve farming methods, introduce new crops, increase production and income, respond to pests, and often support marketing.

7. Land reform is breaking up large land holdings into smaller ones, and transferring land from the powerful to the less powerful. In Africa it usually means a transfer from former colonial settlers to indigenous people. South Africa follows a model of restitution, where land is returned to descendants of the people who were pushed off the land a century before. Zimbabwe has chosen resettlement, where the new farmers are not linked to the historic occupiers.

8. Kenya resettled 50,000 families in 20 years. Lionel Cliffe, "The Prospects for Agricultural Transformation in Zimbabwe," in *Zimbabwe's Prospects,* ed. Colin Stoneman, 309, fn 2 (London, UK: Macmillan, 1988).

9. Klaus Deininger, Hans Hoogeveen, and Bill Kinsey, "Economic Benefits and Costs of Land Redistribution in Zimbabwe in the Early 1980s," *World Development,* 32, no. 10 (2004): 1698. Deininger and Hoogeveen were at the World Bank; Kinsey has run the only long-term study on the 1980s resettlement.

10. Zimbabwe African National Union–Patriotic Front. Known as Zanu during the liberation war, it became Zanu-PF during the 1980 election as part of the Patriotic Front alliance with the other liberation movement, the Zimbabwe African People's Union (Zapu). It returned to the use of just Zanu, then in 1987

merged with Zapu to form Zanu-PF. In this book, we normally use Zanu for the liberation movement and Zanu-PF for the governing party.

11. Joseph Chaumba, Ian Scoones, and William Wolmer, "From Jambanja to Planning: The Reassertion of Technocracy in Land Reform in South-Eastern Zimbabwe," *Journal of Modern African Studies,* 41, no. 4 (2003): 540.

12. Unless noted, interviews took place on farms in 2010 and 2011.

13. G. Pwiti, "Trade and Economics in Southern Africa: The Archaeological Evidence," *Zambezia,* 18, no. 2 (1991): 199–229.

14. Joseph Hanlon and Roger Omond, *The Sanctions Handbook* (Harmondsworth, UK: Penguin, 1987), chap. 22.

15. Kevin Shillington (Ed.), *Encyclopedia of African History* (New York: Fitzroy Dearborn, 2005), 1724–34; Roger Riddell, The Land Question, *From Rhodesia to Zimbabwe,* pamphlet 2 (Gwelo, Zimbabwe: Mambo, 1978), 10.

16. Utete Report, 14, 24 (see fn 5).

17. The Whitsun Foundation, in a report in support of white farmers, gave the number of white farmers in 1980/81 as 4,926 and the number of white farms as 6,034. *Land Reform in Zimbabwe* (Harare, Zimbabwe: Whitsun Foundation, 1983).

18. Sam Moyo, "Three Decades of Agrarian Reform in Zimbabwe," *Journal of Peasant Studies,* 38, no. 3 (2011): 512, Table 4 [Moyo, "Three Decades"].

19. Utete Report, 14.

20. Angus Selby, "Commercial Farmers and the State: Interest Group Politics and Land Reform in Zimbabwe" (PhD thesis, University of Oxford, 2006), 334.

21. This figure is only black owners or leaseholders of entire white farms. One should include 217 "large A2" farmers (see chapter 9), who hold 1.6% of the land. Sam Moyo notes that "if we included those with over 300 hectares, then there are close to 3,000 new large scale capitalist farmers today," Moyo, "Three Decades," 514.

22. Moyo, "Three Decades," 496, 499, 515.

23. Eddie Cross, "Food Crisis in Zimbabwe," Harare *Independent,* April 29, 2011, available at http://www.eddiecross.africanherd.com/ (September 2, 2011).

24. Moyo, "Three Decades," 519, Table 9.

25. Paul Nyakazeya, "Country Average Capacity Utilisation Up 13,5 Percent," *Independent,* November 3, 2011, available at http://allafrica.com/stories/printable/201111041155.html; Bright Madera, "Manufacturing Sector Grows, but . . . ," *Herald,* November 4, 2011, available at http://allafrica.com/stories/201111040199.html (both accessed November 6, 2011).

26. Finance Minister Tendai Biti, quoted in "New Farmers Doing Well: Biti," *Herald,* October 7, 2001.

27. Tendai Biti (Finance Minister), *The 2011 Mid-year Fiscal Policy Review* (Harare, Zimbabwe: Ministry of Finance, July 26, 2011), 18–20, available at http://www.zimtreasury.org/downloads/Mid-Year-Fiscal-Policy-Review.pdf (November 3, 2011).

28. Tabitha Mutenga, "Farmers Decry Input Costs," *Financial Gazette,* October 12, 2011.

29. "Duty on Food Stuffs Restored" (Harare, Zimbabwe: Ministry of Finance, July 27, 2011), available at http://www.zimtreasury.org/news-detail.cfm?News=889 (November 3, 2011).

30. Tabitha Mutenga, "Small-Scale Farmers Boost Tobacco Production," *Financial Gazette,* November 2, 2011, available at http://www.financialgazette.co.zw/national-report/10479-small-scale-farmers-boost-tobacco-production.html (November 6, 2011).

31. "Agreement Between the Zimbabwe African National Union–Patriotic Front (ZANU-PF) and the Two Movement for Democratic Change (MDC) Formations, on Resolving the Challenges Facing Zimbabwe" (Harare, Zimbabwe, September 15, 2008), ¶5.5 (known as the Global Political Agreement, GPA), available at http://www.info.gov.za/issues/zimbabwe/zzimbabwe_global_agreement_20080915.pdf (January 4, 2012).

32. Simon Pazvakavambwa and Vincent Hungwe, "Land Redistribution in Zimbabwe," in *Agricultural Land Redistribution: Toward Greater Consensus,* ed. Hans Binswanger-Mkhize, Camille Bourguignon, and Rogerius van den Brink (Washington, DC: World Bank Publications, 2009), 161. Both Pazvakavambwa and Hungwe are former permanent secretaries of agriculture; neither is subject to sanctions, nor are they on the "Dongo list" as having been leased large farms (see chapter 5).

33. In the UK government, the secretary of state is senior and a member of cabinet, and a minister is junior.

34. Malcolm Rifkind, "The Politics of Land in Rhodesia" (MSc thesis, Edinburgh University, 1968), 196, available at http://www.mct.open.ac.uk/zimbabwe (June 20, 2012).

2

Starting Points

THE COUNTRIES OF EUROPE HAVE MANY SIMILARITIES BUT ALSO EXHIBIT RADICAL DIFFER-ences, shaped by history, geography, culture, and war. Similarly, southern Africa often looks to outsiders to be homogeneous, yet closer observation shows distinctive countries shaped by colonialism, geography, and culture. No one chooses his or her history, but many of us struggle to reshape what we have inherited. Zimbabwe threw off minority rule but 30 years later is still grappling with some of its history. Land reform is an explicit attempt to reverse a historic inheritance. In this chapter we point to eight aspects of Zimbabwe that make it different from its neighbors and from the North, and that have shaped its approach to land reform. Some aspects such as education are positive and have propelled farmers forward. Other aspects, such as endemic violence, are deeply problematic and harmful, and have a long and traumatic history. These starting points have shaped the land reform, and some also present critical challenges for the future.

Education

Zimbabwe has the highest literacy rate in Africa; 93% of adults are literate, according to the United Nations Development Program (UNDP).[1] Even at independence the literacy rate of 78% was then the highest in Africa, but a huge post-independence investment in schooling meant more children going to school and staying on for longer. Figure 2.1 shows that the average number of years of schooling of people over the age of 15 has more than doubled since independence.

Figure 2.1 Increase in Schooling of Adults
Over 15 Years Old Since Independence

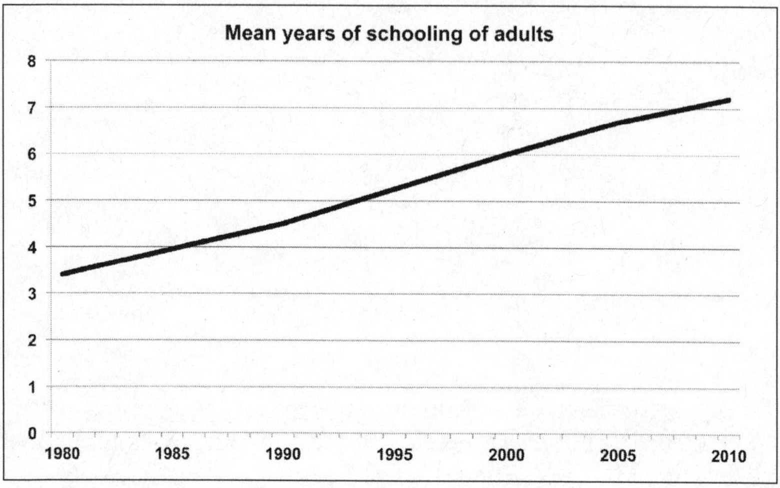

Mean years of schooling of adults

Source: UNDP, International Human Development Indicators, available at http://hdr.undp
.org (July 27, 2011).

This has had a direct impact on farming. The photo on page 21 shows a meeting of women small-scale, land-reform farmers in Goromonzi district; note how many of the women are taking notes. Even small-scale farming is technically sophisticated, with choices of seed varieties, precise planting dates, and complex mixes of fertilizers and pesticides. Tobacco, in particular, requires care and attention in curing and grading.

The high levels of education mean that farmers can take advantage of technical assistance from agricultural extension workers and make informed choices about the mix of crops. We attended a field day for small-scale (A1), land-reform farmers on Kiaora Farm in Mazowe district (see the photo in chapter 13), and were impressed that the farmers discussed the merits and requirements of four different maize varieties, issues around growing soya, and other detailed farm topics.

Farming

Agriculture and land played a much more central role in Zimbabwe's independence struggle and in attitudes toward economic development and accumulation than in some neighboring countries. The leadership of

Photo 2.1 Meeting of women A1 farmers
in Goromonzi, April 15, 2011.

the independence struggles in South Africa and Mozambique was largely urban; the South African uprisings such as in Soweto in 1976 were in the cities. Although Mozambique's guerrilla war was largely waged in rural areas, the Frelimo liberation movement had a modernizing, urban project. Zimbabwe's independence leadership was part of a new, educated, professional generation, but its roots and childhoods on the land play a much bigger role. Displacements of fathers and grandfathers from the land was part of oral history and, often, living memory in Zimbabwe, and regaining the land was central to the independence struggle in a way that was never the case in Mozambique or South Africa.

Colonial history also matters. In Mozambique white farmers were often illiterate peasants sent from Portugal who may have become economically comfortable but were never rich. In Rhodesia white farmers were major commercial farmers who could become wealthy. Even for the Zimbabwean middle class, modern commercial farming can provide a good living. And many in the elite see agriculture as a means of accumulation. Finally, there is something intangible. The Zimbabwean middle and upper classes talk of their rural roots and often want to work on their farm; Mozambique's urbanized elite simply do not think of farming.

Namaacha is a town in the hills 60 km from the Mozambican capital, Maputo. In colonial times it was surrounded by highly productive fruit and vegetable farms. Today the new elite own the farms and use them just as places to visit on the weekend. About the same distance north of the Zimbabwean capital, Harare, is Mazowe, with similar good farmland, again some of it held by the new Zimbabwean elite. But visiting Mazowe still reveals lush, productive farmland; some of the elite have even moved to the farms and go to Harare only when they need to.

War Veterans—And Taking Action

Former US President Dwight Eisenhower (1953–61) was a general and commander of all forces in Europe in World War II and was followed by a Second World War hero, John F. Kennedy (1961–63). The next six US presidents served in the military during World War II. Thus, for 40 years after the war, only veterans were presidents. War veterans in the United States received university or vocational education, special loans to buy homes and start businesses, and other benefits. As a child in the United States in that era, one of the authors remembers the huge political power of the two big veterans organizations the American Legion and the Veterans of Foreign Wars. In Rhodesia white World War II veterans also received land and other benefits.

In a similar way, Zimbabwe gives special status to those who fought for independence, either as guerrillas or as political prisoners of the white regime. Veterans have extra social and political standing, which gives them additional authority and certain privileges—although there are also accusations that some veterans have abused their special standing.

Related is a respect for those who take action to reach their goals, particularly by fighting in the liberation war, or actually occupying land as part of the *jambanja*.

"Fairness" is always subjective, but there is a sense that many Zimbabweans think fairness requires preference for war veterans and that occupiers should receive priority, at least for A1 farms. And that may have some practical content, because there is a hope that giving priority to veterans and those who have taken action is showing preference for more enterprising people in society.

It is hardly surprising that many ministers and senior civil servants are liberation war veterans. They were the dynamic young leadership at independence, they stepped into the shoes of the defeated white minority regime, and they have risen to senior positions. But some of those who fought in the liberation war more than 30 years ago increasingly see their role as defending the values and objectives of that struggle. This led to increasing confrontations with Zanu-PF and the government over land, jobs, and corruption. In 1992, at the inauguration meeting of the Zimbabwe National Liberation War Veterans' Association—a joint association of Zanu and Zapu veterans following the merger of the two parties—the war veterans claimed the party had been hijacked by opportunists and loyalists filling government and party posts. They said Zanu-PF was backing white farmers and they demanded land and said they would take it.[2]

Some military and political leaders argue that the country cannot be commanded by people who did not fight in the liberation war, a point that is particularly targeted at opposition leader and Prime Minister Morgan Tsvangirai, who was a mine union activist rather than a participant in the war. For some, this is just a convenient way to defend their personal positions, but others genuinely believe that they risked their lives to free their country and do not want to see it "lost" to allies of their old oppressors.

But 30 years have passed. The dominant role of ex-combatants leaves little room for a generation too young to have fought in the liberation war. The diminishing number of war veterans runs the risk of creating a new kind of opposition from marginalized youth.

Violence

Zimbabwe's 2008 Global Political Agreement (GPA) notes "the easy resort to violence by political parties, State actors, Non-State actors and others in order to resolve political differences and achieve political ends."

There are high levels of intolerance, and the language of politics is violent and divisive, with use of words such as "sellout" and "traitor" and accusations of tribalism and involvement of spies, which encourages division and violence. Richard Bourne argues that the "culture of violence and impunity were built into the DNA of the state created by Cecil John Rhodes."[3] In a detailed study of what he calls "institutionalized violence," Lloyd Sachikonye traces the roots back to the colonial era.[4] From 1960 on, the colonial government employed torture, repression, severe beatings, extra-judicial murder, and collective punishment against strikes, demonstrations, and anyone thought to support the nascent liberation movement. We went to a talk by one of Zimbabwe's most important environmentalists, Zephaniah Phiri, on his book, *The Water Harvester;* he does not mention it, but he walks with a cane because he was so badly beaten by Rhodesian police five decades ago. By the late 1970s, the regime was using chemical and biological weapons, including poisoned clothing that killed at least 79 nationalist fighters.

But the nationalist movements remained divided from 1960 until 1987, and Sachikonye points to the continuing violence between nationalist groups. Houses were burned and people attacked, and in the sharp splits of the mid-1970s, people were killed. This set an important precedent for violence against political opponents.

After independence, the *Gukurahundi* was a 1982–87 war in Matebeleland[5] against a group of 500 dissidents backed by apartheid South Africa, in which at least 6,000 people were killed.[6] A former Zanu guerrilla defended this, citing the US drone (remotely controlled aircraft) attacks on areas of Pakistan that killed more than 2,000 people as part of the Afghanistan War; the Brookings Institution[7] estimates that 10 civilians are killed for each Taliban militant, and the former guerrilla said this seemed accurate, because he knew how many people it took to hide a fighter, and they knew the risk they were taking. Other former Zanu guerrillas find this abhorrent; Wilbert Sadomfa refers to "atrocities by *Gurkurahundi*."[8] But the point is that violent histories of both the United States and Zimbabwe have created military leaders who find this acceptable.

Violence continued around the 2000, 2002, and 2008 elections. Sachikonye and human rights groups put most (but not all) of the blame on Zanu-PF. Violence around the 2008 election was particularly severe, targeting supporters and activists of the opposition Movement for Democratic Change (MDC). "Violence has been a common response to the exercise of the rights to strike and demonstrate," concluded an International Labor Organization (ILO) Commission of Inquiry. It said it "heard numerous statements that illustrated severe violence against trade unionists and explicit or implicit acceptance by government officials that such violence had occurred." It also noted "many instances in which trade union officials and members were severely beaten and, in some instances, tortured by members of the security forces and the ZANU–PF militia, resulting in serious and long-lasting physical and psychological injuries for many trade unionists, and the death of some."[9] Tsvangirai withdrew from the second round, and the South African Development Community (SADC) came in to negotiate the GPA, which called on the parties "to promote the values and practices of tolerance, respect, non-violence and dialogue as means of resolving political differences." This was promoted at independence day celebrations on April 18, 2011, and was headlined in the Zanu-PF aligned government daily, *The Herald.*

Photo 2.2 Front page of *The Herald,*
Harare, April 19, 2011, opposing violence.

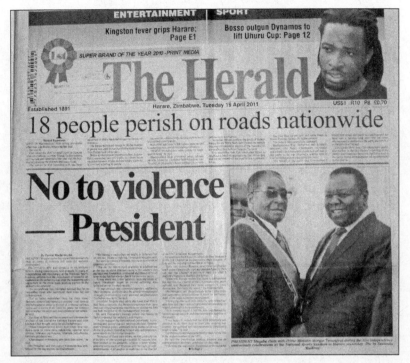

But violence has a long history, and it will take more than a few head-lines and speeches to reverse the culture of intolerance and confronta-tion. Even the opposition is affected. The MDC split in 2005, but even within the main group (sometimes referred to as MDC-T, as it is headed by Tsvangirai), there were fistfights between factions on the floor of na-tional Congress in Matebeleland on April 9, 2011.[10] Reconciliation and a move to normal politics require a change in mind-set, and there have been steps in the right direction: recognition of past violence in meet-ings with the visiting ILO inquiry team, the GPA itself, and headlines like the one pictured.

Corruption and Greed

Many nations have people who say, "I risked my life for my country, and now I deserve to live well," or "I work hard and have special qualities, so I deserve luxury," or "My people expect their chief to live better than they do." Business leaders use political links to bend rules and even break laws to increase their profits. And in a globalized world of conspicuous consumption, some business oligarchs, political leaders, and senior military officials aspire to the standards of the global super-rich. Leaders hire planes to fly to London or Hong Kong for shopping, for example.

Zimbabwe is no exception. Some leaders have used their positions to obtain land improperly and build up wealth, for example, through non-transparent dealings in diamonds and minerals and in foreign currency transactions during the 2006–8 hyperinflation. Zanu-PF itself is divided over how much is acceptable. One senior figure complained to us that "some of them are so greedy that they will take the dirt you are standing on."

Greed is not just an African problem. After leaving office as Britain's prime minister, Tony Blair received millions of pounds in just two years, and he used tax avoidance methods introduced when he was prime minister.[11] In France, former president Jacques Chirac and former prime minister Alain Juppé were convicted of misappropriating more than €1 million.[12] In the United States, Dick Cheney was US secretary of defense from 1989 to 1993, chairman and CEO of the military contractor Halliburton from 1995 to 2000, and US vice president from 2001 to 2009. From 1995, Halliburton paid penalties for 11 instances of misconduct, including three settlements of foreign bribery allegations (one involving Cheney) for which it paid over $600 million in penalties. Kellogg Brown & Root, part of Halliburton until 2007, had 23 instances of misconduct, including six government contract fraud cases.[13]

In rich countries corruption is an affordable tax, but in Zimbabwe and other poor countries, greed and corruption take money and resources that are desperately needed elsewhere. A lack of transparency makes it hard to do any more than guess, but widespread reports suggest that up to signing the GPA and forming the unity government in 2009, corruption had reached levels that had a significant impact on the economy.

British Colonial Models

Zimbabwe students still do English-style O- and A-level examinations, which until 2002 were all done jointly by the Zimbabwe School Examinations Council and University of Cambridge International Examinations, and many independent schools (frequented by the better-off) still use Cambridge exams. This is just one example of the way, despite bitter disagreements with the former colonial power, many colonial models and structures remain in force. The civil service still runs on a British model, and parliament still retains the British structure (although Zimbabwe now has a strong presidential system). However, the new government also took on the authoritarian methods of Ian Smith, particularly his way of dealing with opposition.

At independence, Zimbabwe quickly deracialized legislation and institutions, but their structure was largely left intact. Racial discrimination in land ownership ended just before independence, but the new government did not move to change the inherited system of a few very large commercial farms and most farmers densely packed into what were simply renamed from "Tribal Trust Lands" to "communal areas." The big change, however, was to shift two key colonial institutions, the agricultural extensions services and the Grain Marketing Board, to serve smaller black farmers as well as large farmers.

And, of most importance to this book, the Zanu-PF government eventually adopted colonial and Unilateral Declaration of Independence (UDI) methods to deal with land. The case of Chief Rekayi Tangwena became the model. Tangwena was named chief in the Gaeresi area of Inhanga, Manicaland, in 1966, just after Ian Smith's UDI.[14] He was immediately confronted with an eviction notice by a white farmer who claimed the land, which had been sold in 1905 and 1944 but never occupied. Nevertheless, it was defined as white land, and the 1941 Land Apportionment Act defined as a squatter "an African whose home happens to be situated in an area which has been declared European."[15] Tangwena refused to move, was fined, and then appealed to the High Court, which ruled in 1968 that he had the right to remain. The government then created a key precedent in 1969 when Clifford Dupont, Ian Smith's deputy and another war veteran who had obtained land, simply issued a government order overriding the High Court. Parliament was told that Tangwena had been associating with African nationalists and communist sympathizers, such as author Doris Lessing. Police and army arrived on September 18, 1969, to arrest Tangwena and evict his people; 160 villagers protested outside the police station and were arrested. They were eventually released and reoccupied the village and rebuilt their homes. On October 2, their homes were destroyed and they were again evicted. They reoccupied, rebuilt, and were destroyed again on November 21, but again reoccupied and planted crops as the rains had started. Evicted again on November 24, 1970, people moved up to the Inyanga hills.

Chief Tangwena made contact with Zanu guerrillas in neighboring Mozambique and helped Robert Mugabe, Edgar Tekere (one of the founders of Zanu), and hundreds of others to cross to Mozambique to join
the struggle; then Rekayi Tangwena finally joined them and was made a
senator after independence.[16]

The key point of the story is that World War II veterans Ian Smith
and Clifford Dupont underlined the colonial and UDI precedent that
land is political, that those who occupy land against the will of the state
are "squatters" who are to be forcibly evicted, and that courts do not have
a say on the politics of land.

Government Role

Ruling over a large and increasingly restless majority, then UDI, led the
Rhodesian government beginning in 1931 to take ever tighter control,
especially over the economy and agriculture. It was not just black farmers who were regulated. Increasingly white farmers, too, grew what they
were told to and largely sold to the government. In addition, the government and its agents provided agricultural services. By 1978 maize,
sorghum, groundnuts, soya beans, wheat, coffee, cotton, and tobacco
were government-controlled crops, while tea, fruit, livestock, and dairy
products were controlled by producer associations.[17] Sanctions forced
the government to control foreign exchange and imports and to establish an industrial policy.

Many of these restrictions were kept in place by the independence
government, which allowed it to manage the transition, keep industry
alive, and boost both black and white farmers. Government took a central role in the first land reform and in restructuring the formerly minor-
ity-ruled state. But the second half of the 1980s saw the dominance of
the neo-liberal, free-market model, and the new Zimbabwe came under
increasing pressure from the World Bank and other international bodies
to dismantle the colonial controls and reduce the role of government—
precisely at a time when farmers were clamoring for traditional levels of
support, and the majority population wanted the benefits that before had
gone only to white people. By the mid-1990s, there was a growing sense
that the new model was failing, and the strikes and protests were in part
a popular demand that government become more interventionist. This
led to breaks with the international community and a return to a much
more activist role for the government.

Polarization

Within Zimbabwe and outside, opinion of Robert Mugabe's government is polarized and exaggerated, with little middle ground. In Britain
the position is caricatured by the case of Zimbabwean Gamu Nhengu,
a failed contestant from the television talent contest The X Factor. After
being refused permission to stay in the United Kingdom, she launched
a press campaign, which led to an article in the *Daily Mail* in October
2010 saying, "Don't let me be deported, I will face a firing squad." She
went on to say that if she returned she would be punished by President
Mugabe: "There's a firing squad waiting for us there and they're putting
me in front of it." There are no firing squads in Zimbabwe, but she won
her appeal to stay in Britain in November 2011.[18]

Some of these eight aspects are specific to Zimbabwe and its history,
while others occur in many countries. All aspects, good and bad, have
shaped the land-reform process. Broadly speaking, the negative factors took
an increasingly important role during the hyperinflation period and reduced the effectiveness of the land transfers, while the positive factors have
come to the fore since 2009, allowing the best farmers to move forward.

Notes

1. International Human Development Indicators, available at http://hdrs
.undp.org (July 27, 2011).

2. Zvakanyorwa Wilbert Sadomba, *War Veterans in Zimbabwe's Revolution*
(Woodbridge, Suffolk, UK: James Currey, 2011), 103 [Sadomba, *War Veterans*].

3. Richard Bourne, *Catastrophe: What Went Wrong in Zimbabwe?* (London,
UK: Zed, 2011), 23

4. Lloyd Sachikonye, *When a State Turns on Its Citizens* (Pretoria, South
Africa: Jacana, 2011).

5. Note that there is a shift in the spelling of two southern provinces to
Matebeleland, although the older Matabeleland (with Mata) remains common.

6. Catholic Commission for Justice and Peace in Zimbabwe, "Breaking the
Silence—Building True Peace: A Report Into the Disturbances in Matabeleland
and the Midlands" (1999), available at http://www.zwnews.com/BTS/BTS.html
(accessed July 31, 2011).

7. Daniel L. Byman, "Do Targeted Killings Work?" posted July 14, 2009,
on the websites of *Foreign Policy* (http://www.foreignpolicy.com/articles/
2009/07/14/do_targeted_killings_work) and the Brookings Institution (http://
www.brookings.edu/opinions/2009/0714_targeted_killings_byman.aspx) (July
31, 2011).

8. Sadomba, *War Veterans,* 82.

9. Based on complaints relating to the 2008 election period. "Truth, Reconciliation and Justice in Zimbabwe. Report of the Commission of Inquiry Appointed Under Article 26 of the Constitution of the International Labour Organization . . ." (Geneva, Switzerland: International Labour Office, 2009), ¶545–46, available at http://www.ilo.org/gb/GBSessions/WCMS_123293/langen/index.htm (December 29, 2011).

10. Thabani Ndlovu, "Violence at MDC-T Bulawayo Elections," Bulawayo24news, April 10, 2011, available at http://bulawayo24.com/index-id-news-sc-local-byo-2665-article-Violence+at+MDC-T+Bulawayo+elections+.html (July 31, 2011).

11. David Leigh and Ian Griffiths, "The Mystery of Tony Blair's Finances," *Guardian,* December 1, 2009; Jamie Doward, "Blair Inc's 'Baffling' 40% Rise in Earnings," *Observer,* January 1, 2012.

12. Kim Willsher, "Jacques Chirac Verdict Welcomed by Anti-Corruption Campaigners," *Guardian,* December 15, 2011.

13. Project on Government Oversight (POGO) Federal Contractor Misconduct Database (FCMD), Washington, DC, http://www.contractormisconduct.org/ (July 31, 2011).

14. Henry V. Moyana, *The Political Economy of Land in Zimbabwe* (Gweru: Mambo Press, 1984); chapter 6 gives full details of the Chief Rekayi Tangwena land case.

15. Ibid., 158.

16. Obituary of Senator Chief Rekayi Tangwena, who died June 10, 1984, available at http://www.zanupf.org.zw/index.php?option=com_content&view=article&id=94&Itemid=108 (August 2, 2011).

17. Mudziviri Nziramasanga, "Agriculture Sector in Zimbabwe," in *Zimbabwe: Towards a New Order, Working Papers Vol. 1* (New York: United Nations, 1980), 53.

18. "X Factor Reject Gamu Pleads With Simon and Cheryl: Don't Let Me Be Deported, I Will Face a Firing Squad," London, UK: Mail Online, October 10, 2010, available at http://www.dailymail.co.uk/tvshowbiz/article-1319282/X-Factor-2010-Gamu-Nhengu-begs-Cheryl-Cole-Simon-Cowell-dont-let-deported.html?printingPage=true (November 30, 2011); "X Factor Contestant Gamu Wins Deportation Battle," *Guardian,* November 30, 2011.

3

Land Apartheid

"THE PASSING OF THE LAND APPORTIONMENT ACT, 1930, WAS A DEFINITE MILE-
stone in the history of Southern Rhodesia. It marks the first attempt in
Southern Africa to effect a measure of segregation as between the European and African peoples,"[1] wrote Godfrey Huggins, prime minister of
Southern Rhodesia, in 1935, more than a decade before formal apartheid
was introduced in South Africa. When this was raised in the House of
Commons in London, the British government confirmed that it agreed
with the new law.[2] Thus, in seeing land as racially defined, the government of independent Zimbabwe was—as in many other things—simply
continuing British colonial definitions and practice.

Rhodesian MP Walter Richards warned in 1941, "Without segregation this colony would go 'black' within 50 years and our European
population would be reduced to traders, missionaries and civil servants."[3]

A 1935 article in the *Journal of the Royal African Society* explained
that "the European requires a certain standard of living, he can hardly be
reduced to bare subsistence farming," and thus "areas of good soil, a fair
average rainfall and the altitude and climate are suitable for Europeans."
There are areas that are not "suitable for white settlement" because they
are low-lying, are infested with tsetse fly, or have other problems, and
there is no "real reason why they should not be occupied by Natives."[4]

Land allocation has been a central issue in the country for more
than a century. Settlers began forcibly displacing black Zimbabweans
from their land in 1890, especially after Zimbabweans lost their first war
against the white invaders, the 1896–97 *First Chimurenga*. The Southern
Rhodesia Order in Council, 1898,[5] issued by Queen Victoria, created
Native Reserves, which were "land, the property of the British South

Africa Company, set apart for the purposes of native settlements exclusively." The Order further said, "'Native' means any person not of European descent who is a native of South Africa, or of Central Africa." Further, "a Native Commissioner shall control the natives through their Tribal Chiefs and Headmen," and they will be "guided by native law so far as that law is not repugnant to natural justice or morality." An administrator was given the right to appoint and dismiss chiefs and headmen.

The Land Apportionment Act of 1930 explicitly defined "European" and "native" land areas. The 1930 law gave 51% of the land—naturally the best—to 50,000 Europeans (of whom only 11,000 actually lived on the land[6]), and 30%—the poorer land—to 1 million Zimbabweans. (See Tables 3.1 and 3.2.)

Rhodesia was formally divided into five Natural Regions in 1960,[7] and these have been used ever since to describe land. The definitions are set out in Table 3.2. Natural Region (NR) I is the highlands of Manicaland. NR II is the best general farmland and is concentrated in Mashonaland. NR III has some potential for crops and is mainly in Masvingo and Midlands. Table 3.2 shows that most African lands were NR IV and V.

The 1930 law also established "native purchase areas" (NPAs) whereby black Zimbabweans could buy land and receive titles under European law; 82% of this land was in the drier regions III to V.[8] Africans were charged more for land than whites and could not obtain loans or mortgages, while none of the infrastructure such as wells and dams that were provided for white farmers were made available to black NPA buyers. Also, much of the NPA land was never assigned to black farmers, even though there were many applications.[9] And in something that would be repeated 70 years later, NPA land was often allocated as rewards to civil servants and loyal supporters of the government.[10]

Under the 1930 law, no new "native" land occupations were allowed in European areas, and black Zimbabweans were expected to move to

Table 3.1 Land Apportionment Act, Southern Rhodesia, 1930

	mn ha	%
European Area	19.9	51
Native Reserves	8.5	22
Native Purchase Area	3.0	8
Other	7.5	19
Total	38.9	100

Table 3.2 Natural Regions and Allocations, 1962

Natural Region		Total	European		African	
Farming	Rain per year	ha (mn)	ha (mn)	%	ha (mn)	%
I	Specialized	> 1,050 mm in all months	0.6	0.5	82	0.1	18
II	Intensive crop	700–1050 mm summer	7.3	5.7	77	1.7	23
III	Semi-intensive crop	500–700 mm summer with droughts	6.9	4.4	64	2.5	36
IV	Livestock	450–600 mm summer, infrequent heavy rain & severe dry spells	13.0	6.8	52	6.2	48
V	Livestock	< 500 mm erratic; too low even for drought-resistant crops (also poor soils)	10.3	4.6	45	5.7	55

Sources: Rifkind, "Politics of Land," 200; Kay Muir-Leresche, "Agriculture in Zimbabwe," in *Zimbabwe's Agricultural Revolution Revisited,* ed. Mandivamba Rukuni, Patrick Tawonezvi, and Carl Eicher (Harare, Zimbabwe: University of Zimbabwe Publications, 2006), 103.

"native" areas.[11] Reserves became increasingly overcrowded, and by the mid-1930s there was clear ecological deterioration. The land act was repeatedly changed and the regulations tightened, but in 1941 Prime Minister Huggins told parliament that only 50,000 Africans had been moved into reserves over the previous decade, and there were still 146,475 Africans on European Crown land and 169,023 on European farms.[12] So in 1941, the law was tightened again to provide that "no Native shall acquire, lease or occupy land in the European area"; those Zimbabweans who remained on European land were called "squatters."[13] As Malcolm Rifkind commented, "The Africans concerned were only 'squatters' in a legalistic sense as for the most part they had been on the land for generations before the Europeans had even come to the country."[14] In 1945, the law was tightened further to make it an offense for an owner or occupier of European land, "or his agent," to allow a "native" to occupy European land.

There were regular changes to the land law and the racial labels of land—44 pieces of legislation on land in 35 years, 1931–65—which resulted in endless debates in parliament. But with the new Rhodesia Front government in 1962, a proper survey showed that not only did the one-sixteenth of the population who were European have more than half the land, but they also had the best land (Table 3.2).[15] "Most of the Native Area is poor soil . . . while the European Area contains nearly all the areas of fertile soil in the colony," wrote Ken Brown, a former official in the Native Department, in 1959. "It is quite embarrassing (if you are a European) to drive through a European Area into a Native Area. The change in soil-type coincides almost exactly with the boundary line and is startlingly obvious."[16] In 1949, Prime Minister Huggins admitted "that 30% of the native reserves and about 45% of the native purchase areas are unfit for occupation by natives or their animals because of the total lack of water."[17] Much of the African land was also infested with tsetse flies.[18]

Land acts also dealt with racial segregation. In 1959, major European hotels were allowed to become multi-racial, and the 1961 Land Apportionment Amendment Act stipulated that in the case of mixed marriages, the race of the husband would determine the place of residence.[19]

Great Depression to Green Revolution

The Great Depression of the 1930s had a harsh effect on white farmers: with a sharp drop in sales of tobacco, meat, and maize, many faced bankruptcy. The response was twofold—to support white farmers at the expense of black, and to sharply increase government intervention in white farming. Over the next decades increasing government control effectively turned most white farmers into contract farmers; for example, under the Tobacco Marketing Act of 1936, all tobacco farmers had to be licensed by the government, which also set prices and controlled exports. Tobacco, maize, and dairy control boards were set up as well. The Land Bank, established in 1912 to lend to white farmers, increased loans, and there was a three-year moratorium on all repayments. The maize control acts of 1931 and 1934 ensured that white farmers were paid substantially more for maize than were black farmers. Prosperity returned for white farmers in the late 1930s with the introduction of flue-cured Virginia tobacco, replacing air-dried burley tobacco, and then with the growth of demand during World War II. Until the mid-1930s, Africans and Europeans had been using the same technology—only the scale was different.[20] Indeed, the *Shangwe* people of present-day Gokwe were renowned producers of tobacco in pre-colonial days, and the industry grew in the

1920s, promoted by white traders. But then the government moved to-bacco to be a white crop.[21]

The 1950s brought an agricultural revolution for white farmers, with new seeds and a huge increase in fertilizer use. Between 1948 and the mid-1960s, maize yields per hectare increased 155%, wheat yields 185%, and tobacco yields 300%,[22] driven by tight government control of agriculture, high levels of subsidy, and intensive government research. In 1949, Rhodesia became the second country, after the United States, to release hybrid maize seed for sale to farmers, and by the 1950s there was a strong local seed industry. A rule of thumb is that it takes a decade to develop a new crop variety, test it under farmer conditions, and release it, which requires government support. Mandivamba Rukuni comments, "It took 28 years of local research (1932 to 1960) to develop Zimbabwe's Green Revolution maize variety (SR52)."[23]

Meanwhile, the Rhodesian government had been promoting white immigration since 1903, but the European population was rising very slowly. In part this was because the Rhodesian government wanted only the "right type" of immigrants—British people with some capital—and there was an attempt to ensure that at least 80% of "Europeans" were British subjects. Indeed, Jews fleeing Hitler in the 1930s were rejected, as were Poles and southern Europeans after World War II, even if they had capital to invest.[24] But austerity in Europe at the end of the Second World War, combined with agricultural growth in Rhodesia and the government's desire to actually occupy those areas designated as white, led to a substantial migration.

Special preparations began in 1943 to resettle returning white soldiers on farms, and Prime Minister Godfrey Huggins ruled that year that black ex-servicemen, even those who served on the front lines, were excluded from the scheme. As a result, the government began to push black people off the land to clear it for white veterans. For each farm for a war veteran, a connecting road was built; a basic home was built; land was cleared and fenced; 40 ha were plowed; and essential implements, seed, and fertilizer were provided. A "Soldier Resettlement Scheme" was established as well.[25]

Assisted passage schemes were introduced in 1951 and 1957, targeting in particular retired members of the British military. Settlers were placed on farms for two years of training during which they received rent-free accommodation and free food.[26] The white population jumped from 80,500 in 1945 to 219,000 by 1960. Most went to the cities, but the number of European men working or owning farms almost doubled, from 4,673 in 1945 to 8,632 in 1960. To clear land for the new farmers, in just one decade, 1945–55, more than 100,000 black Zimbabweans were moved, often forcibly, into reserves and inhospitable and tsetse fly–ridden unassigned areas.[27]

Not that much of the land was used. Barry Floyd, who had worked for the Southern Rhodesian government as a land development officer in the African reserves, wrote in the *Journal of the American Geographical Society* in 1962 that "as late as 1955, some four thousand Africans were evicted from the European area. Their abandoned croplands were sometimes farmed after their removal but as often as not lay idle."[28]

Unilateral Declaration of Independence and Sanctions

Not surprisingly, black grievances, protests, and strikes grew. In his 1959 PhD thesis, Barry Floyd notes, "for the reserve native, there are vivid reminders of the injustices of land apportionment every day. Many of the reserves are adjoined by extensive European farms or undeveloped and unoccupied Crown land." Barbed wire fences ran along the physical boundaries between good- and poor-quality land, with Africans densely packed on poor and "over-tired" soils with vast white farms on the good land. "The historic fact that Southern Rhodesia was finally occupied and subdued by force of arms, and that the Europeans are thereby the heirs to land by right of conquest, is also advanced as justification for land apportionment," Floyd notes.[29]

In 1951, native reserves were renamed Tribal Trust Lands, but changing their name did not improve them. By 1960, the government was suggesting rescinding the Land Apportionment Act. The 1962 election was contested on this issue, and the Rhodesian Front was elected on a platform that believed "the pattern and principle of racial differentiation in the ownership, use, and tenure of land established under the Land Apportionment Act must be maintained."[30] Resistance to decolonization and more rights for the black majority then being promoted by the British government led directly to the Rhodesian Front government's making its Unilateral Declaration of Independence (UDI) in 1965. The response was the beginning of the liberation war. Robin Palmer, in his book *Land and Racial Domination in Rhodesia,* comments, "The guerrillas initially obtained their greatest popular support in the Centenary, Sipolilo, and Mount Darwin areas in the northeast, where alienation of land to the

Europeans had taken place only in the past twenty years and the people's resentment was therefore of recent origin."[31]

Two weeks after UDI, the UN Security Council called for voluntary sanctions against Rhodesia; in December 1966, it imposed mandatory sanctions on 60% of Rhodesian exports and 15% of imports, and in May 1968, the Security Council imposed comprehensive mandatory sanctions banning all imports, exports, air links, and diplomatic links.[32] The UDI period had three economic phases—a sharp drop in income in 1966–68 when sanctions were imposed, then six years of import-substitution-led growth, and then a sharp decline from 1975 caused by the escalation of the war and then the withdrawal of South African support.

Several factors were important in Rhodesia's survival—and its collapse. First was tight control of foreign exchange. In 1966, export earnings were cut by a third, so Rhodesia repudiated $250 million in debt to the World Bank and European lenders and cut all profit repatriations, reducing outflows. Import priority was given to essentials—fertilizer, fuel, military equipment—and there was tight import licensing for other goods, so that nothing that could be made locally was imported. The other key factor was sanctions-busting. South Africa invested $650 mn, and both Britain and the United States broke the "mandatory" UN sanctions (in contrast to sanctions imposed on Zimbabwe 35 years later). British companies supplied oil, allegedly with the connivance of the British government.[33] Initially the United States supported sanctions, and on January 5, 1967, President Lyndon Johnson issued an Executive Order implementing the first UN sanctions, and trade quickly stopped. President Richard Nixon (1969–74) opposed Rhodesia sanctions, and in 1971, Congress passed the Byrd Amendment, which allowed US companies to break the sanctions, and in particular to import chrome from Rhodesia. This continued under President Gerald Ford (1974–77), but as soon as Jimmy Carter took office in 1977, he repealed the Byrd Amendment and reimposed sanctions.[34] In 1979, Donald Losman, then a visiting professor at the US Army War College, wrote: "It must be stressed that Rhodesia would have been unable to survive sanctions without enormous gaps in its enforcement. A truly universal embargo, one without loopholes, would have brought quick capitulation."[35]

US historian Gerald Horne documents formal and informal support for UDI Rhodesia in his book *From the Barrel of a Gun*.[36] As the liberation war grew and the United States was withdrawing from Vietnam, several hundred US mercenaries joined the Rhodesian forces. Former mercenaries interviewed by Horne claimed they had support from the

US Central Intelligence Agency (CIA).[37] A Rhodesia lobby in the United States had the support of some in Congress (to whom they contributed campaign funds) and stressed the need to keep Rhodesia white and to fight against "communism." This was confirmed by Ken Flower, head of the Rhodesian secret service, who also commented that it was "international cynicism that helped Rhodesians defeat sanctions."[38]

Rhodesia did well until 1973–75. The liberation struggle intensified, particularly when the guerrillas could have rear bases in Mozambique. This began in 1972, when Frelimo had taken much of Tete province northeast of Zimbabwe, giving access to Manicaland and Mashonaland. After gaining independence from Portugal in 1975, Mozambique gave more open support to Zanu, while more Zimbabweans crossed over to Mozambique to join the liberation movement. Zambia then allowed more space for Zapu, which also sent in more guerrillas. Attacks on roads, railways, economic targets, and the security forces deep inside Rhodesia became more common.

A 1987 study of the sanctions by one of this book's authors concluded that five other factors precipitated the change:

- the economic impact of the worsening guerrilla war, which was costing $1.6 mn per day;[39]
- reduction in sanction-busting, including closing the Zambian border in 1973 and the Mozambican border in 1975 and the United States halting import of chrome in 1977;
- the 1973 oil price rise;
- previously hidden effects of sanctions, including machinery wearing out and not being replaced; and
- South Africa, leaned on by Carter in the United States, and in turn putting pressure on Rhodesia. Eddie Cross, chief economist of the Rhodesian Agricultural Marketing Authority until 1980, said the key element in bringing a settlement and majority rule was "South African economic sanctions against the Rhodesian government."[40] In a brief to the Rhodesian government on June 12, 1979, Ken Flower wrote, "With every month that goes by, sanctions become more debilitating."[41]

The Lancaster House agreement to end the war and bring majority rule was signed on December 17, 1979, and elections were held February 28 and 29 and March 1, 1980.[42] Zanu-PF under Robert Mugabe won 57 of the 80 seats in the House of Assembly (parliament), PF-Zapu under Joshua Nkomo won 20 seats, and UNAC under Bishop Abel Muzorewa won 3 seats. (Both Britain and South Africa supported Lancaster House in part because they expected Muzorewa to win.) Independence was declared on April 18, 1980.

UDI, War, and Farming

From the 1950s, white farmers were encouraged to produce export crops, especially tobacco. But with UDI and international sanctions, these farmers were persuaded to move away from tobacco and into maize, cattle, and cotton. To support white farmers responding to sanctions, the UDI government provided subsidies and loans estimated at $12,000 per farm per year in the mid-1970s,[43] the equivalent to approximately $40,000 per farm per year now.[44] The shift in emphasis squeezed black Tribal Trust Land farmers, whose incomes fell; in the late 1950s, African farmers had produced 32% of marketed production, but this fell to 18% in the late 1960s. Many young people became landless and unemployed and joined the liberation struggle.

From late 1972, the war had an increasing impact on rural people. Villages were bombed by Rhodesian security forces and crops were destroyed and cattle confiscated as a form of collective fines imposed on local people. By mid-1977, one-fifth of the rural population had been forced into "protected villages," where they could spend only a few hours a day in their fields. And most farmers in the Tribal Trust Lands had fewer than the 2.5 ha of arable land, then seen as the minimum to grow food for a family; half owned no cattle.[45] The 1981 Riddell Commission of Inquiry into Incomes, Prices and Conditions of Service noted, "Because of the tremendous pressure on land, peasants have carved up their grazing areas for cultivation and even land which should never be ploughed because of risk of erosion has been planted with crops."[46]

White Farmland: Derelict, Underused, National Disgrace

The scandal of white farming was how little land was actually being used, even as black farmers were being packed ever more tightly into the Tribal Trust Lands. Malcolm Rifkind in his 1968 thesis notes that Rhodesian authorities themselves complained about how little land was being used.[47] A parliamentary committee in 1957 concluded that only 6%–12% of arable European land was actually being farmed.

The three Mashonaland provinces account for 75% of Zimbabwe's prime farmland. In 1965, the chairman of the Rural Land Board wrote: "Just get into an aeroplane and fly over Mashonaland's European farming areas. On practically every farm you will see acres of land lying idle, good grasslands, that was given to these farmers by God and the Rural Land Board. . . . It is a national disgrace that so much land is lying idle and not being used."[48] Fifteen years later, the situation had not improved. In 1981/82, of 1.9 mn ha of arable land in the three Mashonaland provinces, only 440,000 ha (23%) were being cropped, meaning that 1.5 mn ha were lying idle; even making generous allowances for fallow land, white farmers in Mashonaland were using only 34% of their land. The worst province was Mashonaland East, with 15% cropped.[49]

Various estimates have been made of land use, but in 1976, Roger Riddell calculated that only 15% of potentially arable European land was being cultivated. Even in the early 1970s, many white farms were being used only for residential purposes, or as weekend farms.[50] Zimbabwe's *Transitional National Development Plan* in 1982 said, "Utilization of potential arable land in the large-scale and small-scale commercial sectors is about 21 per cent and 18 per cent respectively."[51]

At independence in 1980, according to the Utete Commission in 2003, "The large-scale commercial farming sub-sector of 6,000 white farmers owned 15.5 million hectares, more than half of which lay in the high rainfall agro-ecological regions where the potential for agricultural production is greatest. . . . White commercial agriculture was typically characterised by a lot of land that was unutilised or underutilised, held by absentee landlords or just left derelict for speculative purposes." The report continued: "On the other hand was the small-scale commercial farming sub-sector comprising 8,500 black farmers who held 1.4 million hectares of agricultural land located mostly in the drier agro-ecological regions where the soils are also poor."[52]

Roger Riddell looked closely at agriculture just before and just after independence and found that most white farms were inefficient and only "able to survive because of a wide range of assistance given, both directly and indirectly, to European agriculture in the form of loans, price supports, capital grants, the low wage structure, and 'artificial' land prices."[53] The Rhodesian National Farmers' Union found in 1977 that 30% of all farms were insolvent—kept alive by loans, price supports, and subsidies.

Riddell notes that in the 1975/76 season, 60% of farms (4,023 of 6,682) were not profitable enough to qualify for income tax, while 52% of all taxable income was accounted for by just 271 white farms.

Summing Up: Setting Benchmarks

Policies of the colonial (and UDI) authorities laid the groundwork for actions by the independence government later. Colonial authorities racialized land, defining the good land as "European" and the poorer land as "African" and pushing the vast majority of the people onto the poor half of the country's farmland. And the colonial government set the policy that occupants were to be evicted violently so war veterans and others selected by government could have the land.

The white governments also recognized that white farmers would not thrive on their own. New settler farmers received two years of training. A huge structure of research, training, and marketing boards supported the new farmers but also turned them into virtual contract farmers, growing what the state told them to and selling to state-run or -regulated agencies. To protect white farmers, African farmers were squeezed and marginalized. Even that was not enough, and in the mid-1970s, subsidies and "loans" had reached the equivalent of $40,000 per white farm per year.

But cosseted white farmers did not do very well; 30% were insolvent, another 30% broke even but did not make a profit, 30% made a small profit, and only 5% of farms were very profitable. And white farmers used only between 15% and 34% of their arable land. This gives us a benchmark by which we can judge later land-reform farmers.

Notes

1. Godfrey Huggins, foreword to A. C. Jennings, "Land Apportionment in Southern Rhodesia," *African Affairs*, XXXIV, no. CXXXVI (1935): 296 [Jennings, "Land"]. Huggins was named Viscount Malvern of Rhodesia and of Bexley in the County of Kent (and thus a member of the House of Lords) in 1955.

2. *Hansard*, House of Commons Debate March 26, 1930, vol. 237, 409–10.

3. Malcolm Rifkind, "The Politics of Land in Rhodesia" (MSc thesis, Edinburgh University, 1968), 62 [Rifkind, "Politics of Land"], citing *Legislative Assembly Debates* (*Hansard*) June 24, 1941, col. 1646, available at http://www mct.open.ac.uk.zimbabwe (June 20, 2012).

4. Jennings, "Land," 308–11.

5. Southern Rhodesia Order in Council, 1898, Ordered at the Court at Balmoral by The Queen's Most Excellent Majesty, October 20, 1898, available at http://www.rhodesia.me.uk/documents/OrderInCouncil1898.pdf (accessed January 8, 2012).

6. Jennings, "Land," 310.

7. V. Vincent and R. G. Thomas, *An Agricultural Survey of Southern Rhodesia* (Salisbury, Southern Rhodesia: Government Printer, 1960).

8. John Blessing Karumbidza, "A Fragile and Unsustained Miracle: Analysing the Development Potential of Zimbabwe's Resettlement Schemes, 1980–2000" (PhD thesis, University of KwaZulu-Natal, 2009), citing Roger Riddell, The Land Problem in Rhodesia, *From Rhodesia to Zimbabwe,* pamphlet 11 (Gwelo, Zimbabwe: Mambo, 1978), 51.

9. Rifkind, "Politics of Land," 68, 206.

10. Robin Palmer, *Land and Racial Domination in Rhodesia* (Berkeley, CA: University of California Press, 1977), 214–18 [Palmer, *Land and Racial*].

11. Ifor Leslie Evans, *Native Policy in Southern Africa* (Cambridge, UK: Cambridge University Press, 1934), 121; Palmer, *Land and Racial,* 216, notes that black Zimbabweans were also being pushed off the new Native Purchase Areas and there were 50,000 "squatters" living in NPAs, causing local conflicts.

12. Rifkind, "Politics of Land," 63, citing Huggins speaking to the Legislative Assembly, June 19, 1941.

13. Jennings, "Land," 307.

14. Rifkind, "Politics of Land," 91.

15. Rifkind, "Politics of Land," 200, citing the 1962 Phillips Report; Kay Muir-Leresche, "Agriculture in Zimbabwe," in *Zimbabwe's Agricultural Revolution Revisited,* ed. Mandivamba Rukuni, Patrick Tawonezvi, and Carl Eicher (Harare, Zimbabwe: University of Zimbabwe Publications, 2006), 103 [Rukuni, Tawonezvi, and Eicher].

16. Rifkind, "Politics of Land," 202, citing Ken Brown, *Land in Southern Rhodesia* (London, UK: Africa Bureau, 1959).

17. Rifkind, "Politics of Land," 79, citing Prime Minister Huggins speaking in a parliamentary debate, June 30, 1949.

18. Rifkind, "Politics of Land"; Barry Floyd, "Land Apportionment in Southern Rhodesia," *Geographical Review,* 52, no. 4 (1962): 567 [Floyd, "Land Apportionment"].

19. Rifkind, "Politics of Land," 127, 147.

20. Palmer, *Land and Racial,* 242.

21. Mandivamba Rukuni, "The Evolution of Agricultural Policy: 1890–1990," in Rukuni, Tawonezvi, and Eicher, 43.

22. Patrick Tawonezvi and Danisile Hikwa, "Agricultural Research Policy," in Rukuni, Tawonezvi, and Eicher, 199.

23. Mandivamba Rukuni, "Revisiting Zimbabwe's Agricultural Revolution," in Rukuni, Tawonezvi, and Eicher, 6.

24. Alois Mlambo, *White Immigration Into Rhodesia* (Harare, Zimbabwe: University of Zimbabwe, 2002), 49, 50, 59–67, 70 [Mlambo, *White Immigration*].

25. Asher Walter Tapfumaneyi, "A Comparative Study of Forces Demobilisation: Southern Rhodesia 1945–1947 and Zimbabwe 1980–85" (BA honors dissertation, University of Zimbabwe, 1996), 21–24, 28, 36, 77. One of the many things that annoyed the new government was that at independence it was forced to continue paying pensions and other benefits to white World War II veterans, when black WWII veterans with similar service records were receiving nothing.

26. Mlambo, *White Immigration*, 29.

27. Palmer, *Land and Racial*, 242–43.

28. Floyd, "Land Apportionment," 577.

29. Barry Floyd, "Changing Patterns of African Land Use in Southern Rhodesia" (PhD thesis, Syracuse University, 1959), Lusaka, Zambia: Rhodes-Livingstone Institute, 280–81.

30. Palmer, *Land and Racial*, 244, 249.

31. Palmer, *Land and Racial*, 245–46.

32. Detailed in Joseph Hanlon and Roger Omond, *The Sanctions Handbook* (London, UK: Penguin, 1987), chap. 22 [Hanlon and Omond, *Sanctions*].

33. Martin Bailey, *Oilgate* (London, UK: Hodder & Stoughton, 1979).

34. Gerald Horne, *From the Barrel of a Gun: The United States and the War Against Zimbabwe, 1965–1980* (Chapel Hill, NC: University of North Carolina Press, 2001), 143–54 [Horne, *From the Barrel*].

35. Donald Losman, *International Economic Sanctions* (Albuquerque, NM: University of New Mexico Press, 1979), 122.

36. Gerald Horne is now John and Rebecca Moores Professor of history at the University of Houston.

37. Horne, *From the Barrel*, 25–27, 44–46, 60–61, 75, 150, 220–40.

38. Ken Flower, *Serving Secretly* (London, UK: John Murray, 1987), 70–73 [Flower, *Serving*].

39. Carolyn Jenkins, "Economic Objectives, Public-Sector Deficits and Macroeconomic Stability in Zimbabwe," Centre for the Study of African Economies (CSAE) Working Paper 97-14 (Oxford, UK: CSAE, 1997), 6, available at http://www.csae.ox.ac.uk/workingpapers/pdfs/9714text.pdf (November 15, 2011).

40. Hanlon and Omond, *Sanctions*, 208–9.

41. Flower, *Serving*, 163, 227. He notes that the pressure on South Africa to put pressure on Rhodesia actually started in 1976 under Henry Kissinger, US secretary of state under Ford.

42. On February 14, 1980, there was a separate poll for the 20 seats on the white voters' roll, won uncontested by Ian Smith's Rhodesian Front.

43. Ian Phimister, "The Combined and Contradictory Inheritance of the Struggle Against Colonialism," in *Zimbabwe's Prospects*, ed. Colin Stoneman (London, UK: Macmillan, 1998), 8. Z$8,000 per year, based on data by M. Phillips in a 1984 BA honors thesis at the University of Cape Town.

44. Using the website http://www.measuringworth.com/uscompare/ (October 30, 2011).

45. Roger Riddell, The Land Question, *From Rhodesia to Zimbabwe,* pamphlet 2 (Gwelo, Zimbabwe: Mambo, 1978), 10 [Riddell, "Land Question"].

46. Roger Riddell, *Report of the Commission of Inquiry into Incomes, Prices and Conditions of Service* (1981), 34.

47. Rifkind, "Politics of Land," 204–8.

48. Rifkind, "Politics of Land," 205, quoting "Idle Land a National Disgrace," *Rhodesian Farmer,* April 9, 1965.

49. Dan Weiner, Sam Moyo, Barry Munslow, and Phil O'Keefe, "Land Use and Agricultural Productivity in Zimbabwe," *Journal of Modern African Studies,* 23, no. 2 (1985): 251–85; Sam Moyo, "The Land Question," in *Zimbabwe: The Political Economy of Transition 1980–1986,* ed. Ibbo Mandaza (Dakar, Senegal: Codesria, 1986), 174.

50. Riddell, "Land Question," 13.

51. Republic of Zimbabwe, "Transitional National Development Plan 1982/83–1984/85," Vol. 1 (Harare, Zimbabwe: Government of Zimbabwe, 1982), 65.

52. *Report of the Presidential Land Review Committee,* under the chairmanship of Dr. Charles M. B. Utete (Harare, Zimbabwe: Presidential Land Review Committee, 2003), vol. 1, 14. Volume I, Main Report, available at http://www.sarpn.org/documents/d0001932/Utete_PLRC_Vol-I_2003.pdf, and Volume II, Special Studies, available at http://www.sarpn.org/documents/d0000746/Utete_Report_intro.pdf.

53. Riddell, "Land Question," 11–13.

4

Independence and the
First Land Reform

AT INDEPENDENCE, THE NEW GOVERNMENT IN A SHARPLY RACIALLY DIVIDED SOCIETY
gave top priority to three things:

- First, do not rock the boat and maintain as many of the existing
  systems and economic structures as possible.
- Second, convince the white minority that it still had a place in the
  new Zimbabwe, stressing reconciliation and keeping productive
  white farmers on the land. The government document for donors for the Zimbabwe Conference on Reconstruction and Development (Zimcord) in March 1981 talked of "the experiment
  in moderation and reconciliation which the Government of Zimbabwe is pursuing."
- Third, reduce the huge gaps between white and black, through
  massive expansions of health and education, and shifting agricultural extension to serve black farmers.

Policy seemed more one of "leveling up"—raising the standards for
the black majority rather than challenging the rich minority in one of the
most unequal countries in the world. This included a huge expansion of
education and health. Free primary schooling was introduced and enrollment jumped from 819,000 in 1979 to 2,260,000 in 1986; secondary
school enrollment jumped sixfold.[1] Improvements in health care caused
a dramatic fall in infant mortality, from 120 per thousand in 1980 to
83 in 1982; but there was still a long way to go—white infant mortality
was only 14 per thousand.[2]

A severe three-year drought, destabilization by apartheid South Africa, and less-than-promised support by donors, however, all constrained the space available to the new government.

There was a first land reform, which proved to be the largest in Africa, and it was remarkably successful. But we delay that discussion to set out first the context and limited space in which land reform took place.

Support for Black Farmers

African reserves (known in Rhodesia as "Tribal Trust Lands" and after independence as "communal lands") accounted during the 1970s for only 10%–15% of the country's cotton crop and 5% of its marketed maize production, and only 5% of smallholders were applying chemical fertilizer because the cost was far too high.[3] At independence, government's stress was on promoting farming in the communal areas, where the majority of Zimbabweans live. Government shifted rain-fed maize and cotton production to the communal sectors and pushed the white commercial farmers into more profitable export crops.

"At independence in 1980, the new government threw its political weight behind communal farmers and forced government agencies to remove racial barriers to access to credit, increased the number of extensions officers in communal lands and opened buying points for communal farmers," notes Mandivamba Rukuni.[4] For the 1980/81 season, the government's Refugee Resettlement Programme handed out free seed and fertilizer for at least 1 acre (0.4 ha) of maize to smallholder households whose production had been disturbed by the war. Many peasants used fertilizer for the first time, and with good rains that year, these input packages yielded good results; many smallholders continued to use fertilizer and hybrid seed in the years that followed. As Table 4.1 shows, hybrid seed and fertilizer purchases increased fourfold. This was backed up by the Small Farm Credit Scheme for seasonal production inputs; in

Table 4.1 Modern Inputs Bought by Smallholders

Year	Fertilizer (tonnes)	Hybrid maize seed (t)
1979/80	27,000	4,300
1984/85	127,664	19,500

Source: Masst, "Harvest," 83.

1979/80, loans totaled $1 million, but this jumped to $40 million by 1986/87. The new government immediately restructured Agritex (Agricultural, Technical and Extension Services)[5] to reach most black communal farmers instead of mainly white commercial farmers. The message was changed to help small farmers use new seeds and fertilizers. Mette Masst, who did a study in Kandeya Communal Area, Mount Darwin District, Mashonaland Central Province, found that 60% of communal area farmers attended Agritex training sessions and 78% had contact with extension officers. She also noted that Agritex officers "had a high standing among the peasantry." The final, and perhaps most important, support was that the maize producer price was increased significantly (see Table 4.2), and the Grain Marketing Board (GMB) increased the number of depots from just one in communal areas at independence to 37 by 1991; in the peak year of 1985, it also had 135 special collection points.[6]

The result was spectacular, as Table 4.3 shows. Better fertilizer and seeds, backed by extension services, meant yields doubled, and the area planted also doubled; by 1985, communal farmers were supplying one-

Table 4.2 Producer Prices for Maize and Cotton

Year	Maize $/kg	Cotton $/kg
1979	0.09	0.52
1980	0.13	0.60
1981	0.16	0.56
1983	0.11	0.46
1985	0.11	0.41
1987	0.11	0.48
1989	0.09	0.41
1991	0.05	0.27

Source: Masst, "Harvest," (1996), 86.

Table 4.3 Maize Sales to the Grain Marketing Board From Communal Areas, Tonnes

1980–81	1981–82	1982–83	1983–84	1984–85
66,565	290,488	317,884	137,243	335,130

Source: Esbern Friis-Hansen, *Seeds for African Peasants: Peasants' Needs and Agricultural Research, the Case of Zimbabwe* (Uppsala, Sweden: Nordic Africa Institute, 1995), 63.

third of the maize bought by the GMB.[7] The 1983/84 year was a drought year and production dropped dramatically, yet communal areas, particularly in the Mashonaland provinces, were still selling a significant surplus. High levels of production continued through the 1986/87 season. As Table 4.2 shows, maize prices fell from their 1981 peak, but by then smallholders were so much more productive that they continued high production levels. The best farmers moved over to cotton, and then to burley (air-cured) tobacco, while other smallholders expanded maize production. For Mette Masst, the four most important reasons for the jump in peasant production were

- improved marketing facilities;
- expansion of agricultural extension services;
- improved access to inputs such as seeds, fertiliser, and pesticides; and
- higher producer prices.[8]

The Utete Committee commented: "The small-holder green revolution that occurred in Zimbabwe between 1980 and 1986 due to heavy Government involvement in infrastructure development and input support services is a clear demonstration that sustained public investment in the supply-side of agriculture through institutional capacity development is a critical ingredient for agricultural transformation."[9] A study by the UN Food and Agriculture Organization (FAO) noted, "After independence in 1980, agricultural policy was directed to reducing inequality and to supporting smallholders. The supply response by smallholders was dramatic, and they became the largest suppliers of maize and cotton to formal markets within the first five years (1980–1985) of independence."[10]

Destabilization

Thinking back more than 30 years to the independence period requires understanding a context that is now largely forgotten. Apartheid was still the defining ideology in South Africa, and when Ronald Reagan took office as president of the United States in January 1981, he intensified the Cold War, threw his weight behind South Africa as a bastion against communism, and opposed Zimbabwe as a "communist" state. This effectively gave South Africa a license to destabilize its neighbors. The image of Robert Mugabe, then as now, was highly distorted. Two of the authors remember back to 1981, soon after independence, when we hitched a lift near Mutare with a man who ran a small business. He said to us: "We were told Mugabe was a communist and would nationalise everything. But he's not, you know. Business continues just as before."

Apartheid played a major distorting role over the first decade of independence. There was substantial sabotage, and Zimbabwe was subject to de facto sanctions by South Africa. Most dramatically, South Africa bombed Zanu headquarters at 88 Manica Road, Harare, on December 18, 1981, at a time when a central committee meeting was supposed to be taking place. The meeting had been delayed and the lives of Robert Mugabe and other Zanu leaders were saved, but seven people were killed and 124 injured, mostly Christmas shoppers on the street below. Other South African–initiated attacks included the August 16, 1981, raid on the Inkomo Barracks that destroyed $70 mn in arms and ammunition, and the July 25, 1982, raid on Thornhill Air Base, which destroyed 13 aircraft. Making use of the Zanu policy of reconciliation with the white minority, apartheid South Africa had agents in many key places, including Mugabe's director of close security who was suspected in the Manica Road bomb.[11]

As part of its policy of destabilization, South Africa created or backed armed opposition movements in Angola, Mozambique, Lesotho, and Zimbabwe. In Matebeleland in southwest Zimbabwe, it created "super-Zapu": a group of Zapu dissidents opposed to the very fraught alliance of the two former liberation movements, Zapu and Zanu, into a single army. South Africa used agents inside the dissidents and inside the new Zimbabwe police to cache arms supplied by South Africa and then to "discover" the arms caches, leading to a halt in the integration of the two armies and to the arrest and trial of two Zapu leaders, Dumiso Dabengwa and Lookout Masuku. (Both were acquitted at their trial.) South Africa was able to manipulate the two sides and exploit the already existing tension between Zanu and Zapu, leading to the massive over-reaction that brought the army's Fifth Brigade into Matebeleland for the *Gukurahundi*.[12] It might be easy to dismiss talk of plots and manipulation as simple paranoia, but several senior officials in key positions in the new Zimbabwe police, and several of those who gave evidence against Dabengwa and Masuku at the trial, surfaced in South Africa later in the 1980s and some confirmed they had been South African agents. In 2000, Peter Stiff, who writes detailed and laudatory books about the white security services of apartheid South Africa, largely confirmed South Africa's role.[13]

Zimbabwe is landlocked and South Africa manipulated transport links. The shortest rail links are to Beira and Maputo in Mozambique. South African commandos, and later Renamo[14] guerrillas, repeatedly attacked the two rail links and the oil pipeline to Beira. This forced Zimbabwe to use the longer rail links to South African ports, and South Africa regularly disrupted Zimbabwean shipments, particularly sugar exports and fuel imports. At the end of 1981, Zimbabwe had a backlog of $150 mn worth of exports awaiting shipment. Eddie Cross, then head of the Zimbabwe Cold Storage Commission, estimated in 1984 that Zimbabwe was losing $70 mn per year in higher transport costs due to South African actions. As the attacks increased, Zimbabwe was forced to send soldiers to defend the railway and pipeline to Beira. At one point it had 12,500 troops in Mozambique, at a cost of $3 million per week.

South Africa also ended the preferential trade agreement it had had with Rhodesia, and later imposed duties on Zimbabwean exports such as steel and sent back 40,000 Zimbabwean migrant miners, costing Zimbabwe at least $75 mn per year in lost repatriated salaries and remittances.[15] Finally, hundreds of millions of dollars were smuggled out of Zimbabwe, largely by transfer pricing and other maneuvers by South African companies; just one example was Cone Textiles' paying its South African parent $2 mn extra for dyes imported from the United Kingdom via South Africa.[16]

In a 1998 study, it was estimated that the cost to Zimbabwe of apartheid destabilization was $10 billion (bn), and that Zimbabwe borrowed $3.8 bn to partly cover those costs.[17] The Zimbabwe government inherited a debt of $700 mn from the Rhodesian government, largely spent on fighting a war to maintain white rule, but that the majority government was forced to repay.[18] The Zimbabwe Coalition on Debt and Development has launched a campaign for an audit of Zimbabwe's $7 bn debt and its ultimate cancellation, arguing that most can be traced to borrowing by the Rhodesian government and then borrowing due to apartheid destabilization.[19]

Rain and Drought

Rainfall is highly variable in Zimbabwe, from one year to another and between different parts of the country, which is a major issue for a country that depends on rain-fed agriculture. Figure 4.1 shows the official figures for deviation from the mean rainfall, which shows the variation and indicates that the 15 years after independence had below-average rainfall. From a longer time scale, in the 50 years 1953–2003 there were 14 drought years (rainfall at least 20% below normal), of which five were serious (rainfall at least 50% below normal).[20] This means that farmers must

Figure 4.1 Zimbabwe Seasonal Rainfall, Deviation From the Mean

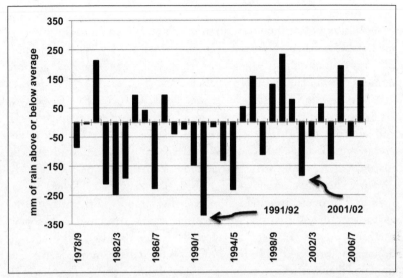

Source: Leonard Unganai, "Climate Change and Its Effects on Agricultural Productivity and Food Security: A Case of Chiredzi District," paper presented at National Climate Change Workshop, Harare, November 23, 2011.

expect a drought every three to four years and a serious drought once a decade. But as the figure shows, bad years often come consecutively.

Drought can have serious political and economic implications. The first three years after independence were all drought years—1981/82 (32% below average), 1982/83 (–50%), and 1983/84 (–31%)—which led Zimbabwe to borrow (with IMF and World Bank encouragement), causing debt problems later. Then 1990/91 was a drought year (–29%), followed by the worst drought of the century in 1991/92 (–77%), which pushed the country into accepting the structural adjustment package (partly due to debt from earlier drought years). The drought years of 1993/94 (–22%) and 1994/95 (–53%) worsened the economic problems caused by adjustment and fed into strikes and disruptions. Then 2001/2, the first year farmers had land under the fast track land reform, was also a drought year (–22%), making it harder for new farmers to become established.

Economic Squeeze

In the UDI period, the Smith government maintained very tight control over foreign exchange, and over the economy in general. Companies were often protected from foreign competition as part of import substitution industrialization, but they were also closely regulated. The new independence government maintained these controls and did not immediately liberalize as happened in South Africa 15 years later. In part this was to maintain independence from South Africa and to promote domestic production and self-reliance.

The sanctioned UDI government had not been able to borrow abroad, so Zimbabwe was considered "under-borrowed" by the IMF and World Bank, which encouraged it to borrow more. Zimbabwe negotiated its first World Bank and IMF loans in 1981. A study by the Oxford University Centre for the Study of African Economies (CSAE) noted, "The expectations of large aid inflows encouraged the government to borrow in anticipation of receiving support in the future [but] as it turned out, very little of these funds was ever received." Donors at the Zimcord in March 1981 promised $1.9 bn, but by 1985 the main donors had provided $574 mn, only 30% of the amount pledged—and much of that was tied to purchases in the donor countries, reducing its value.[21] Zimbabwe also borrowed to meet the costs of defending against apartheid destabilization, paying for increased education and health care, restructuring the economy, and social costs of the three-year drought, which cost the government $480 mn, including $210 mn in food imports.[22] The CSAE study notes that "Zimbabwe's huge foreign debt was accumulated in just three years after independence."[23]

Zimbabwe's relations with the World Bank and IMF were complex. After the first loans, the Bank and Fund increased their pressure. A 1982 IMF agreement collapsed in 1984 when the government restricted payment of dividends on pre-independence investments and allowed the budget deficit to rise to 10%, compared to the IMF target of 5%.[24] Bernard Chidzero, who had been outside Zimbabwe since 1960 and from 1977 to 1980 was deputy secretary general of the UN Conference on Trade and Development, became Minister of Economic Planning and Development in 1980, and from 1985 to 1995 was Minister of Finance. In addition, Chidzero was chairman of the World Bank Development Committee from 1986 to 1990.

He followed the World Bank liberalization line and responded to IMF pressure in 1984 by sharply cutting government spending and reducing protection of local industry, which removed many of the supports for small-scale agriculture. The economy ran into problems in 1987, in part because of debt repayments. In the first four years of independence (1980–83) Zimbabwe received $1.5 bn in new loans, but in the next five years (1984–88) it had to pay back $1.2 bn.[25] The World Bank refused to extend an export revolving fund until Zimbabwe liberalized trade, which it did.[26]

High levels of smallholder maize and cotton production continued through the 1987/88 season. From 1987, economic policy changed and government spending was cut. To try to support the urban poor and communal farmers, the government had a relatively high maize price plus a maize meal subsidy that reached $49 mn in 1982/83.[27] Under World Bank pressure, maize meal subsidies were cut and maize prices were decontrolled, which caused a fall in the maize price (see Table 4.2), which hit farmers. Spending on extension services was reduced and smallholder support diminished, credit and fertilizer purchases dropped, and the GMB cut back the number of collection points, all of which hit small producers. After 1987–88, there was a sharp decline in smallholder production and sales. Maize sales fell as smallholders used less fertilizer on the land. Global cotton prices were also falling, so smallholders used less land for cotton.[28] And it was a repetition of a lesson Ian Smith had learned in the UDI era—farmers need support, and if they are given support, they produce, but production falls when support falls.

But white farmers were supported. In the mid-1980s, the government offered incentives to stimulate export, including foreign exchange allocations in favor of exporters and improvements to air transport. The Horticultural Promotion Council was formed.

Zimbabwe is a major agricultural exporter, the exports are tobacco, cotton, beef, flowers, and sugar. Historically, Zimbabwe was not self-sufficient in food and had to import it, particularly in years of low rainfall. The UDI period saw large government subsidies to switch white farmers to producing food, and Rhodesia came closer to food self-sufficiency, although only in the context of chronic food deficits in the communal areas.[29] The early 1980s policy was a push to self-sufficiency in food produced increasingly by commercial farmers, but by the late 1980s, policy had returned to promoting agricultural exports.

The First Land Reform

In September 1980, just six months after independence, the government announced the Intensive Resettlement Programme to resettle 18,000 families. This target was tripled twice, and by 1982, the Accelerated Resettlement Programme sought to resettle 162,000 families—a target that was not met. But Zimbabwe's first land reform did resettle 75,000 families by 1996, and it was the largest land reform in Africa. Model A, which involved smallholders living in villages, accounted for 85.5% of resettled farmers. Table 4.4, which gives the number of families settled under Model A, suggests that, overall, at least 38,000 families had been resettled by the end of the 1983/84 season—meaning half of all families had been resettled in just four years—and 60,000 by 1988/89.

"The basic objective [of the accelerated program] is to resettle as many people as possible in the shortest possible period of time by minimizing planning, and postponing indefinitely the building of infrastructure. It is assumed that settlers under this programme would make use of the admittedly inadequate infrastructure in adjacent communal areas,"[30] wrote Bill Kinsey at the time.

Top priority for land was given to refugees or others displaced by war, including urban refugees and former inhabitants of "protected villages." Second priority was to the unemployed and residents in communal areas with insufficient land to maintain themselves. Household heads were also supposed to be married or widowed, age 25 to 50, and not in formal employment. Kinsey found that "generally, these criteria seem to have been followed. In this sample, some 90% of households settled in the early 1980s had been adversely affected by the war for independence in some form or another. Before being resettled, most (66%) had been small holders with the remainder being landless laborers on commercial farms, workers in the rural informal sector or wage earners in the urban sector."[31]

Most were settled on small plots, with 5 ha arable land for crops, 0.4 ha for a house, plus land for grazing. (This was known as model A, which was very similar to the fast track land reform model A1 in 2000.)

Male heads of households were expected to be farmers and were not permitted to work on other farms, nor could they migrate to cities, leaving their wives to work these plots. The myth of the self-sufficient peasant has been one of the most contentious issues throughout Zimbabwe's land reform. In communal areas, many families—and the most successful—were worker-peasants, with one member of the family earning a

Table 4.4 Total Number of Families Resettled in Model A

1980/81	81/82	82/83	83/84	84/85	85/86	86/87	87/88	88/89
1,971	10,819	24,819	32,957	36,616	41,332	42,582	48,724	51,411

Source: Friis-Hansen, *Seeds for African peasants*, 61.

salary, which was partly used to invest in the farm. Various studies show that after independence there were marked inequalities in the communal areas, and the main factors creating the difference were draft power (cattle), land, labor, credit, and off-farm income.[32] The need for credit or off-farm income to develop the new resettlement farms became clear, and in 1992 resettlement farmers were officially allowed to hold off-farm jobs. This was also an issue with the second land reform, and we note in chapter 6 the importance of urban work for raising money to capitalize new farms.

In 1983/84, resettlement farmers had only just started, but they accounted for 10% of black farmers' maize production. By 1987/88, they were responsible for 11% of all agricultural production.[33] Bill Kinsey has been following 400 of the resettlement families for nearly two decades,[34] which gives him a unique perspective.[35] By 1997, Kinsey and colleagues concluded that there had been a "dramatic increase in crop incomes observed in these households," which was much larger than the average for Zimbabwe, and "growth in incomes has been shared across all households." He also noted "an impressive accumulation of assets by these households."[36] Notable was the entry by a number of households into the production of higher-value crops such as cotton, groundnuts, and sunflowers. The results were all the more impressive when one considers that much of the land offered for sale for land reform was of poorer quality; of the first 3 mn ha used for resettlement, only 22% was in Natural Region I or II.[37] (See Table 3.2 for definitions of Natural Regions.)

A Reluctant Land Reform

Land had been central to the liberation struggle, and it proved to be a sticking point in the first independence negotiations in Geneva in 1976, and then at the successful talks at Lancaster House, London, September 10 to December 15, 1979. Britain held out to protect white farmers, and the Patriotic Front accepted British demands only after the US and British governments promised money to pay for land.[38]

The draft constitution agreed upon at Lancaster House sets out a "Declaration of Rights," which could not be changed for 10 years, and which includes "Freedom from Deprivation of Property." In particular, it states that "under-utilised land" could be compulsorily acquired for settlement or agricultural purposes only if there is "prompt payment of adequate compensation"; that a "person whose property is so acquired will be guaranteed the right of access to the High Court to determine the amount of compensation"; and that compensation will "be remittable to any country outside Zimbabwe, free from any deduction, tax or charge in respect of its remission."[39] This provision of the constitution was never used. Instead, the government, in negotiation with Britain and other donors, agreed to the "willing buyer, willing seller" principle under which there would be no compulsory purchase, and government would only buy land for resettlement that was offered voluntarily.

But, Lord Carrington, chairman of the Lancaster House Conference, admitted that, although the future government of Zimbabwe "will wish to extend land ownership, . . . the costs would be very substantial indeed, well beyond the capacity, in our judgement, of any individual donor country."[40] Tanzanian president Julius Nyerere commented that it would be impossible for an independent government in Zimbabwe "to tax Zimbabweans in order to compensate people who took [land] away from them through the gun."[41]

Both were right; paying for land was too expensive and it proved impossible for the new government. The 2003 Report of the Utete Committee on Fast Track Land Reform (FTLR) found that "where land was offered to Government, in most cases it was expensive, marginal and occurred in pockets around the country, making it difficult to effect a systematic and managed land reform. Moreover, land supply failed to match the demand for land for resettlement. Added to these complicating factors was the absence of international support to fund land acquisition."[42] Sir Shridath "Sonny" Ramphal, Commonwealth Secretary General at the time of the Lancaster House talks, later said, "Britain let them down. Britain did not fulfil its promises and they found all sorts of ways to wriggle out and that was very unfortunate and that is what has led to some of the bitterness."[43]

The first land-reform program depended on buying land from white farmers, under the "willing seller, willing buyer" principle, which basically dictated that all land had to be offered to the government first, and if the government turned it down, a certificate of "no present interest" was issued, allowing an alternative sale. And the biggest purchases and most resettlement took place quickly, in the first four years, as Table 4.5 shows. In the five years 1980–84, 2.1 mn ha were purchased; in the next six years, only 448,000 ha were purchased.[44] By the mid-1980s, the economic squeeze had hit and there was no money to buy land. In 1986–89, 1,856 farms were offered but the offers were not accepted, because the asking price was almost 10 times the amount being paid by the government

Table 4.5 Land Purchased for Resettlement

Year	Ha	$ mn	$/ha
1979/1980	162,555	4.9	30
1980/1981	326,972	5.3	16
1981/1982	819,155	18.8	23
1982/1983	807,573	21.2	26
1983/1984	173,848	3.5	20
1984/1985	74,848	2.0	26
1985/1986	86,187	2.1	24
1986/1987	133,515	2.3	17
1987/1988	80,554	1.6	20
1988/1989	78,097	3.5	45
Total	**2,743,304**	**65.3**	

Source: John Blessing Karumbidza, "A Fragile and Unsustained Miracle: Analysing the Development Potential of Zimbabwe's Resettlement Schemes, 1980–2000" (PhD thesis, Syracuse University, 1959), 120; Mandivamba Rukuni et al., "Policy Options for Optimisation of the Use of Land for Agricultural Productivity and Production" (report submitted to the World Bank Agrarian Sector Technical Review Group, 2009), 53.

for farms at that time; certificates of no present interest were issued for these.[45] This allowed the sale to other white farmers, often at much lower prices than had been offered to the state, which set a pattern of white farmers who decided to remain collecting several farms.

In his PhD thesis, Angus Selby surveyed 70 white farms in Concession, Mazowe district. None had been sold to the government, but between 1980 and 2000, 52 (74%) had been sold at least once and 14 (20%) had been sold more than once. Multiple farm ownership had increased, and by 2000, the 70 farms had only 51 owners.[46]

Land may have been at the forefront for the guerrillas and in political speeches, but the new government did not give top priority to land reform; in fact, it often seemed distrustful of the idea. Although Lancaster House made land reform difficult, the new government did not take up options available to it; for example, according to the 1981 Riddell Commission, "immediate access to more and better land" was essential for raising incomes of the rural poor, and it called for a land tax to encourage less-used land to be offered for sale, and the creation of land purchase bonds that would guarantee payment in hard currency, but only at a later date.[47] Neither proposal was followed up. Resettlement accounted for only 3% of the investment funds requested at the March 1981 Zimcord.[48]

There was also a broad international view, promoted by some at the World Bank,[49] that big, mechanized farms were more efficient and productive. Diplomats and aid agencies pressured the government to slow down land reform. And many in the new leadership accepted this view, for three different but overlapping reasons. First, they wanted to protect large-scale commercial farming as the driving force for exports, which were becoming increasingly important as Zimbabwe tried to fund its growing budget. Second, they wanted to prevent white flight, as had happened in Mozambique five years earlier, so big white farmers were to be protected. Third, a group in the new government simply wanted to replace some big white farmers with black farmers, rather like Black Economic Empowerment in South Africa a decade later. An estimated 350 black Zimbabweans bought large-scale commercial farms and 600 leased large farms in the 1980s.[50] Large A2 farmers can also be seen as large commercial farmers, and by 2010, there were 1,173 large-scale black commercial farmers with 1 mn ha—3.1% of the land (see Table 1.1)

In 1983, the parliamentary Estimates Committee, chaired by a Rhodesia Front MP who was a white farmer, but with Zanu backing, condemned the land reform and said resettlement officers were "out of control."[51] Bill Kinsey argues that the government's commitment to land reform "dwindled very rapidly."[52] He goes on to argue, "The old compact between government and the white captains of industry and agriculture was replaced by a new political alliance between dominant representatives of the state and black capitalists."[53]

Occupations

The idea that small farmers could be more efficient and productive than large ones may be part of the common wisdom now, but 30 years ago it was marginal and sometimes seen as linked to the far left. Meanwhile, the view was to build up the black majority without pulling down the wealthy white minority. That may have been a sensible position for the new elite, but it was not often accepted on the ground. Many Zimbabweans had been displaced by the war, and there were large movements of people simply occupying land. Not all of these were occupying "white" land; it was also marginal and unallocated land. The 1982 Accelerated Resettlement Programme was "a 'fire-fighting' or phased version of the intensive programme and is aimed at tackling some of the most serious instances of squatting and some of the severe cases of over-population," wrote Bill Kinsey at the time.[54] Dan Weiner concluded in 1989, "Half of all resettled households accessed land as squatters immediately follow-ing independence."[55]

Occupations by landless people had been common in the 1950s and 1960s, notably people evicted from "white" land and children who could not find land in communal areas. Families occupied the margins of com-munal areas, grazing land, and unallocated land. In Manicaland province in the late 1960s, nationalists had called for "freedom farming" and land occupations were directly linked to the growing nationalist movement.[56] The war meant more movements in the 1970s. Independence brought many spontaneous land occupations, particularly of white farms aban-doned in the war and by chiefs trying to regain land that had been taken from them and given to white farmers decades before. Landless families spontaneously settled on wildlife reserves and moved onto white farms bought for official resettlement.

In areas near the Mozambique border, people saw land occupation as similar to the "liberated zones" created by the Frelimo freedom fight-ers in Mozambique, and as a recovery of stolen land, explains Francis Gonese, chair of the National Land Board. He adds, "The colonial set-tlement process itself had in fact shown . . . that the most effective way of taking over land is to physically occupy and effectively utilize."

There seems to have been no complete survey so data must be taken from papers and articles. For example, a study of a wildlife area next to Rengwe communal lands, Hurungwe district, Mashonaland West, found 8,000 people had spontaneously settled by 1982 and this figure had in-creased to 25,000 people in 5,234 families by 2000.[57] In 1985, Manica-land officials reported 50,000 "squatters" in the province.[58]

Jocelyn Alexander studied Manicaland in the 1980s and reported in 1981 in Chimanimani "a large-scale movement onto the vast areas of vacant land in the district, which continued over the next two years."[59] There was supposed to be a formal registration process for resettlement, but of 93,000 forms handed out in Manicaland, only 10,909 were re-turned. People did not trust officials and took the land, often with sup-port of chiefs, local Zanu-PF officials, and even some local government officials; the Provincial administrator defended occupiers as heroes of the liberation war and land-starved peasants. Deputy Lands Minister Moven Mahachi arrived in Chimanimani to explain government policy, stressing that central and not local government would allocate land and that claims would not be based on past evictions or chieftaincies. The prime minis-ter's office released Circular 10 on December 10, 1981, which outlined measures that would be taken against occupiers as well as powers given to police and army to deal summarily with squatters.[60] In 1982, new Deputy Lands Minister Mark Dube declared "total war" on Manicaland squatters, and the secretary of lands said he would "show these people it is the whole of the government against squatting." In 1983, then–Lands Minister Mahachi described squatters as "undisciplined and criminal elements." Yet again, the independence government had taken on the language and policies of the colonial government—"freedom farmers" were now "squatters." Nevertheless, Alexander notes, "Occupations were largely successful" and spontaneous settlers were usually given land.

After 1985, the process did become more centralized, the government position against "squatters" hardened, and evictions increased. Sam Moyo comments, "The brutality with which these evictions were carried out, both by police and farmers, were reminiscent of colonial era evictions."[61] In a process strikingly similar to the eviction of Chief Rekayi Tangwena in Manicaland in 1976, one group of squatters was evicted in Chimanimani in 1988 and their homes were burned. Informal occupations continued, however, and both Sam Moyo[62] and Angus Selby[63] point to the way informal occupiers took over parts of white farms, and where they could not be evicted often stayed with tacit agreement of both the white farmers and local officials.

Summing Up: Optimism Drowned by Debt

The optimism of independence brought a huge transformation in the first half of the 1980s. Major improvements to health care and education made a start on redressing the huge inequities inherited from white minority rule. Support for black farmers in the communal areas made them important commercial producers. The biggest land reform in Africa resettled 38,000 families in four years and eventually resettled 75,000. Reconciliation with the white community was the order of the day, and the dual agriculture system was retained—with big white farms and black smallholders—but the balance was already shifting.

The independence government faced unexpected problems, however. Destabilization by apartheid South Africa disrupted the economy and forced an expansion of the military, a three-year drought hit the new country, and the cost of buying back land that had been stolen three decades earlier mounted up. Donors simply never paid more than $1 bn of the money pledged in a flush of enthusiasm in 1981. By the mid-1980s, transformation was throttled by lack of cash and a sea of debt.

Notes

1. Colin Stoneman and Lionel Cliffe, *Zimbabwe: Politics, Economics and Society* (London, UK: Pinter, 1989), 122, 133 [Stoneman and Cliffe, *Politics*].

2. René Loewenson and David Saunders, "The Political Economy of Health and Nutrition," in *Zimbabwe's Prospects,* ed. Colin Stoneman (London, UK: Macmillan, 1988), 133, 146.

3. Mette Masst, "The Harvest of Independence: Commodity Boom and Socio-economic Differentiation Among Peasants in Zimbabwe" (PhD thesis, Roskilde University, 1996), 65–66, 80 [Masst, "Harvest"], available at http://www.open.ac.uk/technology/mozambique/p11_3.shtml (accessed November 1, 2011).

4. Mandivamba Rukuni, "Revisiting Zimbabwe's Agricultural Revolution," in *Zimbabwe's Agricultural Revolution Revisited,* ed. Mandivamba Rukuni, Patrick Tawonezvi, and Carl Eicher (Harare, Zimbabwe: University of Zimbabwe Publications, 2006), 17–18 [Rukuni, Tawonezvi, and Eicher].

5. Agritex is Agricultural, Technical and Extension Services. In 2003 it was renamed Arex, Agricultural Research and Extension, and then in 2008 changed back to Agritex. We use the acronym Agritex throughout.

6. Masst, "Harvest," 81, 82, 204, 208.

7. Esbern Friis-Hansen, *Seeds for African Peasants: Peasants' Needs and Agricultural Research, the Case of Zimbabwe* (Uppsala, Sweden: Nordic Africa Institute, 1995), 63. However, 15%–20% of communal maize farmers in high rainfall areas generated most of the surplus, according to Mandivamba Rukuni, "Revisiting Zimbabwe's Agricultural Revolution" in Rukuni, Tawonezvi, and Eicher, 12.

8. Masst, "Harvest," 75.

9. Charles Utete, "Report of the Presidential Land Review Committee on the Implementation of the Fast Track Land Reform Programme, 2000–2002" [known as the Report of the Utete Committee, cited here as the Utete Report] (Harare, Zimbabwe, 2003), 74, available at http://www.sarpn.org/documents/d0000622/P600-Utete_PLRC_00-02.pdf (October 23, 2011).

10. Moses Tekere, "Zimbabwe," Harare: Trade and Development Studies Centre, in Harmon C. Thomas, *WTO Agreement on Agriculture: The Implementation Experience* (Rome: FAO, 2003), available at http://www.fao.org/docrep/005/y4632e/y4632e01.htm#bm01 (December 3, 2011).

11. Teresa Smart, "Zimbabwe: South African Military Intervention," in Joseph Hanlon, *Beggar Your Neighbours* (London, UK: James Currey, 1986), 173–77 [Hanlon, *Beggar*].

12. Ibid., 179–83.

13. Peter Stiff, *Cry Zimbabwe* (Alberton, South Africa: Galago, 2000).

14. Renamo was a guerrilla force first created by the UDI regime to oppose the government in the newly independent Mozambique, which was later taken over by apartheid South Africa, and was used particularly to attack transport links.

15. Hanlon, *Beggar,* 185–97.

16. Colin Stoneman, "Zimbabwe: The Private Sector and South Africa," in Hanlon, *Beggar,* 212.

17. Joseph Hanlon, "Paying for Apartheid Twice" (London, UK: Action for Southern Africa, 1998), part of document available at http://www.africa.upenn.edu/Urgent_Action/apic_72798.html (November 4, 2011).

18. Tim Jones, *Uncovering Zimbabwe's Debt* (London, UK: Jubilee Debt Campaign, 2011), 6.

19. Darlington Musarurwa, "Every Zimbabwean Owes US$500," *Sunday Mail,* December 5, 2010, available at http://www.afrodad.org/index.php?option=com_content&view=article&id=395:every-zimbabwean-owes-us500&catid=1:about-us&Itemid=19 (November 4, 2011).

20. Published rainfall and drought reports vary because they depend on which measuring stations are reported and how they are averaged. Figure 4.1 is from Leonard Unganai, "Climate Change and Its Effects on Agricultural Productivity and Food Security: A Case of Chiredzi District," paper presented at National Climate Change Workshop, Harare, Zimbabwe, November 23, 2011. The 14 drought years come from Craig J. Richardson, "The Loss of Property Rights and the Collapse of Zimbabwe," *Cato Journal,* 25, no. 3 (2005): Table 1, averaging data from 93 rainfall stations. Both are based on data from the Zimbabwe Meteorological Services Department. Richardson gives the average rainfall for the 50 years as 755 mm.

21. Roger Riddell, "Some Lessons From the Past and From Global Experiences to Help Move Zimbabwe Forward out of Poverty and Towards Sustainable Development," speech at the Moving Zimbabwe Forward Conference: Pathways out of Poverty for Zimbabwe, Harare, November 30, 2011.

22. Alois Mlambo, *The Economic Structural Adjustment Programme—The Case of Zimbabwe 1990–95* (Harare, Zimbabwe: University of Zimbabwe, 1997), 42. Note that although the official World Bank title is Economic and Structural Adjustment Program, the "and" is frequently dropped in Zimbabwean usage.

23. Carolyn Jenkins, "Economic Objectives, Public-Sector Deficits and Macroeconomic Stability in Zimbabwe" (working paper 97-14, Oxford: CSAE, 1997), 11, 22, available at http://www.csae.ox.ac.uk/workingpapers/pdfs/9714text.pdf (November 15, 2011).

24. Stoneman and Cliffe, *Politics,* 163.

25. The World Bank (http://databank.worldbank.org/) *Global Development Finance* (January 9, 2012) reports Zimbabwe's debt as $5 bn. It reports that in the first four years (1980–83) of independence, Zimbabwe received $1.5 bn in new money in the form of loans. But it has been repaying ever since and is falling behind. In the 26 years 1984–2009, Zimbabwe has made net debt payments of $2.8 bn. (That is, Zimbabwe paid this amount to its creditors, after discounting any new loans. Net = interest payments + principal repayments – new loans.)

Zimbabwe's debt in 1984 was $2.2 bn, yet even after paying more than that to its creditors, by 2009, the total debt had jumped to $4.8 bn.

26. Benson Zwizwai, Admore Kambudzi, and Bonface Mauwa, "Zimbabwe: Economic Policy-Making and Implementation: A Study of Strategic Trade and Selective Industrial Policies," in *The Politics of Trade and Industrial Policy in Africa*, ed. Charles Soludo, Osita Ogbu, and Ha-Joon Chang (Trenton, NJ: Africa World Press/IDRC, 2004), available at http://irsm.gc.ca/geh/ev-71257-201-1-DO_TOPIC.html (November 8, 2011).

27. Godfrey Kanyenze, "Economic Structural Adjustment Programme," in *Post-independence Land Reform in Zimbabwe*, ed. Medicine Masiiwa (Harare, Zimbabwe: Friedrich Ebert Stiftung, 2004), 97.

28. Masst, "Harvest," 78–81, 91, 206.

29. Clever Mumbengegwi, "Continuity and Change in Agricultural Policy," in *Zimbabwe: The Political Economy of Transition 1980–1986*, ed. Ibo Mandaza (Dakar, Senegal: Codesria, 1986), 209.

30. Bill Kinsey, "Forever Gained: Resettlement and Land Policy in the Context of National Development in Zimbabwe," *Africa*, 52, no. 3 (1982): 101 [Kinsey, "Forever Gained"].

31. Jan Willem Gunning, John Hoddinott, Bill Kinsey, and Trudy Owens, "Revisiting Forever Gained: Income Dynamics in the Resettlement Areas of Zimbabwe, 1983–1997" (working paper WPS/99-14, Centre for the Study of African Economies [CSAE], Oxford University, May 1999), version 2, available at http://www.csae.ox.ac.uk/workingpapers/pdfs/9914text.PDF (November 5, 2011) [Gunning, Hoddinott, Kinsey, and Owens, CSAE].

32. Daniel Weiner, "Land and Agricultural Development," in *Zimbabwe's Prospects*, ed. Colin Stoneman, 73, 83 (London, UK: Macmillan, 1988).

33. Daniel Weiner, "Agricultural Restructuring in Zimbabwe and South Africa," *Development and Change*, 20, no. 3 (1989): 405 [Weiner, "Restructuring"], quoting the Central Statistical Office for 1983/84 and *The Herald*, May 8, 1988.

34. "The initial sampling frame was all resettlement schemes established in the first two years of the program in Zimbabwe's three agriculturally most important agro-climatic zones. These are Natural Regions II, III and IV and correspond to areas of moderately high, moderate and restricted agricultural potential. One scheme was selected randomly from each zone: Mupfurudzi in Mashonaland Central (which lies to the north of Harare in NRII), Sengezi in Mashonaland East (which lies south east of Harare in NRIII) and Mutanda in Manicaland (which lies south east of Harare, but farther away than Sengezi and in NRIV). Random sampling was then used to select villages within schemes, and in each selected village, an attempt was made to cover all selected households. . . . Approximately 90% of households interviewed in 1983/84 were reinterviewed in 1997." Gunning, Hoddinott, Kinsey, and Owens, CSAE, 2–3; later published in amended form in *Journal of Development Studies*, 36, no. 6 (2000): 131–54.

35. This is the longest continuous panel study of households ever under-taken in Africa. Marleen Dekker and Bill Kinsey, "Contextualizing Zimbabwe's Land Reform: Long-Term Observations From the First Generation," *Journal of Peasant Studies,* 38, no. 5 (2011): fn 2.

36. Gunning, Hoddinott, Kinsey, and Owens, CSAE, 1.

37. John Blessing Karumbidza, "A Fragile and Unsustained Miracle: Ana-lysing the Development Potential of Zimbabwe's Resettlement Schemes, 1980–2000" (PhD thesis, University of KwaZulu-Natal, 2009), 122 [Karumbidza, "Fragile"].

38. Utete Report, 12–13.

39. "Southern Rhodesia. Report of the constitutional conference, Lancaster House, London, September–December 1979," Cmnd. 7802 (London, UK: HMSO, 1980), Annex C, available at http://www.zwnews.com/Lancasterhouse.doc (October 23, 2011).

40. Utete Report, 13, quoting Lord Carrington, in a statement issued October 11, 1979.

41. Utete Report, 13, quoting Julius Nyerere speaking at a press confer-ence on October 16, 1979.

42. Utete Report, 15.

43. Utete Report, 16, citing an interview on the BBC "HardTalk" pro-gram, March 22, 2002.

44. Sam Moyo, "The Evolution of Zimbabwe's Land Acquisition," in Ru-kuni, Tawonezvi, and Eicher, 146.

45. Karumbidza, "Fragile," 121.

46. Angus Selby, "Commercial Farmers and the State: Interest Group Poli-tics and Land Reform in Zimbabwe" (PhD thesis, University of Oxford, 2006), Appendix 1 [Selby, "Commercial"].

47. Roger Riddell, *Report of the Commission of Inquiry into Incomes, Prices and Conditions of Service, 1981,* 148 [known as the Riddell Commission report].

48. Stoneman and Cliffe, *Politics,* 169.

49. "A Degree of Dualism in Zimbabwe Agriculture Appears to Be the Optimal Solution," in World Bank, *Agriculture Sector Study* (Washington, DC: World Bank, 1983), vi.

50. Sam Moyo and Prais Yeros, "Land Occupation and Land Reform in Zimbabwe," in *Reclaiming the Land,* ed. Sam Moyo and Paris Yeros (London, UK: Zed, 2005), 177.

51. Lionel Cliffe, "The Politics of Land Reform in Zimbabwe," in *Land Reform in Zimbabwe: Constraints and Prospects,* ed. Tanya Bowyer-Bower and Colin Stoneman (Aldershot, UK: Ashgate, 2000), 40.

52. Bill Kinsey, "Zimbabwe's Land Reform Program: Underinvestment in Post-Conflict Transformation," *World Development,* 32, no. 10 (2004): 1671.

53. Bill Kinsey, "Land Reform, Growth and Equity: Emerging Evidence From Zimbabwe's Resettlement Programme," *Journal of Southern African Stud-ies,* 25, no. 2 (1999): 174.

54. Kinsey, "Forever Gained," 101.

55. Weiner, "Restructuring," 402.

56. Jocelyn Alexander, *The Unsettled Land* (Oxford, UK: James Currey, 2006), 87 [Alexander, *Unsettled*].

57. Admos Chimhowu and David Hulme, "Livelihood Dynamics in Planned and Spontaneous Resettlement in Zimbabwe," *World Development*, 34, no. 4 (2006): 732.

58. Alexander, *Unsettled*, 156.

59. Alexander, *Unsettled*, chap. 7.

60. Karumbidza, "Fragile," 136.

61. Sam Moyo, "Land Movements and the Democratisation Process in Zimbabwe," in *Post-independence Land Reform in Zimbabwe*, ed. Medicine Masiiwa (Harare, Zimbabwe: Friedrich Ebert Stiftung, 2004), 203.

62. Sam Moyo, *Land Reform Under Structural Adjustment in Zimbabwe* (Uppsala, Sweden: Nordiska Afrikainstitutet, 2002), 81–83.

63. Selby, "Commercial," 167.

5

Adjustment and Occupation

NELSON MANDELA WAS RELEASED FROM PRISON ON FEBRUARY 11, 1990; SOUTH African de facto sanctions ended and destabilization stopped. But 1990/91 was a drought year (rainfall 29% below average) followed by the worst drought of the century in 1991/92 (rainfall 77% below average). Zimbabwe was forced to accept a World Bank structural adjustment program that deepened poverty and halted resettlement. The independence honeymoon was truly over.

The World Bank Economic and Structural Adjustment Program (ESAP) meant market-oriented reforms and savage cuts in government spending. Zimbabwe had to abandon its import substitution and industrialization strategy, support for black farmers, land reform, and any remaining socialist rhetoric. ESAP involved a rapid devaluation and a floating exchange rate (see Table 6.7); eliminating controls on prices and wages and liberalization of trade and investment; and reducing the civil service and state spending, including health and education, ending subsidies, and privatization of many government-owned businesses. Agricultural marketing was deregulated, and, except for a few commodities, controls on domestic prices were removed.

Post-independence gains were wiped out. By 1992, real wages were lower than at independence.[1] By the end of 1993, between 45,000 and 60,000 people lost their jobs.[2] Job cuts came just as the expanded education system was putting more than 100,000 new high school graduates on the job market each year. Removal of price controls meant that the cost of living for Zimbabwe's lower-income urban families rose by 45% between mid-1991 and mid-1992, and for higher-income groups, it rose by 36%.[3] A study in the high-density Harare suburb of Kambuzuma

67

found that real per capita income for all residents fell by 26% in 1992, and that the poorest quarter of the population had cut real expenditures on food by 15% in 1992.[4]

Meanwhile, the health budget was cut by 20% and the education budget by 14%; fees for hospitals and schools were reintroduced in 1991, leading to a sharp drop in school and hospital attendance, a rise in births outside health facilities, and an increase in maternal mortality. These cuts came just when HIV/AIDS was becoming a serious problem, imposing an extra burden on the health service. But in 1992, Health Minister Timothy Stamps warned that AIDS could no longer be considered "the greatest threat to health." Instead, he said, "The biggest health crisis is the inevitable decline in the standard of living as a result of ESAP." By 1993, a third of Zimbabwe's doctors had left the country and many teachers and other health workers also left, many moving to South Africa and Botswana.[5]

A UN Food and Agriculture Organization (FAO) study noted that "market liberalization reforms led to a tremendous increase in agricultural production costs particularly for stock feeds, fertilizer, transport costs and agricultural equipment."[6]

Poverty levels in Zimbabwe increased from 26% in 1990/91 to 55% in 1995, and then to 72% in 2003.[7]

Even the World Bank's own Independent Evaluation Group (IEG) concluded that "the program did not reduce poverty and unemployment as its architects had hoped."[8] A report for FAO states that "the implementation of the structural adjustment programme in 1990 saw a shift from self-reliance towards trade." It also notes the "negative outcome of the economic reforms on prices and consumer welfare" and that "household food insecurity worsened during liberalization."[9]

But Some Did Well

The poor were being squeezed, but company profits increased by 80% in the seven years to 1996,[10] and white farmers did well. "Most studies have found that it was the large-scale commercial farmers that benefitted from ESAP," noted Godfrey Kanyenze.[11] Angus Selby wrote that "much of this economic growth was skewed towards established capital with international connections, most of which was white-owned. Lower-tier wage earners, smaller businesses and communal producers were left exposed to inflation and reduced government spending."

Horticulture had already become a priority, and the government initially introduced an Export Promotion Programme providing foreign currency for importing inputs. Under ESAP, these export incentives were phased out, but the devaluation of the Zimbabwean dollar throughout the 1990s compensated for that and stimulated exports. The Export Retention Scheme introduced in 1990 was particularly important and was quickly expanded. By 1993, 50% of export earnings could be used for a wide range of imports; foreign exchange transactions were liberalized for individuals in 1993 and companies in 1994; and by 1995, money could be used for holidays and education and profit remission was reopened.[12]

By 1995, one-third of all white farms (more than 1,600 large-scale farms) were exporting horticulture, notably mangetout peas, passion fruit, and flowers.[13] Exports jumped from 14,474 tonnes in the 1989/90 season to 64,650 tonnes in 1999/2000. (See Table 5.1 and Figure 5.1 for more details.) The main export market was the EU, which accounted for 95% of cut flowers exports; 90% of vegetables, herbs, and spices; and 75% of citrus fruit.[14] Vegetables went mainly to the United Kingdom and flowers to the Netherlands. The new farming is capital-intensive; Sam Moyo estimates that 1 ha of flowers in greenhouses costs $100,000 per year.[15] Although the number of permanent farmworkers remained constant, the number of casual and seasonal workers rose from 52,000 in 1983 to 163,000 in 1996, before falling back to 146,000 in 2000; 55% of casual workers were women. By the late 1990s, there were also a number of small-scale horticulture contract farming schemes (which points to the potential for larger land-reform farmers).

Some white farmers did spectacularly well. Selby's study of 70 farms in Concession, Mazowe, Mashonaland Central found half of them had

Table 5.1   Zimbabwe Horticulture Exports, $ mn

	1990	1995	2000	2005	2007
Flower exports	12.8	52.4	67.9	43.6	33.3
Fruit exports	16.2	13.2	29.4	33.4	37.2
Vegetable exports	5.7	19.9	24.5	15.1	12.5
Total	34.7	85.5	121.8	92.1	83.0

Source: UN Comtrade database.[1]

Note: Cited in Stephen Golub and Jeffery McManus, "Horticulture Exports and African Development," paper for the Expert Meeting of LDCs in preparation for the 4th United Nations Conference on Least Developed Countries, October 28–30, 2009, Kampala (Geneva, Switzerland: UN Conference on Trade and Development), available at www.unctad.org/templates/Download .asp?docid=12323&lang=1&intItemID=2068 (December 4, 2011).

Figure 5.1 Flower Exports to the Netherlands, $ mn

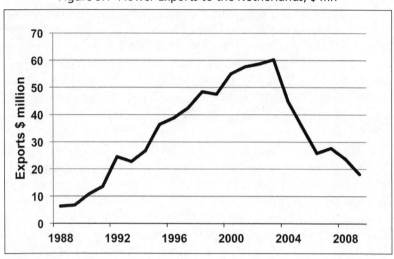

Source: UN Comtrade, www.un.comtrade.org.[1]

Note: Data for Netherlands imports from Zimbabwe. These are more accurate than data for exports from Zimbabwe due to effects of hyperinflation, which make the US dollar values cited for Zimbabwe exports less accurate. On average, Netherlands imports 80% of Zimbabwe's flowers, because Rotterdam is a major European distribution center for flowers.

diversified during ESAP—flowers, horticulture, citrus, ostrich, and tourism. Some were joint ventures with European companies. Farming families sent their children to study abroad, and some returned with new skills and marketing links; some established multimillion-dollar enterprises, including the largest rose grower in the southern hemisphere and the two biggest tobacco producers in the world.

But, Selby admits, "The emergence of young white millionaires against a background of increasing hardships in other sectors implied that the legacies of settler privilege were not abating." Luxury goods such as powerboats were imported. White farmers interviewed by Selby "lamented these ostentatious displays of wealth and identified them as key drivers of class and race resentment." And Selby found that some exporters were moving foreign currency abroad, through transfer pricing—double-invoicing whereby the invoice shown to Zimbabwean officials shows a much lower price for, say, flowers than is actually paid, and the difference goes into a European bank account. As Selby notes, white "farmers misjudged the political debate, partly due to assumptions about their 'indispensability.'" He continues: "Although a black commercial farming class emerged it had little impact on the racial exclusiveness of the sector, which remained its key weakness."[16]

Growing Unrest

But if some white farmers were doing well under ESAP, most Zimbabweans were not. In 1994, there was widespread industrial unrest, including strikes by teachers and medical staff. In August and September 1996, thousands of civil servants went on strike for three weeks. The government abandoned ESAP and adopted a compromise program, ZIMPREST (Zimbabwe Programme of Economic and Social Transformation). Economic unrest continued for the rest of the decade.

War veterans were becoming restless, arguing that they had gained nothing from the liberation war. They began to claim benefits under Rhodesian law written for white soldiers and complained about government corruption. Under the leadership of Chenjerai Hitler Hunzvi, the Zimbabwe National Liberation War Veterans Association (ZNLWVA) held ever-larger demonstrations.

Veterans were demanding $4,000 compensation for all former fighters, plus a $16 per month pension, and in November 1997, President Robert Mugabe unexpectedly acceded to these demands. However much the money was deserved, the huge amount involved was much more than Zimbabwe could afford—in effect, it had to print money to pay the compensation, and in one day the value of the Zimbabwe dollar against the US dollar dropped 73%. This effectively started a process of printing money, which was to cause the hyperinflation and economic collapse a decade later. The decision was also divisive, because this was more money than had been spent on land reform, and it could have been used to satisfy civil service wage demands. This was made worse through extra taxes imposed on workers and farmers to try to pay the bill, causing a split between the war veterans and the Zimbabwe Congress of Trade Unions (ZCTU).

The war veterans were openly challenging Zanu-PF and President Mugabe. They confronted Mugabe dramatically by singing and interrupting him during a speech at Heroes Acre in August 1997.[17] At the age of 15, Margaret Dongo[18] had crossed the border to join the guerrillas in Mozambique, and in 1989 cofounded ZNLWVA. In 1990, sponsored by the war veterans, Dongo became a Zanu-PF MP. Her challenges to the party led her to be deselected, but she was reelected as an independent in 1995. She requested and received a parliamentary written answer, which she published in January 2000, revealing government ministers, judges, generals, and senior civil servants who were leasing large farms from the government, many purchased under the willing seller, willing buyer program.[19]

Land was becoming a much more serious political issue, as unemployed and low-wage workers looked to farming to augment their income or as alternative work. Increasing intensification of white farming, for example, producing flowers in greenhouses, meant that by the mid-1990s, more production and employment was carried out on a relatively small proportion of land.[20] Ever-poorer people looked hungrily at the empty areas of prime farmland. Land had been a central issue in the liberation war, and the veterans successfully took the lead on land reform, using their mobilizing skills from the war to organize peasants and gain support of community leaders. There were 30 occupations in late 1997; some withdrew voluntarily to wait to be resettled by government, and some were evicted.[21] Then there were two higher-profile occupations of white farms in Svosve, Marondera district, Mashonaland East, in June 1998, and Chikwaka, Goromonzi district, also Mashonaland East, in November 1998. Ex-combatant Zvakanyorwa Wilbert Sadomba recorded the detailed preparations, which stretched over several months.[22] The government strongly opposed the occupations, sending state and Zanu-PF vice president Simon Muzenda to Svosve to try to persuade the occupiers to leave. At Goromonzi, police were sent to evict the occupiers, burn their temporary shelters, and arrest the leaders of the war veterans. But the occupation spread to other farms in Goromonzi, and the veterans used their guerrilla war experiences to set up organizational structures to coordinate the growing number of peasant occupiers. The Utete Committee (set up in 2003; see chapter 6) looked back and found that there were "similar and widespread occupations of white commercial farms" in 1998, although in many cases, "villagers reluctantly complied with the Government's order for withdrawal from the occupied farms. The first salvo by a land of hungry and increasingly restless peasantry had however been fired."[23]

Land policy was increasingly confused with inconsistent policies and actions and no single ministry in charge.[24] Parallel attempts to take white land and protect it and ill-defined positions on squatters left both white farmers and landless Zimbabweans to find their own way. Selby comments that "the state did not have a clear or consistent policy on squatters and the nature of the issue was determined more significantly by individual politicians in particular areas and the nature of squatter committees."[25]

Both government and Zanu-PF were divided in two directions. One division dating back to independence was still present: should there continue to be a significant number of large, mechanized white and black farms growing export crops, or should more big farms be broken up for smallholders? The other split involved the land-reform process itself—to move forward with a radical land reform or to try to gain international support for something more gradual.

In 1997, there was more anti-white farmer rhetoric from Zanu-PF hard-liners and the government designated 1,471 farms for possible compulsory acquisition, using the 1992 Land Acquisition Act for the first time. But that was matched by another group whose members still hoped to gain donor support for resettlement, and under their influence in June 1998 the government proposed the Land-Reform and Resettlement Programme–Phase II, which was very similar to the 1980s first resettlement. It called for acquiring 5 mn ha for 91,000 families and explicitly argued that taking 5 mn ha for resettlement would not prejudice the strategic role of the large-scale commercial farming sector. Beneficiaries were to include the landless poor and overcrowded families and youths as well as graduates from agricultural colleges and others with experience in agriculture, who were to be selected in a gender-sensitive manner.[26] The plan was presented to an international donors conference in Harare on September 9–11, 1998, and donors were actually taken to see the occupation at Svosve.[27]

Many in the British government had always been hostile to land reform. At Lancaster House the United Kingdom promised £44 mn (then about $90 mn) for land reform, but it spent only £17 mn.[28] Nevertheless, some in Zimbabwe hoped that the new government of Tony Blair, who took office on May 2, 1997, would be different. But hopes were dashed when, on November 5, 1997, Claire Short, Secretary of State for International Development, wrote a letter to Agriculture Minister Kumbirai Kangai saying, "A programme of rapid land acquisition as you now seem to envisage would be impossible for us to support." She continued: "I should make it clear that we do not accept that Britain has a special responsibility to meet the costs of land purchase in Zimbabwe. We are a new Government from diverse backgrounds without links to former colonial interests. My own origins are Irish and as you know we were colonised not colonisers."[29]

The letter shocked some in Zimbabwe, who saw it as arrogant and a refusal to accept any responsibility as a colonial power. And the hostility continued through the donors conference. Donors agreed that land reform was needed but refused to provide any money. The Zimbabwe government said Britain's "dilatory tactics effectively killed" the plan tabled at the conference.[30]

The seriousness of the problem was obvious. In an academic article in 1999, Bill Kinsey warned, "Those in Zimbabwe most adversely affected by the state's failure to achieve redistribution appear to be increasingly unwilling to sit contentedly and listen, before each election, to phrase-mongers who promise resettlement and then fail to deliver. Civil discontent is on the rise."[31]

In 1999 there was a convention to draft a constitution to replace the one from Lancaster House. The initial draft agreed upon by the convention said that government would provide compensation for land taken for resettlement. War veterans objected, and under their pressure, the section was reversed to read, "the people of Zimbabwe must be enabled to reassert their rights and regain ownership of their land," and any compensation for the land itself should be paid by the former colonial power.[32] Compensation would be paid, however, for improvements.

The opposition Movement for Democratic Change (MDC) was created in 1999 and former ZCTU head Morgan Tsvangirai was elected its president in January 2000. MDC campaigned against the new constitution because it would have increased the powers of an executive president and permitted President Mugabe to seek two additional terms in office. The MDC immediately won support from white farmers who opposed the new land clause in the proposed constitution. Angus Selby comments that "publicity stunts of white farmers handing cheques to the MDC were symbolic gestures of rejection of the ruling party," which proved to be unwise.[33] At the February 12–13, 2000, referendum, the new constitution was defeated, 54% to 46% on a low 26% turnout.

This created a new triangle, with the MDC and the veterans opposed to Zanu-PF, but opposed to each other as well. There was a parliamentary election June 24–25, 2000, and land was a key issue, with white farmers backing the MDC in the hope of reversing land reform. European Union (EU) and other observers accused Zanu-PF of intimidation and violence.[34] Zanu-PF won 47% of the vote and 62 seats, while MDC won 46% of the vote and 57 seats. MDC support was strongest in the urban areas of Harare, Bulawayo, and Matebeleland, while Zanu-PF dominated the countryside.

Jambanja

For the war veterans and the landless, the loss at the donors conference and the defeat of the constitution seemed to imply that there would be no land reform. Mandivamba Rukuni notes that "the land reform programme commenced on the back of a restive peasantry which frequently contested the lack of social justice and the problems of inefficiency that underlay the unequal agrarian structure. Liberal land and agricultural policy reforms in the late 1990s failed to address the land question."[35]

So the veterans began to take action resulting in more than 1,000 occupations in March and April 2000. The occupations were known as *jambanja* ("force" or "action in anger" in Shona). This was a complex process—organizing unemployed people from towns and landless people from communal areas, and then structuring occupation of the farms in an orderly way. Reconnaissance teams tried to negotiate with white farmers and also tried, sometimes successfully, to involve farmworkers. There were relatively few war veterans and they were overstretched, so employed veterans came to help on weekends; there was a big push on Easter weekend, April 21–24. On each farm they tried to have a base and a commander who was a veteran. In some cases veterans were able to organize lorries and other transport to bring occupiers. There seems to have been little support from government, even informally, except in departments where veterans were a presence. Food, fuel, and money came mainly from friends and relatives of the occupiers.[36]

At the local level there was sometimes support from Zanu-PF. A 43-year-old divorcee with three children had been staying in Epworth, a high-density suburb of Harare. She lived in one room with her children, because as an informal trader selling fish and candles, she could not

Photo 5.1 An occupier on Tarka Estates, Chimanimani, Manicaland, in 2004. The name *Third Chimurenga* was adopted by some people to say land occupation was the third liberation struggle.

Photo: Allied Timber Holdings

afford to pay for a second room. She was active in the Zanu-PF women's league, and in July 2000 a meeting was called; people in overcrowded housing were encouraged to occupy farms and transport was arranged (from a private operator with the biggest fleet of buses in the country at the time) for those who wanted to participate in the land occupations in Goromonzi. She is one of 67 plotholders in Zanado Farm in Goromonzi and is proud that she now has a place that she calls "home."[37]

But Zanu-PF at the national level was not sympathetic to the occupations. In March and April, acting president Joseph Msika and Home Minister Dumiso Dabengwa sent police to evict occupiers. But the party began to shift. On April 6, 2000, the government inserted into the old, still valid constitution a new article 16A—the land clause that had been included in the rejected constitution. A new Land Acquisition Act was passed on May 23, 2000. On July 15, 2000, the Accelerated Land Reform and Resettlement Programme, the "Fast Track," was approved. But in August, Lands Minister John Nkomo declared that the occupations had to stop. In Chipinge, Manicaland, war veterans led occupations of Makande and Southdowns estates, but they were driven out violently by anti-riot police in late 2000; even war veterans were beaten.[38] Yet on November 6, 2000, when the white Commercial Farmers Union was challenging the occupations in court, Zanu-PF ran full-page newspaper advertisements saying, "This land is your land. Don't let them use the courts and the constitution against the masses."[39] In mid-2001, parliament passed the Rural Land Occupiers Act, which said any occupations after March 1, 2001, were illegal and must stop (while protecting occupiers from before March 1). However, 42% of occupations took place in 2001 and 2002,[40] most after the law was passed.

Francis Gonese, chair of the National Land Board, comments that "in both colonial and post-colonial Zimbabwe, no 'squatter eviction policy' has ever succeeded, given the underlying politics of land resource, and both white farmers and government officials of the 1980s and 1990s had to learn the hard way."

Realizing the scale of the occupation and farmers' unwillingness to move, Zanu-PF was forced to accept. But this was not a Zanu-PF initiative—it was the war veterans in opposition to Zanu-PF. "Targeting Mugabe for 'confiscating' white land was therefore clearly misplaced, because it was not Mugabe, but the War Veterans who did this," notes Sadomba.[41] Moyo comments, "Both Zanu-PF and the state have followed behind the land occupations movement and tried to co-opt and contain it."[42]

Ian Scoones and his colleagues reported on Masvingo province, which they have been studying since 2000. Occupations started in 1999 and accelerated in 2000. Typically war veterans would establish a base camp on a farm, often in secret initially, and then bring in more people who would build shelters and sometimes even begin to farm. The occupation of Wondedzo farm in Masvingo in late 1999 was coordinated by a war veteran and a farmworker; they first established "bases" on the farm, then went "to the communal areas and moved door to door, asking those who wanted land to come and join them. About 30 people came."[43]

Each occupation was different. "In some cases land occupations were led by organised groups of war veterans, with back-up from the state; in others it was groups of villagers from nearby communal lands who occupied the land. On some occasions farm workers were involved in—or even led—the land occupations; in others they were excluded," Scoones and colleagues report. "The role of the war veterans was certainly crucial in the *jambanja* period. For example, on November 29, 2000, Comrade Hunzvi, then chairman of the ZNLWVA, addressed people at the Chief's Hall in Masvingo town and urged them to invade farms." Political responses were often contradictory, reflecting "long running divisions within Zanu-PF" in Masvingo. "The central state increasingly lost authority and control," Scoones and colleagues conclude.[44]

Occupations were also linked to ESAP. Mr. Katsande was born in Chegutu, a small town, and in 1988, he began working for a textile company, David Whitehead. He married and has four children. In 1996, David Whitehead downsized and Katsande was one of many workers sacked. He could not afford to keep his house in town, so he retreated to his grandfather's communal area in Murehwa, Mashonaland East. But the headman said he did not "know" Katsande since he had never visited his ancestral area, so he could not get land. He considered himself destitute, so when *jambanja* started, he was one of the first to occupy Athlone Farm in October 1999, led by a small group of war veterans. Other occupiers had also lost jobs due to structural adjustment.[45]

Nelson Marongwe studied Goromonzi in Mashonaland East, where 16 large-scale commercial farms had been occupied by March 2000. He tells of the occupation and settlement of Dunstan Farm. A war veteran who had stayed in the area for more than 15 years working as a painter teamed up with other veterans to occupy the farm in February 2000. The pioneer occupiers comprised 25 war veterans and 12 others, but the numbers later swelled to 218, most of whom were ferried onto the farm using hired buses from a private operator. Although the white farmer initially offered stiff resistance, he was eventually forced out of the farm. Marongwe notes that in the A1 study sample in Goromonzi, 89% of the beneficiaries had participated in the land occupations.[46]

Summing Up:
Adjustment Provokes Occupation

The worst drought of the century forced Zimbabwe to accept the World Bank's ESAP, with devastating consequences. Poverty increased dramatically and there were huge cuts in health and education and the reintroduction of fees. Up to 60,000 people lost their jobs, and many teachers and doctors left for South Africa and Botswana. Only white farmers exporting flowers and vegetables benefited.

The economic squeeze caused strikes and unrest. An opposition party, the MDC, was formed. Donors rejected a phased land reform and voters rejected a new constitution that included land reform. War veterans challenged Zanu-PF directly and promoted land occupations, which the government opposed.

Perhaps the only thing Robert Mugabe and the British government agree on is a myth, namely that Mugabe was responsible for the land occupations.

Notes

1. Alois Mlambo, *The Economic Structural Adjustment Programme—The Case of Zimbabwe 1990–95* (Harare, Zimbabwe: University of Zimbabwe, 1997), 85 [Mlambo, *Adjustment*].

2. Nazneen Kanji, "Gender, Poverty and Economic Adjustment in Harare, Zimbabwe," *Environment and Urbanization,* 7, no. 1 (1995): 39 [Kanji, "Gender"].

3. Kanji, "Gender," citing *Sunday Mail,* December 19, 2003. Zimbabwe Congress of Trade Unions put the figure at 60,000 (both public and private sectors), while the Confederation of Zimbabwean Industries put it at 45,000.

4. Kanji, "Gender," 42, 48.

5. Mlambo, *Adjustment,* 83–92.

6. Moses Tekere, "Zimbabwe," in Harmon Thomas, *WTO Agreement on Agriculture: The Implementation Experience* (Rome: FAO, 2003) [Tekere, FAO], available at http://www.fao.org/docrep/005/y4632e/y4632e01.htm#bm01 (December 3, 2011).

7. Government of Zimbabwe, *Zimbabwe 2003 Poverty Assessment Study Survey Summary Report* (Harare, Zimbabwe: Ministry of Public Service, Labour and Social Welfare, 2006), 22; Admos Chimhowu, Jeanette Manjengwa, and Sara Feresu (eds.), *Moving Forward in Zimbabwe: Reducing Poverty and Promoting Growth,* 2nd ed. (Harare, Zimbabwe: Institute of Environmental Studies, 2010), 9. The 1995 and 2003 figures refer to the proportion of people under

the total consumption poverty line; the 1991 figure is not directly comparable because of methodological differences, but it is the accepted figure.

8. World Bank Independent Evaluation Group, "Structural Adjustment and Zimbabwe's Poor" (Washington, DC: World Bank, 1995), available at http://lnweb90.worldbank.org/oed/oeddoclib.nsf/DocUNIDViewForJavaSearch/15A937F6B215A053852567F5005D8B06 (October 31, 2011).

9. Tekere, FAO.

10. Benson Zwizwai, Admore Kambudzi, and Bonface Mauwa, "Zimbabwe: Economic Policy-Making and Implementation: A Study of Strategic Trade and Selective Industrial Policies," in *The Politics of Trade and Industrial Policy in Africa,* ed. Charles Soludo, Osita Ogbu, and Ha-Joon Chang (Trenton, NJ: Africa World Press/IDRC, 2004), citing the Central Statistical Office, http://irsm.gc.ca/geh/ev-71257-201-1-DO_TOPIC.html (November 8, 2011).

11. Godfrey Kanyenze, "Economic Structural Adjustment Programme," in Medicine Masiiwa, *Post-independence Land Reform in Zimbabwe* (Harare, Zimbabwe: Friedrich Ebert Stiftung, 2004), 113 [Kanyenze, "Economic Structural"].

12. Kanyenze, "Economic Structural," 99–100.

13. Sam Moyo, *Land Reform Under Structural Adjustment in Zimbabwe* (Uppsala, Sweden: Nordiska Afrikainstitutet, 2000), 91, 192 [Moyo, *Land Reform*].

14. Tekere, FAO citing "Agricultural Sector of Zimbabwe," *Statistical Bulletin,* 2001.

15. Moyo, *Land Reform,* 93.

16. Angus Selby, "Commercial Farmers and the State: Interest Group Politics and Land Reform in Zimbabwe" (PhD thesis, University of Oxford, 2006), 182, 189–196, 334 [Selby, "Commercial"].

17. Zvakanyorwa Wilbert Sadomba, *War Veterans in Zimbabwe's Revolution* (Woodbridge, Suffolk, UK: James Currey, 2011), 121 [Sadomba, *War Veterans*].

18. It is striking how many people who would now be dismissed as "child soldiers" became important in Zimbabwean politics; many Zimbabwean teenagers understood the importance of the liberation war and joined it.

19. "State Farms Given to Government Officials in Zimbabwe," Agence France Presse–English, March 29, 2000. The Dongo list is posted at http://www.zwnews.com/dongolist.xls and an explanation is at http://www.zwnews.com/dongolist.cfm (November 9, 2011).

20. Selby, "Commercial," 335.

21. Sam Moyo, "Land Movements and the Democratisation Process in Zimbabwe," in Medicine Masiiwa, *Post-independence Land Reform in Zimbabwe* (Harare, Zimbabwe: Friedrich Ebert Stiftung, 2004), 204 [Moyo, "Land Movements"].

22. Sadomba, *War Veterans,* 123–35, 155.

23. Charles Utete, *Report of the Presidential Land Review Committee on the Implementation of the Fast Track Land Reform Programme, 2000–2002,* Harare,

2003, 15, available at http://www.sarpn.org/documents/d0000622/P600-Utete_PLRC_00-02.pdf (October 23, 2011).

24. John Blessing Karumbidza, "A Fragile and Unsustained Miracle: Analysing the Development Potential of Zimbabwe's Resettlement Schemes, 1980–2000" (PhD thesis, University of KwaZulu-Natal, 2009), 177; Mandivamba Rukuni, "The Evolution of Agriculture Policy: 1890–1990," in *Zimbabwe's Agricultural Revolution Revisited,* ed. Mandivamba Rukuni, Patrick Tawonezvi, and Carl Eicher, 49 (Harare, Zimbabwe: University of Zimbabwe Publications, 2006) [Rukuni, Tawonezvi, and Eicher].

25. Selby, "Commercial," 168.

26. United Nations Development Programme, "Zimbabwe: Land Reform and Resettlement: Assessment and Suggested Framework for the Future," Interim Mission Report (New York: UNDP, 2002), 6, available at http://www.eisa.org.za/PDF/zimlandreform.pdf (November 9, 2011).

27. Jocelyn Alexander, *The Unsettled Land: State-making & the Politics of Land in Zimbabwe, 1893–2003* (Oxford, UK: James Currey, 2006), 184.

28. The United Kingdom provided £20 mn for land, only £17 mn of which was used because Britain imposed extra conditions. Britain argues that the £27 mn it provided as general budget support between 1980 and 1985 should also be considered support for land reform. Paul Boateng (British High Commissioner in South Africa), "Zim Broke Land Reform Deal," *The Star* (South Africa), June 18, 2007.

29. http://politics.guardian.co.uk/foi/images/0,9069,1015120,00.html (October 23, 2011).

30. "Background to Land Reform in Zimbabwe," Embassy of Zimbabwe in Sweden (and other embassies), n.d., available at http://www.zimembassy.se/land_reform_document.htm (January 2, 2011).

31. Bill Kinsey, "Land Reform, Growth and Equity: Emerging Evidence From Zimbabwe's Resettlement Programme," *Journal of Southern African Studies,* 25, no. 2 (1999): 195.

32. Sadomba, *War Veterans,* 156–59.

33. Selby, "Commercial," 297.

34. European Parliament, "Account of the Mission to Observe the Parliamentary Elections in Zimbabwe 24–25 June 2000," July 6, 2000, 9, available at http://www.europarl.europa.eu/intcoop/election_observation/missions/20000624_zimbabwe_en.pdf (November 9, 2011).

35. Mandivamba Rukuni, "Revisiting Zimbabwe's Agricultural Revolution," in Rukuni, Tawonezvi, and Eicher, 13.

36. Sadomba, *War Veterans,* 170–81.

37. Nelson Marongwe, "Interrogating Zimbabwe's Fast Track Land Reform and Resettlement Programme: A Focus on Beneficiary Selection" (PhD thesis, Institute for Poverty, Land and Agrarian Studies [PLAAS], University of the Western Cape, 2008), 213–15 [Marongwe, "Interrogating"].

38. Phillan Zamchiya, "A Synopsis of Land and Agrarian Change in Chipinge District, Zimbabwe," *Journal of Peasant Studies,* 38, no. 5 (2011): 1063.

39. "Zimbabwe Farmers Launch Challenge," BBC, November 6, 2000, available at http://news.bbc.co.uk/1/hi/world/africa/1009463.stm (December 28, 2011).

40. Sam Moyo et al., *Fast Track Land Reform Baseline Survey in Zimbabwe* (Harare, Zimbabwe: African Institute for Agrarian Studies, 2009), 20.

41. Sadomba, *War Veterans,* 161.

42. Moyo, "Land Movements," 207.

43. Ian Scoones et al., *Zimbabwe's Land Reform* (Woodbridge, Suffolk, UK: James Currey, 2010), 45–47.

44 Ibid., 43, 45.

45. Shingirai Mandizadza, "The Fast Track Land Reform Programme and Livelihoods in Zimbabwe: A Case Study of Households at Athlone Farm in Murehwa District," Livelihoods After Land Reform in Zimbabwe, Working Paper 2 (Cape Town, South Africa: Institute for Poverty for Land and Agrarian Studies [PLAAS], University of the Western Cape, 2010), available at http://www.larl.org.za.

46. Marongwe, "Interrogating," 211, 213.

6

The Second Land Reform

CONTINUING LAND OCCUPATIONS; A SERIES OF LAWS, AMENDMENTS, AND REGULATIONS; and a constitutional amendment in 2000 created the "fast track" land reform, but it happened so quickly that politicians and government officials struggled to keep up. Many occupiers farmed in the 2000/1 season even if land was not allocated until the next year. When teams were sent to mark out plots, some occupiers had to move to new plots. Nevertheless, by 2003, nearly 135,000 families had been given land, and by 2010 the number was up to nearly 169,000. In just three years, the bulk of Zimbabwean farmland that had been in the hands of white farmers passed to black smallholders, finally redressing a century of colonial domination. Taking into account the 1980s land reform, 245,000 families (more than 1.5 million Zimbabweans) were living on their own farms.

Fast track continued the division between big commercial farms and smallholdings, which has characterized Zimbabwean agriculture since the colonial era, with two models, A1 and A2. As a World Bank report commented, "One of the objectives of the Fast Track was to enable local indigenous people to exercise control of the large-scale commercial farming sector. It targeted not only poor people, but wealthy people willing to venture into commercial farming."[1]

A1 is the smallholder model for previously landless people, with a typical white farm being divided into 40–45 A1 farms (see Table 6.1). This allows 6 ha of good farmland (more in poorer areas) and usually some communal grazing land, which is important since most farmers use cattle for plowing. This is similar to the 1980s resettlement model A. Settler selection and placement for A1 was the responsibility of the

Table 6.1 Size of Farms Before and After Resettlement, 2003

	White farms			Resettled farms		
	no.	ha	avg. size (ha)	no.	avg. size (ha)	no. per white farm
A1						
Manicaland	246	195,644	795	11,019	18	45
Mash. East	382	302,511	792	16,702	18	44
Mash. West	670	792,513	1,183	27,052	29	40
Mash. Central	353	513,195	1,454	14,756	35	42
Midlands	306	513,672	1,679	16,169	32	53
Mat. North	258	543,793	2,108	9,901	55	38
Mat. South	226	683,140	3,023	8,923	77	39
Masvingo	211	686,612	3,254	22,670	30	107
A2						
Manicaland	138	77,533	562	463	167	3
Mash. East	319	250,030	784	1,646	152	5
Mash. West	568	369,995	651	2,003	185	4
Mash. Central	241	230,874	958	1,684	137	7
Midlands	106	181,966	1,717	229	795	2
Mat. North	65	142,519	2,193	191	746	3
Mat. South	65	191,697	2,949	271	707	4
Masvingo	170	753,300	4,431	773	975	5

Note: Mat. = Matebeleland; Mash. = Mashonaland; avg. = average; no. = number.
Source: Data from Utete Report, 24.

Provincial and District Land Identification Committees. Plots tended to be pegged out by extension officers. Roughly half of settlers were *jambanja* occupiers, and the rest came through formal and informal application processes. The Utete Committee reported that in 2003, 97% of A1 farmers given land had taken up their plots.[2] Government did try to help the new A1 farmers, but Utete found that A1 farmers "required inputs such as seed, fertilizer and tillage services and that during the last cropping season [2002/3], inputs had been given in a haphazard manner and in inadequate quantities." Also, "budgetary allocations for the Programme remained woefully inadequate."[3]

The A2 model sought to create larger black commercial farms and was based on splitting a white farm into three to seven A2 farms. Applications had to be submitted to the Ministry of Lands, Agriculture and Rural Resettlement and required recommendations by the Provincial and District Land Identification Committees. The Ministry placed advertisements in the main national newspapers inviting people to apply, and application forms required a business plan setting out cash flow and budgets as well as specifying the applicant's income, property, experience, qualifications, and training. Applicants were required to have their own resources for farming without government support. Special consideration was given to war veterans, war collaborators, ex-detainees, and women.

Former academic Dr. Charles Utete was chief secretary to the President and cabinet, and when he retired in April 2003, he was appointed to head the Presidential Land Review Committee on the Implementation of the Fast Track Land Reform Programme, the first detailed report on fast track land reform.[4] Often billed as a close advisor to Robert Mugabe,[5] he is subject to international sanctions[6] and is on the Dongo list for having been leased a 3,350-ha farm in Lomagundi, Mashonaland West, by the government on October 1, 1991. Despite, or perhaps because of, his political status, his report was detailed and set out unflinchingly some of the problems of the fast track. In particular, he was outspoken about disorganization and bureaucratic and political infighting, which seemed to have played a big role for A2 farms.[7] The Integrated Regional Information Network (IRIN) commented that the report "lauded the goal of the government's fast-track programme, but said agrarian reform was tarnished by bureaucratic bungling and irregularities."[8]

Half of A1 and A2 farms were formally assigned in 2000 and 2001, a quarter in 2002, and then smaller numbers through 2006. Most A1 and A2 farmers started farming in the year the land was allocated, and nearly all had started by the year after allocation.[9]

Five surveys give us a good picture of land-reform farms and farmers and paint a relatively similar picture. Three were national:

- The Utete Committee in 2003.
- A set of *A2 Land Audit Reports* for each province done for the Ministry of Lands, Land Reform and Resettlement in 2006,[10] which surveyed 10,513 farms, representing 79% of the allocated A2 farms.
- The *Baseline Survey* by Sam Moyo and his team at the African Institute for Agrarian Studies, who interviewed 2,089 resettlement households (1,651 A1 and 438 A2) in early 2006 in six districts, one in each of six provinces.[11] This is still the most widely cited survey. (The Moyo team also interviewed 760 farmworkers; see chapter 12.)

In addition, two surveys cover specific geographic areas:

- The Masvingo survey was done by a team involving Ian Scoones of the Institute of Development Studies, Sussex; Nelson Marongwe in Harare; Crispen Sukume, formerly of the Department of Agricultural Economics, University of Zimbabwe; and Blasio Mavedzenge of Agritex, Masvingo, and is published as *Zimbabwe's Land Reform: Myths & Realities.*[12] The team has been studying 400 fast track farmers in Masvingo province since 2000; although this is only one province, it still gives an excellent picture of resettlement farmers.
- A 2004 survey conducted by a team headed by Prosper Matondi, which looked closely at Mazowe district, Mashonaland Central, and compiled data from 19 former white farms divided into A1 plots and 13 divided into A2 farms.[13]

Take-Up and Use Rates

These surveys allow us to draw a picture of how rapidly the new farmers took up their land, and how much is being used.

The Utete Committee found that 2,652 farms with 4.2 mn ha had been allocated to 127,192 households under the A1 resettlement model as of July 31, 2003. The take-up rate by beneficiaries was a very high 97%.[14] By 2010, the total was 145,800 beneficiaries with 5.8 mn ha (see Table 1.1).

Although the A1 resettlement went relatively smoothly, the A2 model was more complex and moved more slowly. In part this reflected the serious drought in 2001/2 (Figure 4.1) that hit new farmers just as they were occupying their land,[15] and that seemed to have had more impact on capital-intensive A2 farms. Raising the required investment capital, even if it only required mortgaging a house, caused delays. And there were political problems, discussed in more detail in chapter 9. For A2, Utete found that 1,672 former white farms with 2.2 mn ha had been allocated to 7,260 applicant beneficiaries, with an average take-up rate of 66% nationally. "This failure by some 34% of applicants to take up their allocations implied a considerable amount of land lying fallow or unused while, ironically, thousands of would-be A2 beneficiaries were pressurising the authorities to be allocated land," the Utete Committee said.[16]

By 2006, the number of beneficiaries was up to 15,607. The *A2 Land Audit* showed only 7% of A2 plots were vacant because they had not been taken up, but another 15% were vacant and not yet allocated.[17] By 2010,

A2 land had increased to 3.5 mn ha and the number of A2 farmers had jumped to 22,917. (This includes 217 with large plots, totaling 509,000 ha, who should really be treated as black, large-scale commercial farmers; see Table 1.1.)

Both the *Baseline Survey* and the *A2 Land Audit* looked at land use in 2006. The *Baseline Survey* (Table 6.2) shows that a quarter of new farmers were already using nearly all of their arable land. More than half of A1 farmers and 43% of A2 farmers were using more than 40% of their arable land. As white farmers had been using only between 15% and 34% of their land,[18] this suggests that the new farmers had very quickly begun to use more of their land than their predecessors. The *Baseline Survey* also found 14% of A1 farmers and 28% of A2 farmers using irrigation. But one-fifth of all farmers were not using their land.[19] The *A2 Land Audit* found 55% of new A2 farmers productive or highly productive, 37% under-using their land, and 7% not using it at all (see chapter 9).

Who Received Land?

The way the questions were asked, and the extent to which people had to choose a single attribute for themselves, varied between surveys. Tables 6.3–6.6 give a variety of descriptions of land-reform beneficiaries. What is striking is that the various surveys give quite similar results.

For smallholders, Tables 6.3 and 6.5, giving the origins of resettlement farmers from the *Baseline Survey* and the Masvingo study, both show most A1 farmers came from the communal areas; both surveys also find that 1% came from 1980s resettlement or purchase farms. Both also show a significant group of urban poor. Tables 6.4 and 6.5 also show a

Table 6.2 Arable Land Use in 2006

Land use rate	A1	A2
0	21%	18%
1%–20%	11%	22%
21%–40%	15%	17%
41%–60%	14%	13%
61%–80%	12%	8%
81%–100%	27%	22%

Source: Moyo et al., *Baseline Survey,* Table 4.5.

Table 6.3 Origin of Land Recipients, Baseline Survey

	A1	A2
Communal land	66%	53%
White farm	9%	4%
Urban	20%	35%
Employed elsewhere	3%	8%
Other	2%	1%

Source: Moyo et al., *Baseline Survey,* Table 2.6.

Table 6.4 Previous Employment, Baseline Survey

	A1	A2
Not employed & farmers	40%	36%
Employed		
Private		
Skilled, managerial	3%	5%
Semi-skilled	14%	7%
Unskilled	7%	5%
Civil service		
Skilled, managerial	2%	3%
Semi-skilled	2%	5%
Unskilled	1%	1%
Army, police	11%	9%
Other	19%	29%
Number of farms	1,651	438

Source: Moyo et al., *Baseline Survey,* Table 2.11.

significant group of new smallholders from the military and civil service. The Masvingo sample of A1 farms, where the recipients were identified from lists, found that 66% were "ordinary"[20] (Table 6.5).

The *Baseline Survey,* the *A2 Land Audit,* and the Masvingo study asked questions about A2 farms in different ways, making it hard to summarize the results together, although it is clear that many A2 farmers are "ordinary" people. A large share of A2 farmers came from urban areas, reflecting the need to mobilize finances. The *Baseline Survey* found that while 77% of A1 farmers lived on the farm and only 17% still lived in urban areas, only 60% of A2 farmers lived on their farms and 34% lived

Table 6.5 Settler Profile of Masvingo Sample

	A1	A2
"Ordinary" from rural areas	54%	12%
"Ordinary" from urban areas	12%	44%
Civil servant	17%	26%
Security services	4%	2%
Business people	5%	10%
Former farm workers	8%	5%
Number of farms	266	57
Of whom, war veterans	9%	9%

Note: Security services includes army, police, and Central Intelligence Organisation.
Source: Scoones et al., *Land Reform,* Tables 2.6 and 2.7.

in urban areas. The *Baseline Survey* also found that 45% of A2 farmers retained other jobs (17% working for the government)—underlining the need to continue to raise money to develop A2 farms.

The surveys also provided a range of other information. The *A2 Land Audit* showed that education levels were quite high: 17% of A2 farmers had formal agricultural training and another 13% had university degrees.[21]

Initially, there was some instability. The *Baseline Survey* found that 14% of A1 farmers and 11% of A2 farmers had been threatened with eviction, and 5% of A1 farmers and 4% of A2 farmers actually were evicted—mostly by local or national government, but also by soldiers and war veterans. Of the locations surveyed, the biggest problems were in Goromonzi, which is close to Harare and where there was intense competition for land.[22] However, Prosper Matondi in a survey of Mazowe district found much lower levels—only 3% of A1 farmers and 1% of A2 farmers had been threatened with eviction.[23]

Elites and Cronies?

One of the frequent complaints about the land-reform program is that large amounts of land (often cited as 40%) have gone to "Mugabe's cronies." Table 1.1 shows that 13.5 mn ha of former white land have been transferred to black farmers since independence. Of that, 9.5 mn ha (71%) went to smallholders—1980s resettlement and A1 farmers. Another 3 mn ha (22%) went to small A2 farmers, and 1 mn ha (7%) to large A2 farmers and black, large-scale commercial farmers.[24]

Since independence, Zimbabwe has followed the colonial dual agricultural strategy of big, commercial farms and smallholders. Although A2 farms are smaller than the old white farms, they are still large and capital-intensive, and applicants had to prove they had money to invest. Many of the holders on the black, large-scale commercial farms bought their farms. By definition, this is an elite; these are relatively well-off or even wealthy people. One cannot support continuation of large-scale commercial farming, as most of the international community does, and then object that the farms are in the hands of an elite.

Just as in the colonial era the white regime gave land as rewards to its supporters, the independence government has done the same thing. Indeed, politics in most countries (including Europe and the United States) has a certain amount of patronage, rewarding key supporters of winning political parties.

With both A2 and whole farms, being in Zanu-PF or having friends among the right people must have helped. But does this make all 23,000 A2 and large-scale farmers "Mugabe cronies"? We are not willing to dismiss such a large group of people so easily, even though some people at the top have multiple farms that are among the largest and best. If we are to object to big farms being held by an elite, it means objecting to the whole system of having A2 and large-scale farms, because only an elite can afford the investment. Similarly, applicants for A2 farms had to show they had money to invest, so it is not surprising that most A2 farmers have urban links (see Tables 6.3 and 6.5). Blasio Mavedzenge, a member of Ian Scoones's research team and an agricultural extension officer, is also an A1 farmer and says, "I am a government worker, but I am not a crony, and I think that applies to many people."[25]

In this context, "cronies" could be described as people who received large or multiple farms mainly because of their close links to Zanu-PF or the government, and who would not have qualified otherwise. Unquestionably, some "cronies" have received land—and some of the best land, and they often received tractors and other support not available to ordinary land-reform farmers. Table 6.6 shows that 130 A2 farms, about 1.2% of all A2 farms surveyed, went to people in the office of the President and cabinet, and another 38 farms went to ministers. And according to the Dongo list,[26] among large farms that have been leased to individual farmers by the state, there is quite a sprinkling of generals, ministers, judges, and others with obvious political or military links. And several hundred people have multiple farms, or farms that are larger than

Table 6.6 Settler Profile, *A2 Land Audit Reports,* 2006

Background of A2 settler	% of settlers	Number of farms	Detail of government settlers %	Detail of government settlers Number
"Ordinary"	37	3,936		
War veterans	17	1,974		
Businesspeople	9	916		
Government	27	2,862		
of which				
Civil service			17	1,822
Security services			7	787
Office of the President & Cabinet			1.2	130
Ministers			0.4	38
Other politicians			0.8	85
Traditional leaders	0.5	48		
Other & unspecified	7	777		
Total farms		10,513		

Note: War veterans includes detainees, collaborators, etc.; government includes retired people in those sectors; other politicians includes MPs and provincial and local politicians; and traditional leaders includes chiefs, spirit mediums, and pastors. Beneficiaries chose their own designations and had to choose one, even though they might have been both a war veteran and a civil servant and businessperson.

Source: A2 Land Audit Reports.

the maximum sizes set in 2001[27] (see Tables 9.1 and 9.2). There are no precise figures, in part because the "comprehensive, transparent and non-partisan land audit . . . for the purpose of establishing accountability and eliminating multiple farm ownerships" called for in the Global Political Agreement (GPA) (¶5.9) has not been carried out.

It is important to remember that self-funded, large-scale farming ensures that all big farmers are in the elite. But not all are "cronies." For example, on the Dongo list, there are also significant numbers of agronomists and professional farmers as well as engineers, doctors, and other professionals. We estimate that less than 5% of new farmers with under 10% of the land are "cronies."

In chapters 7 and 9, we ask the other question: Are these elite farms being used productively?

Sanctions

Responding to the Fast Track Land Reform (FTLR) and the violence around the 2000 elections, the United States, European Union (EU), and Australia imposed sanctions on Zimbabwe in 2002 and 2003 and modified them in subsequent years. By 2011, EU sanctions included an asset freeze and travel ban on 163 people (covering entry or transit) and 31 firms linked to the Zanu-PF and government leadership. EU sanctions specify that "no funds or economic resources shall be made available directly or indirectly to, or for the benefit of" persons or companies on the list.[28]

The US sanction is stricter than the EU sanction; it "prohibits US persons, wherever located, or anyone in the United States from engaging in any transactions with any" person on this list, or "entities they control," or "immediate family members," or anyone "acting on behalf of a sanctions target."[29] This covers 118 individuals and 11 companies, including several major banks—Agribank, Infrastructural Development Bank, and ZB Bank, apparently because the state owns shares in them. Also on the list is a major parastatal company, Zimbabwe Iron & Steel Company (Zisco). WikiLeaks revealed that Finance Minister Tendai Biti sought the removal of the three banks from the US sanctions list arguing that this would aid the country's economic reforms. This was backed by US ambassador Charles Ray in December 2009[30] but rejected by the US government. The inclusion of banks has a very wide effect, because it makes it difficult for US citizens and companies to do business with Zimbabwe. For example, Zimbabwe is one of the few countries not served by PayPal, an online payment system,[31] and the US Treasury reportedly has told PayPal not to deal with Zimbabwe.[32]

Finally, neither the EU[33] nor the United States will allow aid to be used for land-reform farmers. And the United States and United Kingdom blocked any World Bank or IMF assistance to Zimbabwe.

One thing that is striking is how much more serious the United States is about sanctions against Zimbabwe, compared with its sanctions against white-ruled Rhodesia (see chapter 3).

The Harare-based Trade and Development Studies Centre (TRADES Centre) in 2010 compared the response of Rhodesian and Zimbabwe governments to sanctions.[34] Rhodesia took tight control of foreign exchange and restricted imports, especially of anything that could be produced locally; import substitution industrialization was encouraged (drawing in part on domestic savings that could not be sent abroad);

and money supply was tightly controlled to prevent inflation. Zimbabwe did just the opposite: with no import controls, imports increased; there was no support for domestic industrialization and deindustrialization, which started under ESAP, continued; and "money printing was the order of the day resulting in the country plunging into a hyper inflation mode which destabilized every other sector of the economy." The report hints that the Zimbabwe government may have been trying to fight on too many fronts at once: where the Rhodesian government gained support from the business community, the Zimbabwe government was "fighting [the] private sector. The private sector was viewed as an arm of the opposition."

Hyperinflation and Divisive Politics

Land reform did not start at the most auspicious time. Two years of drought hit the new farmers. The Zimbabwe dollar, which had been Z$19 to the US$1 in 1997, had fallen to Z$55 to the US$1 by 2000. It reached Z$1,000 to US$1 in mid-2002. Gideon Gono was named governor of the Reserve Bank in November 2003, and his policy was to expand the economy by printing money and subsidizing local production and key goods, while using administrative means to try to control inflation and speculation. This heterodox policy failed and led instead to corruption and hyperinflation. By January 2006, the exchange rate was Z$100,000 to US$1, and by mid-2007, the parallel (unofficial) rate was Z$100,000,000 to US$1. By mid-2008, the parallel rate for the US dollar was equivalent to the Z$ with 13 zeros and prices were doubling daily; by the end of 2008, it was 22 zeros (see Table 6.7).

This was one of the worst cases of hyperinflation ever[35] and caused chaos for everyone, including farmers. Corruption became more serious as members of the elite could exchange money at meaningless official rates, and thus build mansions for a few thousand dollars; by mid-2007, the parallel exchange rate was 1,000 times the official rate. Sporadic government interventions in agricultural input and output, transport, interest rates, and the foreign exchange markets only exacerbated the crisis. Controlled prices of inputs (seeds, fertilizer, fuel) and services such as tillage provision at levels far too low to cover costs of production or repairs (in the case of machinery) led to shortages and low production because suppliers could not cover their costs. At the same time, a parallel high-priced market emerged. National fertilizer production fell from 505,000

Table 6.7 Exchange Rates of Zimbabwe Dollar to US Dollar,
          Selected Dates

	Official rate	Parallel rate
1980	0.68	
1983	0.96	
1984	1.50	
1990	2.64	
1991	5.05	
1994	6.82	
1997	10.50	
1999	36.23	
Jan. 2001	55	70
Jan. 2003	55	1,400
July 2003	824	3,000
Jan. 2004	4,196	5,000
Jan. 2005	5,730	6,400
July 2005	17,600	25,000
Jan. 2006	99,202	150,000
Aug. 2006	250,000	550,000
Jan. 2007	250,000	6,000,000
July 2007	250,000	300,000,000
Jan. 2008	30,000,000	6,000,000,000
May 6, 2008	187,073,020,880	200,000,000,000
June 30, 2008	11,378,472,550,240	40,928,000,000,000
Sept. 30, 2008	1,322,500,000,000,000	10,000,000,000,000,000
Oct. 29, 2008	6,195,200,000,000,000	900,000,000,000,000,000
Nov. 24, 2008	441,825,000,000,000,000	12,000,000,000,000,000,000,000

Note: This is the rate for the original Zimbabwe dollar; new currencies with fewer zeros were issued on August 1, 2006; August 1, 2008; and February 2, 2009.

tonnes in 1999 to 166,000 tonnes in 2007.[36] Government intervention in the transport sector, both road and rail, also did not work.[37] Hyper-inflation brought sudden benefits for some people—for example, when diesel or fertilizer had to be sold at an official price and cost pennies in real terms, those who could gain access (which sometimes included ordinary farmers) could use the input or swap it for something else. Farmers moved to informal marketing and barter for both sales and inputs and increasingly depended on relatives sending money from abroad. Shingi-rai Mandizadza, who was staying on Athlone Farm in Mashonaland East doing interviews in 2008, reports traders passing through selling clothing and household goods such as soap; a skirt cost three buckets of maize. Cattle were also being traded for inputs and equipment.[38]

Government attempts to use force to halt inflation hit land-reform farmers. Breakup of white farms and changed settlement patterns caused a radical change in trading patterns, with many new small traders mar-keting beef and other goods, and with the opening of informal markets closer to where people were living on resettlement farms. In 2005, gov-ernment launched Operation Murambatsvina to try to eliminate the huge informal trading sector that had grown up under liberalization. The new unregistered markets serving resettlement farmers were destroyed. "In many urban areas, this campaign was directed against opposition sup-porters, and became highly politicised, displacing many people. But in the new resettlements, this was not the case, with Zanu-PF supporters and war veterans suffering as much as others," notes Ian Scoones and his team, reporting that even an appeal by a war veteran leader of an oc-cupation was unsuccessful in protecting a local market.[39] It was only in 2009, with dollarization, that the local markets were restored.

Similarly, in colonial times and in the first years of independence, the beef trade had been tightly controlled by the government and the Cold Storage Commission (CSC).[40] But with ESAP and land reform, a new large network of small traders began to dominate the cattle trade. In 2007, the government announced price controls on beef, closed pri-vate abattoirs, and required that all meat be marketed through the CSC. Youth brigades of the National Youth Service, known as "green bomb-ers," after the color of their uniforms, supported by the security services, "went from butcher to butcher, shop to shop, checking on prices and arbitrarily fining or arresting those who contravened the regulations. Of course with real prices increasing at an exponential rate due to inflation the price controls were meaningless before they were published, and no-one could afford to sell beef through regular channels. The black market increased further. . . . The price control policy quickly descended into chaos, with the security services closing businesses, extracting bribes and imposing fines, while the beef market moved underground," reported Blasio Mavedzenge and a research team in Masvingo.[41]

It is estimated that by 2007, 2 million people had left Zimbabwe, half of them for South Africa—continuing a migration that had started under structural adjustment. They were sending back an estimated $500 million per year. But UNDP noted that "the impact of the brain drain on public service delivery has been devastating. For example, in the case of health care, it is estimated that more than 80% of the doctors, nurses, pharmacists, radiologists and therapists who trained since 1980 have left."[42]

Our interviews in 2011 showed two surprising responses. First, the recovery with dollarization was so rapid that people did not much mention the hyperinflationary period and were looking forward. Second, when asked, farmers were not so negative about hyperinflation. They did receive some supplies from the government, for example, in 2005/6, one-third of A1 farmers obtained some seed from the government.[43] Negative real interest rates meant that loans were repaid at a fraction of their real cost, and inputs, when available, were almost free. Under dollarization, they complained, loans had to be repaid, and inputs were always available but too expensive. Nevertheless, farmers are voting with their hands and producing and selling more under dollarization.

Political Crisis

On the political front, in 2005, the opposition split into two factions, MDC-T under Morgan Tsvangirai and MDC-M under Arthur Mutambara.

At the end of March 2007, the Extraordinary Summit of Southern African Development Community (SADC) Heads of State and Government in Tanzania mandated that South African president Thabo Mbeki facilitate negotiations aimed at resolving the governance crisis in Zimbabwe. There had been some political violence in 2007 and early 2008, reported EISA, the Johannesburg-based Electoral Institute for Sustainable Democracy in Africa, pointing to "attacks on supporters, members and leaders of the MDC in particular. There also were instances of MDC attacks on Zanu-PF, but these were far fewer than the other way around." Talks stalled in late 2007 and presidential and parliamentary elections were held on March 29, 2008. EISA "noted the peaceful environment that prevailed" around the election period itself. "The general short-term pre-election conditions of peace, calm and conditions that were conducive to the expression of political preference were better than in preceding elections."[44]

Results were delayed until May 2. The Zimbabwe Election Commission said Tsvangirai had won 48% and Mugabe 43%, and a second round would be held on June 27, 2008. For the House of Assembly (parliament), MDC (the original MDC headed by Morgan Tsvangirai, sometimes referred to as MDC-T) won 100 seats, Zanu-PF 99 seats, MDC-M (the breakaway group initially headed by Arthur Mutambara) 10 seats, and there was one independent. Senate results were Zanu-PF 30 seats, MDC 24, and MDC-M 6.

The mood changed after the inconclusive elections. Key Zanu-PF officials started accusing the opposition of being "traitors," "sellouts," "witches," and "prostitutes." Just before the first election, Zimbabwe Defence Forces Commander Constantine Chiwenga had said, "The army will not support or salute sellouts and agents of the West before, during and after the presidential elections. We will not support anyone other than President Mugabe."[45] Mugabe himself said he would never allow "the land that we fought for to be taken by the MDC and given to the whites."[46] Later he noted, "Soon after the March elections war veterans approached me and said that they would take up arms if Tsvangirai won the elections in order to protect their farms and nation's sovereignty. . . . A ballpoint pen [used to mark a ballot paper] cannot argue with a bazooka. The veterans will not allow it."[47]

The observer mission of the Pan-African Parliament (part of the African Union [AU]) found that "political tolerance in Zimbabwe has deteriorated to the lowest ebb in recent history. . . . The prevailing political environment throughout the country was tense, hostile and volatile as it has been characterised by an electoral campaign marred by high levels of intimidation, violence, displacement of people, abductions, and loss of life. . . . Houses burnt down, people assaulted and sustained serious injuries. Violence disrupted normal life of ordinary Zimbabweans and led to internal displacement of people. . . . A number of cases of abduction, some of which resulted in deaths, were reported." The observers' report continued: "The Mission was able to attend star rallies organised by the Presidential candidate of Zanu-PF. However, it noted with grave concern that the MDC Presidential candidate was not accorded the opportunity to hold rallies. The Mission was disturbed by the numerous arrests that the MDC Presidential candidate was subjected to."[48]

Tsvangirai withdrew from the second round on June 22, citing violence against his party's supporters. On June 22, then–UN Secretary-General Ban Ki-moon issued a statement saying he "deeply regrets that, despite the repeated appeals of the international community, the Government of Zimbabwe has failed to put in place the conditions necessary for free and fair run-off elections. . . . The campaign of violence and

intimidation that has marred this election has done a great disservice to
the people of the country and must end immediately."[49] The election
went ahead and Mugabe was elected.

In June, a complaint was made to the International Labour Organization, which sent a three-person Commission of Inquiry: Judge Raymond
Ranjeva (Madagascar, chair), Prof. Evance Kalula (Zambia), and Bertrand
Ramcharan (Guyana), a former acting UN High Commissioner for Human Rights. Its report said that "the Commission witnessed a country
in deep crisis" and cited "the scale and duration of the systematic and
systemic violations of trade union and human rights," including "a clear
pattern of arrests, detentions, violence and torture by the security forces."
The report continued: "The Commission is particularly concerned by
the fact that it appears that, in rural areas in particular, ZCTU officials
and members were systematically targeted by vigilante mobs," and about
"the routine use of the police and army against strikes, . . . leading to injuries and deaths." Perhaps most striking was that "the Government of
Zimbabwe accepted that 'things' had happened, that these 'things' were
regrettable, and that it was important to ensure that such 'things' did not
happen again." The Commission rejected the government's explanation
"that the reason that the ZCTU was targeted was due to its involvement
in politics which exceeded its proper trade union role."[50]

The election result was tainted and the economy was in crisis due to
hyperinflation, so negotiations resumed, with AU and SADC support. A
Memorandum of Understanding was signed on July 21, 2008, by Robert
Mugabe (as president of Zanu-PF), Morgan Tsvangirai and Arthur Mu-
tambara (as presidents of "the two Movement for Democratic Change
[MDC] formations"), and South African president Thabo Mbeki (as
SADC facilitator). This led to the September 15, 2008, GPA. On Feb-
ruary 11, 2009, Morgan Tsvangirai was sworn in as prime minister of
Zimbabwe in a new Government of National Unity (GNU).

In December 2008 and January 2009, foreign currencies were legalized and the South African rand (in the south) and the US dollar (in
most of the country) became the normal currencies; soon civil servants
were paid in US dollars, the Z$ was abolished in April 2009, and the
government switched to accounting in US dollars.

A 2011 analysis by the South African–based African Centre for the
Constructive Resolution of Disputes (ACCORD) said that "since the
conclusion of the GPA, there have been visible changes [but] the coalition government is at a critical juncture and it faces multiple challenges
in Zimbabwe's political and economic terrain." It continued: "Although

the GNU has been welcomed by many as the antidote to Zimbabwe's crisis and much has been celebrated about its achievements, the Zimbabwe conflict is still very fluid as conditions shift everyday due to the belligerent nature of the relationship between Zanu-PF and the MDC."[51]

The report cites a number of outstanding issues. "The sanctions debate in Zimbabwe has also become polarised, with ZANU PF on one side accusing the MDC of reneging on its promise to have these restrictive measures removed, and the MDC on the other hand arguing that the removal of such measures is dependent upon visible democratic reforms by ZANU PF. Against this background, regional and international sentiments are fundamentally divided on the issues of sanctions on the ZANU PF leadership as both the AU and SADC have remained resolute in calling for the removal of all forms of sanctions on Zimbabwe while the international community disagrees."

Another issue had to do with the reappointment of Reserve Bank Governor Gideon Gono on November 26, 2008, and the appointment of Johannes Tomana as attorney general on December 18, 2008. MDC said these appointments of people seen as Zanu-PF loyalists violated the GPA, and SADC, at an extraordinary summit on January 27, 2009, agreed that "the appointments of the Reserve Bank Governor and the Attorney General will be dealt with by the inclusive government after its formation."[52] Despite agreeing to this at the summit, President Robert Mugabe declined to reverse the appointments.

Summing Up: Progress Despite Tensions

Under the fast track land reform, 169,000 farmers have received land since 2000. Most are small farmers under model A1, but the fast track also includes model A2 with land for wealthy people prepared to invest in larger-scale commercial farming—maintaining the dual agriculture policy that had continued since the colonial era. The 146,000 A1 farmers moved quickly onto their land and are using more of the land than their white predecessors. A2 farm allocation was more competitive and politicized, while the need for capital slowed the A2 farmers' occupation of their land. The bulk of settlers are "ordinary" people, with 17% of A1 farmers and 18%–27% of A2 farmers coming from the civil service (which includes teachers and agricultural extension officers as well as an elite). Undoubtedly some are political elites or what are sometimes called "cronies," which we guess to be 5% of farmers and 10% of land.

Sanctions have been imposed on Zimbabwean leaders and banks. Most aid agencies will not work with land-reform farmers. Hyperinflation in 2005–8 was the result of printing money and had a devastating effect on the economy. Elections in 2008 were violent, which led to AU- and SADC-sponsored talks, which eventually led to a GPA in 2009 with opposition leader Morgan Tsvangirai becoming prime minister.

In January 2009, the US dollar became the currency, which ended hyperinflation and brought a rapid economic recovery.

Notes

1. Simon Pazvakavambwa and Vincent Hungwe, "Land Redistribution in Zimbabwe," ed. in *Agricultural Land Redistribution: Toward Greater Consensus,* ed. Hans Binswanger-Mkhize, Camille Bourguignon, and Rogerius van den Brink (Washington, DC: World Bank Publications, 2009), 157 [Pazvakavambwa and Hungwe, World Bank].

2. Charles Utete, *Report of the Presidential Land Review Committee on the Implementation of the Fast Track Land Reform Programme, 2000–2002* (Harare, Zimbabwe, 2003), 24 [known as the Report of the Utete Committee, and cited here as Utete Report], available at http://www.sarpn.org/documents/d0000622/P600-Utete_PLRC_00-02.pdf (accessed October 23, 2011).

3. Utete Report, 22, 30.

4. Appointed May 14, 2003, reported October 2003.

5. David Masunda, "Double Blow for Bob," Johannesburg *Mail & Guardian,* April 18, 2003.

6. He was placed on the EU sanctions list specifically as "Chairman of the Presidential Land Review Committee."

7. Utete Report, 21–22, 31.

8. "Zimbabwe: Focus on Utete Committee Report on Agrarian Reform," IRIN, November 6, 2003, available at http://www.irinnews.org/report.aspx?reportid=47101(November 10, 2011).

9. Sam Moyo et al., *Fast Track Land Reform Baseline Survey in Zimbabwe: Trends and Tendencies, 2005/06* (Harare, Zimbabwe: African Institute for Agrarian Studies, 2009), 18, 19, 51 [Moyo et al., *Baseline Survey*].

10. Ministry of Lands, Land Reform and Resettlement & Informatics Institute, *A2 Land Audit Report* (Harare, Zimbabwe, 2006); the report was completed in eight volumes, one for each province, issued at different times during 2006 [*A2 Land Audit Report*].

11. Moyo et al., *Baseline Survey.*

12. Ian Scoones et al., *Zimbabwe's Land Reform: Myths & Realities* (Woodbridge, Suffolk, UK: James Currey, 2010) [Scoones et al., *Land Reform*]. The team studied 400 farmers in four districts: Gutu (Natural Region III with poor

soil and some rain, 73 A1 and 12 A2); Masvingo (NR III/IV with poor sandy soils, 194 A1 and 4 A2); Chiredzi (NR V, dry with heavy soils, but also including sugar estates, 29 A2 and 57 informal); and Mwenezi (NR V, very dry and heavy soils, 24 A1, 26 informal, and 14 A2).

13. Prosper Matondi, "Mazowe District Report—Findings on Land Reform, Volume II" (Harare, Zimbabwe, 2005) [Matondi, "Mazowe"].

14. Utete Report, 5.

15. Mandivamba Rukuni, "Revisiting Zimbabwe's Agricultural Revolution," in *Zimbabwe's Agricultural Revolution Revisited,* ed. Mandivamba Rukuni, Patrick Tawonezvi, and Carl Eicher (Harare, Zimbabwe: University of Zimbabwe Publications, 2006), 14.

16. Utete Report, 5.

17. *A2 Land Audit Report.*

18. See chapter 3.

19. Moyo et al., *Baseline Survey,* 64.

20. Matondi, "Mazowe."

21. Nelson Marongwe, "Interrogating Zimbabwe's Fast Track Land Reform and Resettlement Programme: A Focus on Beneficiary Selection" (PhD thesis, Institute for Poverty, Land and Agrarian Studies [PLAAS], University of the Western Cape, 2008), 154.

22. Moyo et al., *Baseline Survey,* 44–45.

23. Prosper Matondi, "Juggling Land Ownership Rights in Uncertain Times in Fast Track Farms in Mazowe District," 2011.

24. It would appear that the "40%" comes from the fact that A2 land is 38% of the total 9.2 mn ha in the fast track land reform, and then claiming that all A2 land went to "Mugabe cronies."

25. Interviewed by Martin Plaut, "Crossing Continents: Farming Zimbabwe," BBC Radio 4, December 1, 2011, and December 5, 2011, available at http://www.bbc.co.uk/programmes/b017mvx6#synopsis (December 6, 2011).

26. See chapter 5. The Dongo list is posted on http://www.zwnews.com/dongolist.xls, and an explanation is at http://www.zwnews.com/dongolist.cfm (n.d., accessed November 9, 2011).

27. Pazvakavambwa and Hungwe, World Bank, 157, 159.

28. The Council of the European Union, "Council Decision 2011/101/CFSP of 15 February 2011 Concerning Restrictive Measures Against Zimbabwe," *Official Journal of the European Union,* 16 (February 2011).

29. Legislation is on the US Treasury website: http://www.treasury.gov/resource-center/sanctions/Programs/Pages/zimb.aspx, and the list of sanctioned individuals and companies is on the website of the US embassy in Harare, http://harare.usembassy.gov/uploads/GA/r_/GAr_mydP5GsiV8xOy-zfcQ/SDN_List1.pdf (both accessed November 11, 2011).

30. "Biti Sought Sanctions Removal—WikiLeaks," *NewsDay,* September 20, 2011, available at http://www.newsday.co.zw/article/2011-09-20-biti-sought-sanctions-removal-wikileaks (November 11, 2011).

31. PayPal serves 188 countries, but not Zimbabwe; see https://www.paypal.com/uk/cgi-bin/webscr?cmd=_display-country-functionality-outside (November 11, 2011).

32. Walter Nyamukondiwa, "Sanctions: US Blocks Couple's US$30 000 Transfer," *The Herald,* March 9, 2011.

33. "No EU Farm Aid . . . Until Land Audit," *Zimbabwean,* July 30, 2010, available at http://www.thezimbabwean.co.uk/news/33149/no-eu-farm-aid--until-land-audit.html (November 11, 2011).

34. James Hurungo, "An Inquiry Into How Rhodesia Managed to Survive Under Economic Sanctions: Lessons for the Zimbabwe Government" (Harare, Zimbabwe: TRADES Centre, 2011), available at http://www.tradescentre.org.zw/index.php?option=com_docman&task=doc_download&gid=62&Itemid=8 (December 24, 2011).

35. The Hungarian pengo in 1946 had an extra 29 zeros compared to its value a few years earlier. In the more famous hyperinflation of Weimar Germany, the mark added only 14 zeros between 1921 and 1924. Wikipedia has the best table of Zimbabwe dollar exchange rates, http://en.wikipedia.org/wiki/Zimbabwean_dollar#Exchange_rate_history (December 1, 2011).

36. Tendai Murisa, "Farmer Groups, Collective Action and Production Constraints: Cases from A1 Settlements in Goromonzi and Zvimba," Livelihoods After Land Reform in Zimbabwe, Working Paper 10 (Cape Town, South Africa: PLAAS, University of the Western Cape, 2010).

37. Kingstone Mujeyi, "Emerging Agricultural Markets and Marketing Channels Within Newly Resettled Areas of Zimbabwe," Livelihoods After Land Reform in Zimbabwe, Working Paper 1 (Cape Town, South Africa: PLAAS, University of the Western Cape, 2010), available at http://www.larl.org.za [Mujeyi, "Emerging Agricultural Markets"].

38. Shingirai Mandizadza, "The Fast Track Land Reform Programme and Livelihoods in Zimbabwe: A Case Study of Households at Athlone Farm in Murehwa District," Livelihoods After Land Reform in Zimbabwe, Working Paper 2 (Cape Town, South Africa: PLAAS, University of the Western Cape, 2010), available at http://www.larl.org.za. See also Philani Moyo, "Land Reform in Zimbabwe and Urban Livelihoods Transformation," Livelihoods After Land Reform in Zimbabwe, Working Paper 15 (Cape Town, South Africa: PLAAS, University of the Western Cape, 2010).

39. Scoones et al., *Land Reform,* 210.

40. Later the Cold Storage Company, but still state-owned.

41. Blasio Mavedzenge et al., "The Dynamics of Real Markets: Cattle in Southern Zimbabwe Following Land Reform," *Development and Change,* 39, no. 4 (2008): 620, 633.

42. Dale Doré, Tony Hawkins, Godfrey Kanyenze, Daniel Makina, and Daniel Ndlela, "Comprehensive Economic Recovery in Zimbabwe" (Harare, Zimbabwe: UNDP, 2008), 109–12, available at http://www.humansecuritygateway.com/documents/UNDP_Zimbabwe_ComprehensiveEconomicRecovery.

pdf; Daniel Makina, "Survey of Profile of Migrant Zimbabweans in South Africa," 2007, 2, available at http://www.idasa.org/our_products/resources/output/survey_of_profile_of_migrant/?pid=states_in_transition (both accessed November 11, 2011).

43. Mujeyi, "Emerging Agricultural Markets," 9.

44. EISA, "Election Observer Mission Report: The Zimbabwe Harmonised Elections of 29 March 2008," Election Observer Mission Report, No. 28 (Pretoria, South Africa: EISA, 2008), 27, 41, available at http://www.eisa.org.za/PDF/zimomr08.pdf (November, 4, 2011).

45. *The Language of Hate* (Harare, Zimbabwe: Media Monitoring Project Zimbabwe, 2009), 7, 20, quoting, "I'll Only Salute Mugabe, Not Sellouts: Chiwenga," *The Standard,* March 9, 2009.

46. "Safeguard Revolution—President," *Herald,* June 13, 2008, quoted in *The Language of Hate* (Harare, Zimbabwe: Media Monitoring Project Zimbabwe, 2009), 51.

47. "Maize Imports Supported," *Sunday Mail,* June 22, 2008, quoted in *The Language of Hate* (Harare, Zimbabwe: Media Monitoring Project Zimbabwe, 2009), 56.

48. "The Pan-African Parliament Election Observer Mission to the Presidential Run-off and Parliamentary By-elections in Zimbabwe—Interim Statement" (Johannesburg, South Africa: Pan-African Parliament, June 29, 2008, available at http://www.pan-africanparliament.org/PrintNews.aspx?Search=1&Lang=en-US&ID=352 (November 4, 2011).

49. Ban Ki-moon, "Opposition Withdrawal From Zimbabwe Election 'Deeply Distressing' Development," press statement SG/SM/11650 (New York: UN Department of Public Information, June 22, 2008), available at http://www.un.org/News/Press/docs//2008/sgsm11650.doc.htm (November 3, 2011).

50. "Truth, Reconciliation and Justice in Zimbabwe. Report of the Commission of Inquiry Appointed Under Article 26 of the Constitution of the International Labour Organization . . ." (Geneva, Switzerland: International Labour Office, 2009), ¶542, 560, 574, 593, 594, 600, 606, 608, available at http://www.ilo.org/gb/GBSessions/WCMS_123293/lang--en/index.htm (December 29, 2011).

51. Martha Mutisi, "Beyond the Signature: Appraisal of the Zimbabwe Global Political Agreement [GPA] and Implications for Intervention," *Policy & Practice Brief* 4 (Umhlanga Rocks, South Africa: ACCORD, 2011), available at http://www.accord.org.za/downloads/brief/policy_practice4.pdf (January 4, 2011).

52. "Communiqué: Extraordinary Summit of the SADC Heads of State and Government: Presidential Guest House, Pretoria, Republic of South Africa—26–27 January 2009," available at http://www.un.int/wcm/webdav/site/zimbabwe/shared/documents/statements/Communique%20SADC.pdf (January 14, 2012).

7

Tomatoes, Maize, and Tobacco

"MY FATHER WAS A PEASANT FARMER. BUT THIS IS DIFFERENT. THIS IS PURE BUSINESS," explains Fanuel Mutandiro, who has become one of the most success-ful A2 farmers, sending thousands of 8-kg boxes of tomatoes a month to market in Harare. As he takes us around the 60 ha that are his part of what was Normandale Farm, Mazowe district, he makes clear that toma-toes are the core business, but he is investing the tomato profits to diver-sify. He shows us potatoes, soya beans, and maize to feed the chickens he is starting to grow, and the new fish tank (for bream tilapia). And he is planning a cold store. We also look at his wife Dorothy's vegetables; she is now growing on a commercial scale, and there is clearly a family rivalry here. Next we look at the cattle—"my bank," says Fanuel. After a bad season in 2009, he sold 25 cattle to get the money for inputs and diesel for the tractors, and to pay the workers until the tomato profits began to come in.

Fanuel was a security guard, but in the late 1990s, he began to do vegetable trading, buying from white farmers and selling in Harare. With the fast track land reform, he applied for land and was given this piece of Normandale, which was not being farmed and had no infrastructure. He admits he knew little about farming, so he asked for advice. "When I started, I had help from the agricultural extension service, Agritex. Then I started to do my own experiments—and if I failed, I tried again. Now I could teach them." And he talked to white farmers, one of whom gave him a key piece of advice: "Don't buy a truck until you have two trac-tors. You can't plow with a truck, but you can use a tractor to carry."

So he mortgaged his house in Harare, bought a used tractor and some irrigation pipes from the white farmer leaving Normandale, and installed electricity. He used the tractor to clear the land and drill bore-holes for water. When his tomatoes began producing, he used his tractor and a trailer to make 70 trips to Mbare Market in Harare, 45 km along a main road. "Some people laughed at me," he says. But mostly the driv-ers who were caught up behind him remembered him. Then he bought a bigger tractor. He continued to expand, setting up a system of plant-ing 1 ha of tomatoes each month to ensure that he was in continuous production, and drove the bigger tractor and trailer to Harare. Finally, he was able to buy a truck. Since then, he has built a house for his fam-ily. And Fanuel experiments: he tried a new variety of tomatoes one year in the wet season, but it was less resistant to mold and he lost a whole crop. But other trials have succeeded, as he learns from experience.

Tomatoes may be profitable for Fanuel, but maize and tobacco are the crops on which land reform will be judged—tobacco is the biggest export and maize is the main staple and has been subject to extensive re-search and breeding, as we noted in chapter 3. Peasant and resettlement farming is quite sophisticated with hybrid maize seed, chemical fertiliz-ers, and various pesticides and, sometimes, herbicides. Maize yields vary substantially with rainfall, but in the late 1990s and early 2000s, com-munal farmers had yields of 1 to 1.5 tonnes per ha (t/h), 1980s resettle-ment farmers about 2 tonnes, and commercial farmers about 5.[1]

Standing in the maize in Esther Makwara's A1 farm in May 2011 is impressive—tall, dense with large maize cobs and excellent weed control. The Agritex officer with us estimates that she will harvest 8 t/h—better than most of the old white commercial farmers. Esther was a teacher, but her grandfather was a purchase farmer and she grew up on a farm. She started in 2002. Her husband still worked in Harare and stayed there but provided the money to hire a tractor and buy some inputs, while other inputs came from the government. Using not only her own 6 ha, but an-other 9 ha from farmers not ready to start yet, she produced 100 tonnes of maize and made enough profit to buy a tractor. Now she grows two crops a year, with irrigated sugar beans or wheat in winter and rain-fed maize in the summer. In the succeeding years, she continued to reinvest profits, buying various implements, more irrigation pipes, a second trac-tor, and even a small car. Asked how she bought all these things, she leans over and picks up a handful of dirt—purchases came from the profits of the farm. On her small farm, she now has six full-time workers, plus ad-ditional seasonal workers.

Esther's house is in the old white farm compound of Craigengower Farm, in Mazowe district; twenty-five kilometers down the road is

Normandale Farm. When we visited in May 2011, the living room was filled with sacks of soya beans, outside was a full maize crib, and in the kitchen was Esther's new peanut butter maker, which she bought to deal with the 2 tonnes of groundnuts she produced. Craigengower had been broken up into 74 A1 farms, each about 6 ha. In chapter 1, we cited MDC policy coordinator Eddie Cross's view that "the majority of [former white] farms have become largely defunct, their homesteads and farm buildings derelict and their arable lands have returned to bush." Eddie should visit Craigengower. Driving into the old white farm compound, one arrives at a hub of activity. Every building is in use—grain and machinery stores, houses for some farmers, and a house for the agricultural extension officer who serves this and two other farms. Indeed, all he needs to do is to use Google Maps satellite pictures to show how intensively Craigengower is used. But Eddie is right about one thing. One item in the compound is derelict: the old swimming pool is empty and filled with weeds.

A Spectrum of Farmers

This is some of the best land in Zimbabwe, and Esther and Fanuel are among the best of the new farmers. After visiting Esther's fields, and

Photo 7.1 Esther, right, discusses maize
with her neighbors, Craigengower Farm.

slowly collecting other curious farmers as we walk around, we go to other fields in Craigengower. Stephen Chigodza is vice chair of the village, and his maize, too, is impressive, with good weed control. The Agritex officer with us predicts 5 t/h. But the adjoining field is filled with stunted maize and weeds. This, our group agrees, is a really poor farmer; he still lives in Harare and is not paying attention to his land. "He needs a push," says the Agritex officer.

Next we walk up the track to Milca Changwa's field. She gave up teaching to take over her father's land. She admits she is not doing well this year and will be lucky to get 3 t/h. But she is committed and is learning. "Esther is our role model," she says. "I can turn to her."

At Normandale, Fanuel says he has already filled his land and now borrows 20 ha of a farm up the road—an indication that many new farmers still do not use all their land. And he becomes angry when he talks about another A2 farmer up the road who had political connections, received land, and was given a tractor with all the implements. "But he sold the implements and does not even use the tractor," Fanuel says. And he points to the farm nearby, also part of Normandale, which is obviously overgrown: "He is in government, and has done nothing since he received the land." But then we go to another farm on Normandale. When we arrive, the farmer is next to the maize-shelling machine, with a pile of husks and cobs on one side and a pile of unshelled maize ears on the other. As he comes over to greet us, he is covered with bits of maize husk; even his glasses are flecked with maize bits. He is a general in the army, but he lives on the farm. When he took up his 50 ha of Normandale, it had 3 ha of roses. The white farmer ran the roses for the first year, then introduced the general to the exporter so he was able to keep the contract. Production continued for another two years but was then hindered by hyperinflation. Because of the way euros were converted to Zimbabwe dollars, export farmers without good foreign contacts lost out, because money was worth so much less when they tried to buy inputs. And the plastic sheeting for the greenhouses was not available. So he had to abandon roses; but, like all good farmers, he switched to something else, and has now moved to integrated production, with maize and soya beans to feed chickens and chicken manure and soya to feed fish.

We note that the word "farm" can be confusing, because there are now farms on farms. White large-scale commercial farms all had names, and these are still used to identify the larger community. Thus, Esther's A1 farm or plot is defined as part of Craigengower Farm, the old white name. We try to make clear whether we are referring to new or old farms.

Photo 7.2 Maize shelling on an A2 plot on Normandale Farm.

Tobacco Versus Maize

As with the white farmers before them, only a small group of land-reform farmers have become very profitable commercial farmers. But many are successful on a smaller scale. Tobacco, cotton, and contract farming have played a big role in the post-dollarization period.

Mrs. Chibanda, whom we mentioned in chapter 1, is proud of her 6-ha plot on Bellevue Farm in Goromonzi. "We were living on my father's farm in the Mutoko communal area when the war veterans came and said, 'If you come with us, you will get land,' so we did. The white farmer blocked the road and tried to stop us, but we occupied. We were allocated this plot. There was nothing but bush here when we arrived." A decade later, she and her husband and two children have a two-room brick house and a traditional round brick Shona kitchen. They grow most of their own food, with a half-hectare of maize plus a garden. But their main concern is 1.5 ha of tobacco and two new tobacco-curing barns, built on credit by Northern Tobacco, using bricks made by the Chibandas. Curing the tobacco is the most difficult part of the process—it needs to remain soft and not brittle, and it takes a week to cure, during which time the fire in the base of the barn must be kept burning at the right level. The Chibandas slept in front of the barn to ensure that the fire did not go out during the night. Their profit, after deducting input costs, was likely to be over $1,000 in 2011; not a huge amount, but enough to make them commercial farmers.

Enisi Madzimbamuto has an A1 farm on Springdale Farm in Macheke. Her husband still works in a factory in Harare, and she smiles when she says she earns more than he does. She has cattle, and from the profits of the farm, she has bought plows, cultivators, a harrow, and a cart. She tried tobacco but gave it up—it is just too much work. Instead she just plants maize and can run the 6-ha farm mostly by herself, with some seasonal labor. From her 5 ha of maize, she harvests more than 3 t/h—not up to the high levels of some farmers, but still enough to give her a profit of $2,000 per year, which, she points out, is better than the tobacco farmers are earning. And she has time to grow her own food on the other hectare.

Thus, it seems possible for average A1 farmers to be serious commercial farmers, and even to earn a good living from maize rather than tobacco.

1980s Success—but
It Takes a Generation and Support

We should not be surprised by the success of A1 farmers, because the best study of the 1980s resettlement concluded that "access to land enabled resettlement farmers to grow rapidly at a time when the Zimbabwean economy stagnated."[2] Bill Kinsey, who has been interviewing 400 resettled households since 1983/84, finds "that both production levels and productivity rise substantially following resettlement,"[3] leading to "a dramatic increase in crop income" from a mean income of $200 per family in 1982/83 when they were first on the farm to $1,100 per family by the 1995/96 season.[4] His team was able to draw comparisons with a group that remained in the communal areas, and found the resettlement group farmed twice as much land (3.5 ha compared to 1.7 ha) but was more than three times as productive ($250/ha compared to $80/ha).[5]

They also acquired assets more quickly; for example, cattle herds increased 16% per year. By 1995, half of the land-reform farmers had bank accounts. But Kinsey notes that in an inflationary environment, cattle were "an investment that would have outperformed every financial instrument available in the Zimbabwean economy."[6]

In the early 1980s, land reform beneficiaries received significant support. Bill Kinsey and colleagues report that "extension coverage and access to credit were both universal in the initial stages and marketing facilities, schools, clean water supplies and other infrastructure were provided." They note that the researchers "have been made very aware just how much beneficiaries value in noneconomic terms the opportunities made available to them." And "beneficiaries for the most part became better farmers."[7] One estimate of support was $597 per family for the actual farm ($119 for training, extension, land preparation, and so on, and $478 in credit) plus $763 per family for infrastructure ($592 per family to build a school and $171 for other infrastructure such as roads, water, and dip tanks). On top of that, land and acquisition costs were $2,684—more than was actually spent on the new farm.[8] This is already much less than the subsidy to white farmers in the 1970s (see chapter 3).

Kinsey and colleagues also looked at the internal rate of return for resettlement and found rates of 15% to 20%, even when the cost of land was taken into account, which is very high for agricultural projects.[9] Nevertheless, support was reduced once structural adjustment began.

One lesson is that it does take a generation for land-reform farmers to learn to make the best use of their farms. Kinsey and colleagues wrote: "In the early 1980s, it was not uncommon to see three people working with an ox team and plough: one handling the plough; one leading the team with a rope; and the third walking alongside with a whip exhorting the oxen to behave and do what is wanted. Fifteen years later, one sees a single man ploughing by himself and controlling the animals entirely through whistles and voice commands. More generally, it is entirely likely that these households have acquired significant 'learning by doing.' The land these households settled on in the early 1980s was entirely unfamiliar to them. Over time, they will have learnt what crops grow best on which plots, the appropriate methods for growing new crops and so on."[10] Kinsey adds that "just like people, oxen 'learn by doing.' Over time, they become used to the commands of the individual leading them and learn what is required of them." He continues: "Much of the arable land allocated to the settlers in the early 1980s had lain uncultivated for many years." It had to be cleared, but the new settlers also had to plant, so full clearing and stumping took several years. Then there were ongoing investments in soil conservation and water control, as well as buying and learning to use new equipment.

Indeed, there is ample evidence internationally that any benefits from human resettlement take at least a generation to appear.[11]

But how do we assess the land reform overall? Proponents of land reform will point to Fanuel Mutandiro and his tomatoes, while opponents will point to the empty land across the road. As we saw at Craigengower, few farmers are as good as Esther, and there is a spectrum of farmers, from good to bad, and most somewhere in the middle. And a handful of examples, good or bad, proves nothing. In chapter 8 we look more closely at A1 farmers, and in chapter 9 at A2 farmers. Those chapters draw on the extensive data on fast track land reform to try to establish the actual position a decade after the occupations. In this chapter we look specifically at successful land-reform farmers and ask what makes them successful—and we try to establish some criteria for success, comparing the history of white farmers, production in the 1990s, and expressed goals of land reform. We argue that the same characteristics apply to both A1 and A2 farmers.

Six Criteria for Success

From a broad range of research and our own interviews, the most successful land-reform farmers seem to have six characteristics:

1. Money and Knowledge to Start
New farmers receive no financial help and they need some resources to start. For an A1 farmer, it may be cattle they bring from the communal areas, or a partner with a job in the city. Some A2 farmers have mortgaged houses in the city to pay for a tractor, pump, seeds, and so on. We did not find one successful farmer who really started with nothing. Similarly, some knowledge is essential—having grown up on a farm or taken a course. White farmers who were given land in the 1940s and 1950s were sent on courses and forced to do a one- or two-year apprenticeship on a farm before they could occupy their own land.

2. Training, Looking, and Experimenting
Many of the successful A2 farmers took courses, before or after obtaining land, and a number are sending their children to agricultural colleges. Looking for help, often from a friendly white farmer or other experienced person, makes a difference. And talking to other farmers and watching what they are doing seems essential. To Lucia Madzimbamuto, a successful A1 farmer, it was obvious: "If you are a farmer, you always look at other farms." Agritex extension officers have played an essential

role for both A1 and A2 farmers in improving farming techniques and in introducing new crops and methods. Enisi Madzimbamuto, a neighbor of Lucia, is an A1 farmer who is more successful than her neighbors in growing maize; when asked why, she says it is because she follows the instructions of the Agritex officer, puts on the right amount of fertilizer, and weeds the maize. The Kinsey studies showed that one or two visits per year by an agricultural extension officer raised production by 15%.[12]

And good farmers look for new ideas. One A2 farmer was raising pigs and trying to become self-sufficient in feed; when we asked how he found out what to feed the pigs, he laughed and said, "the Internet." Finally, experimentation makes a huge difference. Every good farmer has had failures, and the good farmers all told us how they were learning from mistakes and trying to do better next year.

3. You Have to Have a Plan

We heard that phrase so often from farmers it became a litany. But it wasn't rhetoric—the successful farmers all had plans—what to do next season and the season after, what to do if this crop failed or that crop was a success. The successful farmers were like chess players, always thinking several moves ahead. We met an ex–air force commander who is now a pig farmer, and his plan is to be self-sufficient, growing all his own feed. Over several years he has developed sunflower and bought a press, selling the oil and using the oil cake in the pig feed, and building silage tanks. When we were at his farm he was looking to use the pig waste to produce biogas. And he sells his own pigs, mostly to local gold miners. Esther, described earlier, grows three different varieties of maize, each of which is better under different rainfall conditions, to take advantage of Zimbabwe's variable climate.

4. Reinvestment

All successful farmers plowed substantial money back into their farms. Zimbabwean farming, both A1 and A2, is seriously capital-intensive. Seeds, fertilizer, plowing, electricity, and wages all have to be paid before the crop is sold. All of the successful farmers, both A1 and A2, bought their inputs for the next season as soon as they sold their crop. There are many claims on money—children's clothing, school fees, roof repairs, and an endless list of other needs—and if money from crop sales is spent on those "essentials," then there is not enough left for the next season. That creates a downward spiral, which we saw often enough, of people not having enough money for fertilizer, so they get a poor yield, and thus earn less from sales, so they have even less money for fertilizer the next season, and so on. The other half of reinvestment is buying farm equipment—plows, planters, cattle, perhaps tractors—and steadily equipping the farm over a decade or more. Here the plan becomes essential. Farmers need to know what they are going to plant in the next season so they buy the right seeds and fertilizer, and they need to be able to think long term about what equipment to buy next—a pump or planter this year? One of Bill Kinsey's studies shows that three things had the strongest impact on increased crop yield per hectare: tools and equipment (oxplows, oxcarts, harrows, planters, etc.), trained oxen, and extension services.[13] Putting income back into the farm by buying equipment has a high rate of return.

5. Hard Work—and Living on the Farm

Farming is harder work than many resettlement farmers realize when they first apply for land. And all of the successful farmers, A1 and A2, work extremely hard. Some of the elite try to be what are cynically called "cell phone farmers," who stay in Harare and keep in touch with a manager by mobile telephone. The air force commander admitted to us, "I was a cell farmer for three years, but it didn't work. You must live on the farm." So he retired and moved to the farm.

6. Understanding Farming

The final characteristic is something intangible, which some farmers have and others do not, about understanding farming and the land—people who look at other farms and actually see, who can take away the lessons of the Agritex officer, who can hold the soil in their hands and know what will grow. Most people can grow enough food to survive, but being a successful farmer requires something extra.

Again the Kinsey data provided a useful guide. In 1995, agricultural extension agents were asked to rate the ability of the farmers, and they found 36% poor or below average, 39% average, 17% above average, and 8% excellent. And farmers ranked above average or excellent were, indeed, more productive, with 40%–50% higher output per hectare.[14]

Contract Farming

Buying enough inputs for the next season, not just to grow the same amount but to expand production, is key to the success of small farmers.

And lack of money to buy inputs was one of the biggest complaints we heard, in part because there are so many demands on the money earned from crop sales. Contract farming has made a major difference for small farmers, because they are able to obtain inputs and technical assistance on credit. The contract farming company deducts the costs from the sale price and the cash handed to the farmer is all profit, which he or she is then free to use for household and family expenses, which reduces some of the management problems.

"The contract growing and marketing scheme, which is now about to enter into its eighth successive season, has played an important role in maintaining tobacco production in the country," according to Minister of Agriculture, Mechanisation and Irrigation Development Joseph Made in November 2011. Previously white farmers sold their tobacco at government-regulated auctions, but in 2004 the government introduced a dual marketing system, which allowed contract sales to operate concurrently with the auction sales. In 2011, 56% of all tobacco was produced on contract.[15] Thousands registered to grow only tobacco in 2010 and 2011 and are still mastering the crop, so the quality is not yet high enough; in 2011, 7% of bales were rejected by the auction houses.[16] Tobacco Marketing Board chair Monica Chinamasa pointed to high post-harvest losses in 2011 and said there was need for a concerted effort to train growers to reduce handling losses.[17] China is the biggest buyer of tobacco, taking one-quarter of the crop in 2011.[18]

Contract farming is not just for small farmers. Emmaculate Gweshe is chair of the Goromonzi women farmers group and has an A2 farm on Bellevue Farm. She grows maize and vegetables, but tobacco is done on contract with Northern Tobacco, which provides two full-time managers and all inputs and equipment. In 2010/11, Gweshe's farm produced 154 tonnes of high-quality tobacco. The Northern managers on her farm are also responsible for A1 contract farmers in the neighborhood.

The other big contract crop is cotton. A 2010 regulation requires that all cotton buyers (of which there were 13 in 2011) and all those doing contract cotton farming must register with the Agriculture Marketing Authority. The regulation also tightens penalties against "side-selling" by growers—selling to someone other than the company that provided inputs on credit. And a system of agreed-upon minimum prices has been established. Cottco[19] is the largest buyer and now obtains 98% of its cotton from farmers on contract. Sino-Zim Development Company registered 180,000 cotton farmers for the 2010/11 farming season and provided inputs to cover 130,000 hectares.[20]

Contract farming is being expanded to other crops as well. Lunar Chickens, owned by Reserve Bank Governor Gideon Gono, contracts A1 farmer groups to grow soya for chicken feed.

Seven A1 farmers on Kiaora Farm are part of a contract farming scheme for winter barley. The brewery, Delta, will not deal with individual small farmers, so the white farmer who formerly had this land, John Sole, operates a contract scheme as an intermediary. Delta provides the initial financing, which is used for inputs and plowing, and pays $85 per month to the seven farmers and $70 per month to 15 workers. Water is pumped from a nearby lake and the seven farmers rotate the use of the irrigation pipes, trying to take account of electricity cuts, to ensure that all get water. The total profit for the seven farmers in 2010 was $20,000.

What Do We Mean by *Successful*?

In this chapter, we have been judging resettlement "success" by production—are resettlement farmers producing more than the white farmers they displaced and more than the people left behind in the communal areas? But that may be too narrow a view.

The liberation war was fought in part to reclaim the land, so simply taking it back is an important goal. And, as in Europe, the United States, and Rhodesia after the Second World War, land is seen as a reward for those who risked their lives or suffered in the war. But land is an important economic asset for Zimbabwe and should be used productively. Many donors and some in the Zimbabwe government wanted to use land primarily to reduce poverty; this led to the dual strategy that big modern farms—an agribusiness sector—would be expanded to build export production, but some land would be distributed to the poorest citizens. At first, the 1980s land reform sought to benefit the poorest, but by the second half of the decade, emphasis shifted so less stress was on beneficiaries being poor, and more was on having experience and being productive. This became a central issue in the failure of the donor conference in 1998—government emphasized productivity, while donors were divided, but with many stressing poverty reduction. A World Bank report noted, "The British government insisted on making financial resources available to acquire land on a WSWB [willing seller, willing buyer] basis and anchored its support for land distribution in its poverty reduction strategy."[21] Tension with the international community was also heightened by the Zimbabwe government's more assertive position on national control of resources and increasing calls for indigenization and local ownership.

Tension runs through all land reform, not just in Zimbabwe, between welfare and production. Should the land be given to the poorest and most in need to provide immediate help to them? Or should the land be given to those who can make best use of it, to increase production and create jobs and economic growth through multiplier effects, as new production is sold and the earnings are used to buy more goods locally, thus creating jobs both on the farm and in town? In general, the poorest are relatively less productive on the new land. So, do we try to reduce poverty directly by giving poor people land, or indirectly by raising production and creating markets and jobs?[22]

How should we react to the A1 farmers, many of whom are women, who do not use their entire 6 ha but produce enough to live much more comfortably than they did in the communal areas, and now have enough money to send their children to school and even for advanced training? Should we say this is an anti-poverty success, or should we look to the unused land and say it could be more productive? This must also be seen in the context that land reform is once and for all; there will be no more land to redistribute, so we are reducing some poverty now, but what will the long-term impact be?

Fast track A1 may, accidentally, have hit the right balance. By stressing occupation, which required action, farmers were self-selected and are likely to be the most dynamic. But these individuals were also largely landless or unemployed, and thus poor. Kinsey also notes that younger farmers achieved higher levels of productivity, perhaps because they are more innovative and more willing to adopt new technologies.[23] That would probably also apply to those willing to occupy land as part of *jambanja*.

A2 is more production-biased, and that is built into the requirement that farmers have money and experience. But that makes it hard to argue against elites' gaining many A2 farms, as they are precisely the people who have the money to invest.

The Masvingo study (see chapter 6) found that resettlement land "carries with it quite different meanings for different people. For some it is a source of private accumulation, a useful asset as part of a wider range of activities; for others it is the first time they have had productive land and is their main source of livelihood; for others it is a source of security for later in life or for their children; and for others still it has particular symbolic value, an achievement from long term political struggle. Constructions of 'success,' 'viability' and 'impact' therefore vary significantly in the new resettlements and may not tally with those in the minds of the technocrats and planners."[24]

Interestingly, Kinsey notes that the 1980s resettlement farms were twice as productive as communal areas, but because of their success, they attract more people to the household—11 per household compared to 7 in communal areas. So that resettlement did do both—production rose and, as more people were attracted to the households, poverty was reduced.[25]

In practice, land reform cannot be judged by a single criterion—it must do two things at the same time: increase productivity and bring new land into production while also reducing poverty by both giving people land and creating jobs. And, of course, it should transfer land from white to black and reward those who fought for liberation. The mixed goals mean it will never be "fair" in the sense of simply picking names out of a hat, or only giving land to the very poorest. But we can ask that it both increase production and reduce poverty.

Summing Up: Success

There is no single measure of "success" for a land-reform farmer. It is a mix of higher productivity, poverty reduction, and redressing the colonial inheritance; A1 farmers will be judged differently from A2, although the best A1 farmers are already serious small commercial farmers. And the history of the white farmers, and then the 1980s land reform, is that it takes a generation—and substantial support—for new farmers to become established. Fast track farmers had less support than white or 1980s reform farmers, so they are only partway down the road toward developing their farms.

The farmers we talked with and other research have identified six factors that seem important for the success of both A1 and A2 farmers: (1) money and knowledge to start; (2) training, looking, and experimenting; (3) "you have to have a plan"; (4) reinvestment and buying inputs (which makes contract farming increasingly important); (5) hard work; and (6) an intangible understanding of farming.

Notes

1. Kingstone Mashingaidze, "Maize Research and Development," in *Zimbabwe's Agricultural Revolution Revisited,* ed. Mandivamba Rukuni, Patrick Tamonezvi, and Carl Eicher (Harare, Zimbabwe: University of Zimbabwe, 2006).

2. Jan Willem Gunning, John Hoddinott, Bill Kinsey, and Trudy Owens, "Revisiting Forever Gained: Income Dynamics in the Resettlement Areas of Zimbabwe, 1983–97," *Journal of Development Studies,* 36, no. 6 (2000): 133 [Gunning, Hoddinott, Kinsey, and Owens, 2000].

3. Bill Kinsey, "Zimbabwe's Land Reform Program: Underinvestment in Post-Conflict Transformation," *World Development,* 32, no. 10 (2004): 1682 [Kinsey, 2004].

4. Gunning, Hoddinott, Kinsey, and Owens, 2000, 136.

5. Bill Kinsey, "Land Reform, Growth and Equity: Emerging Evidence From Zimbabwe's Resettlement Programme," *Journal of Southern African Studies,* 25, no. 2 (1999): 184 [Kinsey, 1999].

6. Kinsey, 2004, 1686.

7. Ibid.

8. Ibid., 1682; Klaus Deininger, Hans Hoogeveen, and Bill Kinsey, "Economic Benefits and Costs of Land Redistribution in Zimbabwe in the Early 1980s," *World Development,* 32, no. 10 (2004), 1707 [Deininger, Hoogeveen, and Kinsey, 2004], citing Anne-Sophie Robilliard, Crispen Sukume, Yuki Yanoma, and Hans Löfgren, "Land Reform and Poverty Alleviation in Zimbabwe: Farm-Level Effects and Cost-Benefit Analysis" (mimeo, 2001).

9. Deininger, Hoogeveen, and Kinsey, 2004, 1707.

10. Jan Willem Gunning, John Hoddinott, Bill Kinsey, and Trudy Owens, "Revisiting Forever Gained: Income Dynamics in the Resettlement Areas of Zimbabwe, 1983–97," Working Paper 98 (Oxford, UK: Centre for the Study of African Economies, May 1999 version), 8.

11. Kinsey, 1999, 175.

12. Trudy Owens, John Hoddinott, and Bill Kinsey, "The Impact of Agricultural Extension on Farm Production in Resettlement Areas of Zimbabwe," *Economic Development and Cultural Change,* 51, no. 2 (2003): 338.

13. Ibid., 344.

14. Ibid., 339, 351.

15. Tabitha Mutenga, "Small-Scale Farmers Boost Tobacco Production," *Financial Gazette,* November 2, 2011, available at http://www.financialgazette.co .zw/national-report/10479-small-scale-farmers-boost-tobacco-production.html (accessed November 6, 2011).

16. Reginald Sherekete, "Tobacco Grower Profile Shifts," *Zimbabwe Independent,* November 3, 2011, available at http://allafrica.com/stories/printable/ 201111041161.html (November 6, 2011).

17. Ibid.

18. Ibid.

19. Cottco is the Cotton Marketing Board, which was privatized in 1994. It is 100% owned by the Zimbabwe-based AICO Africa Limited, which also owns 51% of Seedco (formerly Seed Co-operative Company of Zimbabwe, privatized in 1996) and 49% of Olivine. The largest shareholders are state agencies and Old Mutual. Cottco claims to be Southern Africa's leading cotton-buying,

-processing, and -marketing organization; see http://www.thecottoncompany
.com/ and http://www.aicoafrica.co/.

20. "Chinese Company Subcontracts 180,000 Zimbabwean Cotton Farmers," *Herald,* October 10, 2010.

21. Hans Binswanger-Mkhize, Camille Bourguignon, and Rogerius van
den Brink, *Agricultural Land Dedistribution: Toward Greater Consensus* (Washington, DC: World Bank Publications, 2009), 150.

22. There is a good discussion of this debate in Nelson Marongwe, "Redistributive Land Reform and Poverty Reduction in Zimbabwe," n.d., available at
http://lalr.org.za/zimbabwe/redistributive-land-reform-and-poverty-reduction-
in-zimbabwe (December 26, 2011).

23. Kinsey, 2004, 1688.

24. Ian Scoones et al., *Zimbabwe's Land Reform* (Woodbridge, Suffolk, UK:
James Currey, 2010), 9–10.

25. Kinsey 1999, 184; Kinsey 2004, 1685.

8

New Smallholders

"PRODUCTION IS GOING UP, AND I AM TAKING FARMING AS A BUSINESS," EXPLAINS Winnett Dembo. "And when I sell my crops, the first money goes for school fees, but then I buy all my inputs for the next season." It has taken her a decade, but she is the most successful small farmer in her area. Her 5-ha farm does not seem small to her, because when she was in Domboshava communal lands she had less than 1 ha of land. Her husband was looking for work at the Iron Duke Mine in Mazowe, Mashonaland Central, and it was the time of *jambanja*. She and her husband became part of the group of 29 families linked to the mine that took over empty land between the mine and the citrus estate. They have never received formal permission to occupy, partly because the government is worried that the mine has polluted the local water supply, but they are receiving support from the local Agritex extension officer, they are building houses, and production is growing. We were shown around several immaculate compounds, with flowers around the houses and spectacular views of the nearby hills; they will be unwilling to leave now.

Winnett's 5 ha are carefully divided into 2 ha for cotton, 2 ha for maize—from which she is obtaining an excellent yield of 4 t/h—and now 1 ha for tobacco. She has built a barn to dry her burley (air-cured) tobacco and the quality seems good. Indeed, production is so good that she now hires workers (all women) to weed the maize and cotton and for the tobacco, including the woman bundling tobacco in the picture on page 122.

Winnett is seen as the most successful of the Iron Duke settlers. In the rest of this chapter we look more closely at A1 farmers.

Photo 8.1 Tying bundles of tobacco leaves to dry,
Bindari Farm near Iron Duke Mine, Mazowe.

Looking More Closely at Three A1 Farms

We draw in this book on a range of studies from across Zimbabwe, but for our own more detailed research we looked at some of the richest farmland, in Mashonaland in three districts—Mazowe (particularly Kiaora and Craigengower farms), Murehwa (Springdale Farm, Machecke), and Goromonzi (Brookmead and other farms). We also had a survey conducted of all A1 farmers on Kiaora, Springdale, and Brookmead farms, concentrating on the period since dollarization at the beginning of 2009. Figure 8.1 gives the gross incomes of the 102 farms surveyed for the 2010/11 season, which included the winter 2010 crop. This is gross income, and agriculture in Zimbabwe is based on purchased inputs, so costs of fertilizer, plowing, and so on, need to be deducted. On the other hand, these farmers grow most of their own food, which is not sold, so is not included.

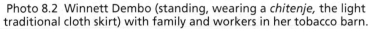

Photo 8.2 Winnett Dembo (standing, wearing a *chitenje,* the light traditional cloth skirt) with family and workers in her tobacco barn.

To interpret this data, we need to look at costs. Seedco, the Zimbabwean seed company, suggests using about two 50-kg bags of fertilizer for each tonne of maize to be produced.[1] In mid-2011, fertilizer cost $31 per bag, and the Grain Marketing Board (GMB) was paying $275 per tonne for maize (roughly the world market price). GMB was also trading maize for fertilizer, which made the effective cost $14 per bag for farmers who could take advantage of the offer. Some farmers have oxen, as was the case with Enisi Madzimbamuto, or even tractors, and can plow their own land, but many must hire someone to do it, which can cost up to $60 per hectare. In addition, seed must be purchased. Good maize production requires good weed control, which often means buying herbicide or paying farmworkers to weed. Roughly speaking, if a farmer grows 3 tonnes of maize per hectare, the first tonne goes to pay input costs.[2] (Most families also keep 1 tonne of maize for their own consumption.)

Figure 8.1 Gross Crop Income From Three Sets of
A1 Farms in Mashonaland, 2010/11

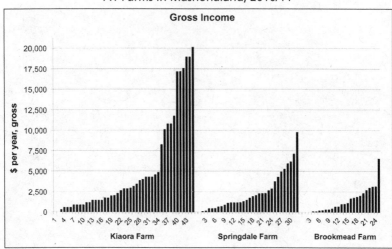

For other crops, the ratios seem similar. For example, input costs for tobacco are at least $650 per hectare,[3] and sales should exceed $2,000 per hectare. Soya beans require $787 per hectare in seeds and chemicals.[4] Winter crops require irrigation, which means paying for electricity. We take as an approximate rule of thumb that one-third of gross income is costs, and two-thirds is profit. Thus, the bars in Figure 8.1 should be lowered by about one-third to obtain net income.

At the time of the survey, a teacher earned $150 per month[5] or $1,800 per year, and rural teachers grew some of their own food. A1 farmers grow most of their own food, so it could be said that any farmer with a net income of more than a teacher's wage is a successful small-scale, commercial farmer.

Based on that, we take a gross income of $2,500 as the boundary line—above that, farmers are earning more than teachers and we treat them as being serious (albeit small) commercial farmers. At the other end of the scale, the absolute minimum investment cost is more than $100 per hectare, and our interviews show that a gross income of below $1,250 per year is proving to be too little to buy necessary inputs and pay school fees and other necessary costs, and input purchases fall in a declining spiral. Farmers in this group are often in trouble, with output declining each year. A study by Precious Zikhali in Mazowe found that households with more children used less fertilizer per hectare and that "having a lot of children arguably strains the household's resources."[6]

One-fifth of our survey farmers are in the middle, with gross incomes between $1,250 and $2,500. They seem to be a mix, with some simply comfortable at this level and with enough food to live better than in the past, while others are moving up to be serious commercial farmers, sometimes with the support of contract farming.

Table 8.1 shows the distribution of our three groups for the three farms in 2010/11, which is also shown in Figure 8.1. In Kiaora, most farmers are "commercial" in our sense, and in Springdale, one-third of them are. The middle group remains at around one-fifth. Brookmead has a number of farmers who received land recently and are only starting, but some of them are obviously in trouble (one-third have maize yields below 1 t/ha). Table 8.2 shows average gross income over three years.

We now look more closely at these farms, to see what characterizes the successful farmers. The obvious point is that there is no "typical" farmer; all are different and often do widely differing things with similar land. Kiaora is probably one of the richest A1 farms in Zimbabwe, and its crop distribution is shown in Figure 8.2. Eleven farmers stand out, nine of whom grow both a rain-fed summer crop and an irrigated winter crop. Contract farming for seed soya in the summer and wheat or barley (see chapter 7) in the winter is key to high income.

Earnings from the crops each farmer in Springdale grows are shown in Figure 8.3. There is relatively little irrigation and there are few winter crops. The chart shows the importance of tobacco. The most profitable farmers grow both tobacco and maize, while a middle group has chosen

Table 8.1 Percentages in Gross Income Groups, 2010/11

Gross income	Kiaora	Springdale	Brookmead
>$2,500	53%	31%	20%
$1,250–$2,500	20%	25%	20%
<$1,250	27%	44%	60%

Table 8.2 Average Gross Income, $

	2008/9	2009/10	2010/11
Kiaora	1,773	2,157	5,166
Springdale	1,543	3,156	2,409
Brookmead	712	811	1,347

Note: Kiaora farmers who grew wheat in 2008, the height of hyperinflation, bartered it rather than sold it, so the value is not included, and the $1,773 average is only for maize sold under dollarization. Rainfall in the 2010/11 season was quite variable and was poorer at Springdale than at the other two farms.

Figure 8.2 Kiaora Farm Gross Crop Income, 2010/11 $

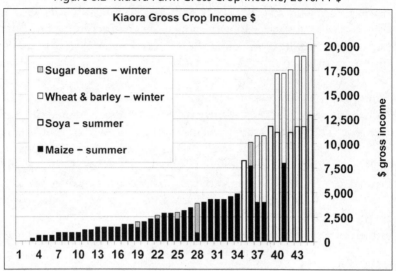

to concentrate on tobacco instead of maize. Several farmers have significant earnings from other crops, notably groundnuts, sweet potatoes, and sugar beans. Pauline Murema (number 24 in Figures 8.3 and 8.4) earns her money from tobacco as well as sweet potatoes and horticulture (counted together as "other" in Figure 8.3), and not maize.

Maize productivity is sometimes seen as a measure of a person's quality as a farmer, and high maize yields make the middle group in Kiaora (Figure 8.2) much more profitable than a similar group in Springdale. But Figure 8.4, which compares maize yields with total income for Springdale, suggests a more mixed picture. Several farmers, including Enisi Madzimbamuto, mentioned earlier (number 25 in Figures 8.3 and 8.4), have made as much from maize as others have from tobacco. But other high earners have low maize productivity.

The transformation post-dollarization is particularly notable, as is the importance of contract farming for tobacco, barley, soya, seed maize, and other crops, which has expanded since dollarization.

These groups of farmers are all individuals making different choices and getting different results. Pauline and Enisi are examples of serious A1 commercial farmers. The leader of a group of barley farmers on Kiaora Farm is a former textile supervisor, who says he earns much more from farming than he did in the factory. He points out that the barley farmers were doing better because they agreed to form a group, which many A1

Figure 8.3 Springdale Farm Gross Crop Income, 2010/11 $

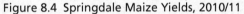

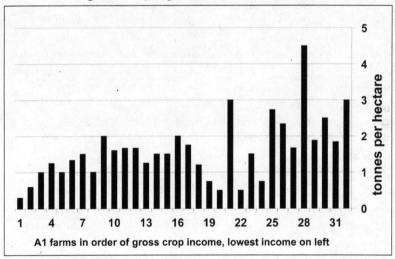

Figure 8.4 Springdale Maize Yields, 2010/11

Note: Farms are in order by gross income and are in the same order in Figures 8.3 and 8.4.

farmers are reluctant to do; his organizing skills from his factory days probably made the difference.

Jane Mupaso on Bellevue Farm is an example of someone in the middle who seems to be moving up. She only received her plot in 2007 (having been moved around a bit, after her previous A1 plot was incorporated into an A2 farm). Initially she and her husband and their three children lived in the old farmworkers' compound and she grew maize; she did not use the whole plot, but is producing 2.5 t/h of maize, and in 2010 sold 4 tonnes to the GMB (and kept 1 tonne for herself). She has five cattle and does her own plowing. Her plot is dominated by two new tobacco barns and this is her first season. She has moved onto the plot to be close to the tobacco barn, and we sit on mats outside her new one-room wood house. She had already sold seven bales of tobacco for $1,550, which is a good price, but most of it will go to Northern Tobacco for the inputs and barn. She expects to sell more maize than last year to GMB; it is hard work and slow going, but Jane is clearly moving up.

And at the bottom are two different kinds of people. Grace's sons teach building so they have built her a nice brick house. It is a pleasant compound with fruit trees, on land she occupied in *jambanja,* and over the decade her cattle herd has increased from 5 to 15. But her sales last year comprised 3 tonnes of maize and $60 worth of paprika. She does not use her whole 6 ha ("No one can," she says), largely because she has no money for inputs. Her sweet potatoes were eaten by termites because she cannot afford pesticides. She lives comfortably, but will never be a small commercial farmer. And down the road is another farmer who took the land during *jambanja.* She has 3 ha of maize but could not afford inputs so she has spread fertilizer for 1 ha across the 3; not surprisingly, her yield is poor and will not even cover her own consumption. It would have been less work and more productive to have grown 1 ha or even half a hectare of maize and concentrated the inputs. She has no cattle and has to hire oxen to plow and uses only part of her land. Can she survive this downward spiral?

Our group is only a small sample, so it is useful to compare to others. The first benchmark was the one set by the white farmers at independence, whom the international community considered highly successful: they used less than 34% of land, and 30% of farmers were failing, 30% just getting by, and a small group was doing very well (see the end of chapter 3). The new farmers are definitely using more of the land, although less intensively. And after just a decade, the distribution of these farmers into success or income groups seems quite similar to that of the white farmers.

In the following three sections we look at other research on fast track farmers and on the 1980s land reform.

Masvingo

The most detailed study of fast track land reform is the Masvingo province study, which has been studying 400 resettlement farmers since
2000.[7] The research team is composed of Ian Scoones of the Institute of
Development Studies, Sussex, United Kingdom; Nelson Marongwe and
Crispen Sukume of the University of Zimbabwe; and three resettlement
farmers: Blasio Mavedzenge, Felix Murimbarimba, and Jacob Mahene-
hene. Mavedzenge is also an Agritex extension officer and Murimbarimba used to be. Masvingo province is very different from the lush and
well-watered land of Mashonaland, which we have looked at in detail.
Masvingo is one of the poorer agricultural areas, with lower rainfall and
sandy soils that had been largely used for ranching, but the new settlers
were now turning it into farms, although it also includes the irrigated
sugar estates. The research sample contained 266 A1 farmers, 53 who saw
themselves as A1 but whose plots were not recognized by the government
(similar to Iron Duke), and 57 A2 farmers. Also, the researchers' book,
Zimbabwe's Land Reform: Myths & Realties, was published in 2010, so
their data only covers up to the 2009 harvest, which means their information ends under hyperinflation and does not include the dollarization
period, on which we concentrate. Despite the differences, however, their
findings are very similar to ours.

The Masvingo team developed two typologies. One uses community self-ranking techniques to divide resettlement farmers into three
"success groups" (SGs), of which SG1 was "doing well, improving"; SG2
was "getting on, but with potential"; and SG3 was "asset poor, often
struggling." The team also finds that "the top 40% of households (SG1
and some SG2) are producing the majority of outputs and selling the
most."[8] This roughly corresponds to the three groups we identified in
Mashonaland.

Maize is a useful production marker, although Masvingo production
is almost entirely rain-fed. The 2007/8 season had very poor rainfall,
so national production of maize was only 470,000 tonnes, whereas the
next year, 2008/9, had exceptionally good rains, and national production
was nearly triple that of the previous year, at 1,242,600 tonnes. Maize
is the staple grain in most of Zimbabwe, and the average family needs 1
tonne per year; sorghum is a staple in the driest parts of Masvingo. The
Masvingo researchers found that only one-quarter of households did not
produce enough grain to feed their families in 2008/9, although in the

previous dry year, nearly three-quarters of households had to purchase some grain.[9] Table 8.3 shows again how the better farmers sell considerably more maize, and that even in a poor agricultural area, 42% of the best farmers sold more than a tonne of maize in 2009 (the end of the hyperinflation period).

The other Masvingo typology uses four categories defined by the researchers.[10] In the lowest category they find 10% of A1 farmers "dropping out." Above that, there are 35% "hanging in" but not doing well. Above that, with 21%, is a category they call "stepping out"—that is, diversifying into gold panning or trade, or receiving remittances (this was during hyperinflation), and thus not totally dependent on their farm. And in the highest category, they find 34% "stepping up"—these are the serious and profitable A1 commercial farmers. The stepping-out and stepping-up groups are accumulating and investing and often employ labor.

Many farmers, especially in the hyperinflation era and in drought years, earn money from a range of activities off their own farm—as laborers on other farms, in urban jobs, through crafts such as pottery or carpentry, by trading meat and crops with other farmers, and by selling goods in shops and markets. Local agricultural processing is also growing, such as pressing oil, making peanut butter, or processing soya beans. The Masvingo study notes that local markets have sprung up in resettlement areas, although this was disrupted by Operation Murambatsvina in 2005, when the government destroyed informal, non-registered trading areas across the country.[11] The 1980s resettlement program banned any work off the main farm, but the ban was withdrawn after a serious drought. And it is clear for the fast track resettlement farmers that other income can be quite important, for investing in the farm, and for some farmers as part of a diversified livelihood strategy. Migration to South Africa and remittances were particularly important during the hyperinflation period.

Table 8.3 Maize Sales by A1 Farmers, Masvingo, 2009

Success group	No. of A1 farmers	Maize sales		
		None	< 1 tonne	> 1 tonne
SG1	77	35%	23%	42%
SG2	80	53%	31%	16%
SG3	87	65%	21%	13%

Source: Scoones et al., *Land Reform*, 110.

Other Fast Track Comparisons

Two other studies of fast track farmers are relevant. Fast track "beneficiaries achieved higher land productivity than communal farmers," according to a 2007 study by Precious Zikhali that compared 161 fast track
families in Mazowe with 222 families in the nearby Chiweshe communal
area.[12] She found that the fast track farmers averaged 2.4 t/h of maize,
compared to 0.8 t/ha in communal areas—still below the 1999 commercial average of 4.4 t/ha, but a major advance in a short time. Fast track
farmers are proving to be better farmers, and Zikhali credits their productivity gain to three factors:

- fast track farmers use twice as much fertilizer and their fertilizer
  use is twice as productive as the communal farmers',
- they use oxen and tractors more effectively, and
- the old white farmland in Mazowe is much better than in the
  communal areas.

Easther Chigumira[13] looked at two farms divided into A1 farms in
Kadoma district, Mashonaland West, which had one of the highest number of farm occupations in 2000, and both of these farms had been occupied. Chigumira interviewed the former white owner of Molina Farm,
T. Lubbe, who said that this was 1 of 13 farms he owned, and that he
used only 3% of Molina Farm.[14] Chigumura interviewed a sample of
27 of the 125 A1 farmers in Molina. Most came from the Mhondoro
communal area, and 11 were part of the initial occupation; however, 6
of the 27 plots went to Rural District Council members and 1 to a local
chief. The other farm was Lenteglos, where Chigumira interviewed 22
A1 farmers; 6 had been communal farmers, 7 had been farmworkers, and
the rest had urban jobs; only 2 had been part of the initial occupation.

Molina and Lanteglos are in Region III—adequate land but not the
best—and the 2003/4 season was only the third for most of the farmers. By December 2004, when the thesis research was completed, the 27
families interviewed on Molina had cleared 328 ha of this largely unused
farm for cultivation. In 2003/4, they produced on average 6.8 tonnes of
maize and 11.2 bales of cotton per family. On Lanteglos Farm, Chigumira surveyed 22 plots that had been allocated 108 ha of land, 78 ha of
which had been virgin land that had not been used by the white farmer
and had to be cleared. In December 2004, 71 ha (65%) were being

farmed, and 39 ha still had to be cleared. For the 2003/4 season, the average harvest was 3.8 tonnes of maize and 5.2 bales of cotton. Chigumira commented that the Molina farmers "reported that in the 2003/2004 season, they had generated more money from farming . . . than they had in previous periods. . . . They were therefore able to invest their money in assets for the farm or bank it, whereas previously they could not."

1980s Land Reform

In the previous chapter we noted that it takes a generation for new farmers to become established. The fast track farmers have been in place for only a decade, and part of that was disrupted by hyperinflation. But we can use Bill Kinsey's data on farmers resettled in 1982–84 after 15 years, because they were very similar to A1 farmers. He found that the average (mean) gross crops sales in 1995/96 for his resettlement farmers was $1,100 with a maximum of $3,300; resettlement households sold 78% of what they produced, and total income (including the remaining 22% of crops consumed in the family and some off-farm income) was $1,640 for the year. In addition, the average farm had cattle worth $1,100. Gross cash income from crops, per hectare, was $260.[15] So it would appear that the A1 farmers are doing better than the 1980s land-reform farmers were at roughly the same point in their history.

Two students also did research on 1980s resettlement areas in the late 1990s. Average Chigwenya looked at resettlement in Gutu South, Masvingo, and found that 17% of farmers had yields between 1.5 and 2 t/h of maize, and 18% had more than 2 t/ha; in an adjoining communal area, no one had more than 1.5 t/ha.[16] Knowledge Chikondo's study in the Masasa Ringa Model A scheme in Mashonaland East found 42% produced more than 3 t/ha.[17] Chikondo also looked at differentiation and found four categories by gross value of production (i.e., sales plus consumption). The poor group (<$580) accounted for 27%; the middle group (between $580 and $1,160) 48%; the upper middle (between $1,160 and $1,740) 12%; and a rich group (>$1,740) 12%. She found that a third of farmers in her sample did not realize the equivalent of the urban minimum wage. She also found that half of farmers used recommended levels of fertilizer, and half used less.[18] Again, our A1 farmers seem similar but are doing a bit better.

Investment

Investment is a key issue. In chapter 3, we said we could use white farmers as a benchmark and noted that white farmers in the mid-1970s were
being subsidized by the equivalent of $40,000 per farm per year—in ad-
dition to huge extension support and guaranteed markets, tightly controlled by the state. The result was that one-third of white farmers were
still failing; one-third were breaking even; and some had become highly
productive, while a few became spectacularly profitable.

We offer two different estimates based on the $40,000 per farm.
Since white farms, on average, were broken into 48 A1 farms or 4 A2
farms, that is equivalent to $800 per year per A1 farm, or $10,000 per
year per A2 farm. Alternatively, we note that white farms in Mashonaland
that were listed for seizure in a "Government Gazette Notice" (widely
referred to as "gazetted") averaged 490 arable hectares, which would give
about $80 per arable hectare per year,[19] and would be about $500 per
year per A1 farm. In the previous chapter we noted Bill Kinsey's estimate
of investment in 1980s resettlement farms of $579 in the actual farm.
Spread over a decade, this is one-tenth of what was spent on white farmers. Fast track farmers have received even less support.

Despite not having the support given to their white predecessors,
land-reform farmers have made substantial investments using their own
money rather than outside investment or loans. Looking at his 1980s resettlement farmers, Kinsey compared assets of different groups, drawing
lines at the 25th percentile (i.e., the poorest 25% are below this line),
the median, and the 75th percentile. He also created a score of consumer
durables such as bicycles, chairs, and lamps, and found that at the poor
end (25th percentile) in Mupfurudzi, the family owns 4 cattle and has a
durable score of 7, the median has 7 cattle and a durable score of 16, and
at the 75th percentile there are 12 cattle and a durable score of 28—so
the family at the 75th percentile has roughly three times the assets of the
person at the 25th. Also, the person at the 25th percentile has the same
assets as the average person in the communal area.[20] But Kinsey's data also
show "quite modest asset accumulation overall but dramatic gains on the
part of some households."[21] Since his data also show that equipment has
quite a high return, this suggests that there is a top group of smallholders
who are becoming serious and profitable commercial farmers.

The Masvingo team estimates that average investment in the first
seven years was $2,161. Of this, housing and buildings accounted for

$631, cattle $612, land clearance $385, and farm equipment $198 at 2009 prices.[22] This is significant investment of more than $300 per year; if all A1 farmers were making that size investment, it would be around $50 mn per year. It is also clear that the most successful farmers are those who started with some assets, particularly cattle and plows, and that those who are dropping out simply never accumulated enough capital. Nevertheless, nearly all farmers significantly increased assets such as ox-plows.[23]

Summing Up: Successful Small Commercial Farmers

A significant percentage of A1 farmers have become serious small, commercial farmers, earning more than teachers and thus most civil servants. The resettlement process takes a generation, and A1 farmers were held back by hyperinflation; nevertheless, more farmers are moving to being commercial. There is no single model for commercial farming and there are many possible cash crops, including maize, tobacco, and barley, and contract farming helps.

There is, of course, a spectrum of farmers, with many in the middle who are better off than they were before, but not commercial farmers. And there is a group doing poorly. This picture is very similar to that of the white farmers and of the 1980s land-reform farmers.

The big difference is lack of support for new farmers. We estimate that in the UDI era, white farmers had subsidies that were equivalent in current money to $500 to $800 per year per A1 farm. Resettlement farmers are forced to use their own money and invest from below—and they do, to build houses and acquire equipment.

Notes

1. For each tonne of maize to be produced, Seedco recommends one 50-kg bag of basal fertilizer Compound D (8:14:7 NPK) before planting and one 50-kg bag of top dressing ammonium nitrate (34.5% N) when the plants are four to six weeks old (*Seed Co Agronomy Manual,* March 11, 2011), available at http://seeds.seedco.co/products (October 4, 2011).

2. For larger commercial farmers trying for higher yields, input costs will be higher. The *Financial Gazette* estimated for the 2011/12 season, "To produce one hectare of maize, a farmer would need 25kg of seed, six 50kg bags

of Ammonium Nitrate and eight 50kg bags of Compound D, costing a total of approximately $480. This does not include tillage, fuel, labour, pesticides, herbicides and harvesting" (Tabitha Mutenga, "Farmers Decry Input Costs," *Financial Gazette,* October 12, 2011) [Mutenga, "Farmers Decry"].

3. A small tobacco barn costs $1,500 and is built on credit, repaid over three years.

4. Mutenga, "Farmers Decry."

5. Increased to $220 per month in mid-2011.

6. Precious Zikhali, "Fast Track Land Reform and Agricultural Productivity in Zimbabwe," EfD Discussion Paper 08-30 (Washington, DC: Environment for Development Initiative, 2008), 20 [Zikhali, "Fast Track"], available at http://www.efdinitiative.org/research/publications/publications-repository/fast-track-land-reform-and-agricultural-productivity-in-zimbabwe/files/EfD-DP-08-30.pdf (accessed December 15, 2011).

7. Ian Scoones et al., *Zimbabwe's Land Reform: Myths & Realities* (Woodbridge, Suffolk, UK: James Currey, 2010) [Scoones et al., *Land Reform*].

8. Ibid., 123.

9. Ibid., 103, 111.

10. Ibid., 228.

11. Ibid., 217.

12. Zikhali, "Fast Track."

13. Easther Chigumira, "An Appraisal of the Impact of the Fast Track Land Reform Programme on Land Use Practices, Livelihoods and the Natural Environment at Three Study Areas in Kadoma District, Zimbabwe" (MSc thesis, Rhodes University, January 2006), 116–63.

14. Ibid., 116–17.

15. Bill Kinsey, "Land Reform, Growth and Equity: Emerging Evidence From Zimbabwe's Resettlement Programme," *Journal of Southern African Studies,* 25, no. 2 (1999): 184, 186 using exchange rates from Mandivamba Rukuni, Patrick Tawonezvi, and Carl Eicher (eds.), *Zimbabwe's Agricultural Revolution Revisited* (Harare, Zimbabwe: University of Zimbabwe Publications, 2006), xxiii: 1992 (Z$5.48 = $1), 1995 (Z$9.34), 1996 (Z$10.84), and 1997 (Z$18.61).

16. Bill Kinsey, "Zimbabwe's Land Reform Program: Underinvestment in Post-Conflict Transformation," *World Development,* 32, no. 10 (2004): 1669–96 [Kinsey, 2004], citing Average Chigwenya, "An Assessment of Environmental Impacts of Resettlement Programmes in Zimbabwe With Specific Focus on Gutu South Resettlement Scheme" (BSc honors thesis, Department of Rural and Urban Planning, University of Zimbabwe, 2001).

17. Kinsey, 2004, citing K. Chikondo, "Production and Management of Natural Resources in Resettlement Areas in Zimbabwe: The Case of Masasa-Ringa" (MSc thesis, Agricultural University of Norway, 1996) [Chikondo, "Production and Management"].

18. Kinsey, 2004, citing Chikondo, "Production and Management."

19. Sam Moyo, "Three Decades of Agrarian Reform in Zimbabwe," *Journal of Peasant Studies,* 38, no. 3 (2011): table 1, 496; Sam Moyo, *Land Reform Under Structural Adjustment in Zimbabwe* (Uppsala, Sweden: Nordiska Afrikainstitutet, 2000), annex table 2.4.3, 187.

20. Jan Willem Gunning, John Hoddinott, Bill Kinsey, and Trudy Owens, "Revisiting Forever Gained: Income Dynamics in the Resettlement Areas of Zimbabwe, 1983–97," *Journal of Development Studies,* 36, no. 6 (2000): 151.

21. Kinsey, 2004, 1687.

22. In 2009, a cultivator cost $220, a plough $150, a bicycle $115, and an ox $425.

23. Ian Scoones et al., *Land Reform,* chap. 4.

9

New World of Commercial Farming

IT WAS ONLY WHEN HE WAS SHOWING US HIS PIGS THAT WE NOTICED THAT TUCKED INTO his muddy boots were pinstripe trousers. This farmer is a former diplomat, but living on his farm in Mazowe district, he no longer needs his old suits, so they have become a different kind of work clothes. He has a medium-sized A2 farm, with 150 ha arable. The former incumbent had used this farm for export horticulture, and the ex-diplomat decided to continue in the same way. The European buyer was initially reluctant to deal with a land-reform farmer and said he would buy only if the new farmer could prove clear title. Under the land-reform law, new farmers do not pay for land but must buy the equipment on it. Using money saved from his diplomatic postings, the new farmer bought the equipment, and the former white farmer gave him a letter saying that he had been paid. The surprised European buyer accepted the handover and entered into a contract for pea production. The contract involved quite precise instructions—plant 1 ha this week, one-half ha next week, use these fertilizers and these chemicals. The ex-diplomat built a packing shed to process the peas for European supermarkets. Within a couple of years, he had a large area under peas. But by 2004, inflation had become an issue and there was a major fall in horticulture exports (see Table 5.1 and Figure 5.1). The big problem was that hard currency receipts had to be converted to Zimbabwe dollars and then converted back to hard currency to buy inputs. And the former diplomat, along with many others, found that currency exchange meant that export horticulture simply was no longer profitable. He tried potatoes and seed maize, but they, too, proved unprofitable in the difficult economic climate.

At that point, after a big rethink, he moved into more integrated systems, doing more of his own processing. He argues that the middlemen, many of them former white farmers, take all the profit, and he can survive as a commercial farmer only by capturing some of that profit. He uses all the buzzwords, "value added" and "value chains," but actually does put them into practice.

He began by growing maize, sunflower, and soya. He grinds and packs maize meal, presses sunflower for oil, and presses soya to produce the emulsifier lecithin. The next step was to start processing for neighboring farmers, for cash or a share of the maize meal, oil, or oil cake. Then he took on pigs, using the oil cake left after pressing as part of their food. And then he moved on to marketing—finding people with electricity and a freezer, particularly near mining camps, who would sell his pork. When we interviewed him in August 2010, he claimed to have an entirely integrated production. "It has taken time and some experimentation," he said. He started with just a few pigs and expanded slowly. "I now make all my own feed and have proper growth rates in the pigs." The next step is to use the pig waste to produce biogas—a process he had seen when he was a diplomat.

None of it has been easy and there are still problems, the biggest of which is very irregular electricity. In rural Mazowe there is usually only electricity at night, often from 10 p.m. to 6 a.m. So his workers must come in at night to grind and pack maize meal and press oil. Indeed, he had to buy a second oil press because he could not run the first one for enough hours.

This story would not seem unusual in most parts of the world, but it is important in the context of Zimbabwe. Without any of the training and financial support given to white farmers 50 years ago, the diplomat is succeeding—and satisfies the six criteria we noted in chapter 7. His own investment has been important—he says he received only a single tractor and harrow in one of the government's equipment distributions, but all the other equipment he bought. Finally, his story highlights several points we elaborate further in the following sections: the cooperative role of some former white farmers, the disaster of hyperinflation and continuing electricity problems, the need to be flexible in the face of difficulties, the importance of contract farming even for big farmers (as it had been for white farmers before), and the fact that simply growing things is not enough and there must be other income streams.

A2 Farmers

The story of A2 farmers is much more mixed than that of A1 plotholders. A2 farms were intended to be commercial, and farmers were expected to bring money and experience. They were allocated in three sizes—small, medium, and large[1]—and were subject to area limits that were, in general, smaller than white commercial farms (see Table 9.1 on page 140). Government also announced a one-person, one-farm policy, and in late July 2003, the President himself in the ruling party's top decision-making body, the Politburo, told "top Zanu-PF officials with multiple farms to relinquish them within two weeks." At least 25,000 ha were recovered after second farms were released;[2] however, neither rule has been completely enforced.

There was very broad electronic and print media advertising and publicity encouraging people to apply for land. Six criteria were used to score A2 applications. Five gave 20 points each—income, property, cash flow, experience, and qualification and training—and there were an extra 10 points for women. The application form says that applicants must "provide proof of availability and/or ability to mobilise adequate resources." The applicant also had to supply a cash flow projection and "proof of training or experience in the agri-industry."[3]

To obtain an A2 small-scale farm required at least 30 points; medium, 60; and large, 90. Application forms were processed at provincial levels by mainly civil service teams. Nelson Marongwe, who looked closely at the Mashonaland provinces, and particularly Mashonaland East, for his PhD, reports that "for Mashonaland East Province, this was carried out at Pumpkin Hotel in Mutoko district over a two week period," July 15–29, 2001, by a team of 23 government officials from various departments, plus one representative of the war veterans. This part was largely technical, but it became political later.

Politics of A2

The A2 allocation process was much more political than the A1 distribution, in part because of the intense competition for land and for the best and biggest farms, and because of the leadership's real desire to create a new class of black commercial farmers. The Utete Report found that in Mashonaland East, 1,646 A2 plots had been allocated by mid-2003, but there were 35,000 applicants on the waiting list.[4] Although the application process was technical, the final decision-making process was political and somewhat disorganized. Allocations were done by the Ministry of Lands in Harare on the recommendation of the Provincial Land Identification Committee, which was chaired by the governor and consisted mainly of provincial-level representatives of government ministries and

Table 9.1 Maximum A2 Farm Sizes (ha) Set by Government in 2001

Natural Region	Small-Scale Commercial	Medium-Scale Commercial	Large-Scale Commercial
I	20	100	250
IIa	30	200	350
IIb	40	250	400
III	60	300	500
IV	120	700	1,500
V	240	1,000	2,000

agencies, but also, according to Nelson Marongwe, included representatives of the army, police, Zanu-PF as a political party, war veterans, and chiefs. In his PhD thesis, Marongwe notes that "applications for A2 farms were, in some cases, submitted through one's place of employment," including the Ministry of Defence, President's Office, police, and ministries. "Thus, a list of potential beneficiaries marked 'from the army' etc. would be submitted for consideration" by a committee with people from the army and Zanu-PF. "Political bias in the selection criteria was therefore inevitable." The issue was compounded by the way the Ministry of Lands also allocated land without reference to the provincial committees.[5]

The 2003 Report of the Utete Committee was outspoken in saying that "politicians and war veterans used their positions to influence the allocations" and committee members allocated land to themselves.

Provincial governors told Utete "that there was no uniform mechanism for the selection of beneficiaries for the A2 resettlement model with offer letters being generated from the Head Office of the Ministry of Lands, Agriculture and Rural Resettlement, the Provincial Governors' Offices, or even the District Administrators' Offices." Utete reported "political interference" in allocations and that Provincial and District Land Identification Committees had difficulty working because of "conflicting instructions and directives from central Government Ministers and even junior officials of key Ministries." Governors allocated land irregularly, and "prominent politicians" and war veterans exerted improper influence to allocate plots, particularly A2.[6]

There were "double allocations, multiple allocations, and favouritism in land allocation." The report cites the case of Hurungwe in Mashonaland West where the district administrator "did not post 341 offer letters to the beneficiaries, but instead, issued his own offer letters to favoured people."[7]

One reason for very low take-up of A2 offers in Mashonaland East was that 721 offer letters, some dating back to November 2001, had not been distributed before the March 31, 2003, deadline had expired. This may not have been accidental, because "it was discovered that most of the plots had been allocated to at least two different applicants."[8]

Knowing the system helped, although the application process was difficult even for those who were in an advantageous position. A district agronomist with Agritex who has a diploma and degree in agriculture nevertheless attributes her allocation of land to the fact that at the time she was involved in planning A2 farms. Because of her job, she knew the system and, without this knowledge and interaction, she thinks that she probably would not have gotten the farm. She had applied for land in 2000 but got nothing, and it was only after being transferred to Goromonzi and becoming involved with the land demarcation that she was successful.

Another woman was very determined, but admits she "copied and pasted" her farm plan and cash flow on her application, adding individual details as necessary. She admits, "I exaggerated as I actually had nothing, but am very capable and was determined to get some land to farm on. Life is very challenging with lots of problems and I needed to supplement my income." She comments that "it is not clear how much these applications were scrutinised." She was allocated 34 ha in Mazowe and in fact she had some experience—her father and grandfather had small African purchase farms, in a dry, infertile area—and now she is doing well.

And we saw the other side. A woman who falsely claimed to be an ex-combatant had gained an A2 farm with the old farmhouse perched on top of a small hill. She is producing relatively well but has used the money to buy the three new cars in her driveway and has never bought a tractor. One neighbor commented on her sense of entitlement: "She thinks tractors and combine harvesters come free." Indeed, she complained about the lack of resources, and asked us: "Don't you know someplace to get donors to help us?"

In his PhD thesis, Nelson Marongwe looks closely at A2 farms. He alleges that in some cases senior political figures displaced already settled A1 farmers to obtain a large farm. He cites four cases in Mazowe district, Mashonaland Central: a Zanu-PF party Central Committee member, a cabinet minister, and two senior Zanu-PF officials. However, in at least two cases, the Provincial Land Allocation Committee recommended withdrawing offer letters to the political A2 settlers.[9]

He looks at large farms in Mashonaland West, a province that is mostly in regions II and III, but with significant parts in IV and V. Two-thirds of the farms are under 50 ha and thus fit within the small-scale commercial criteria. However, 55 of the farms are over 500 ha, which suggests that some farms may be too large (see Table 9.2). Marongwe notes that 104 farms in the province were distributed as whole farms, 9 of which could be identified as part of the political elite: two ministers and a former minister, three MPs, a retired army commander, a retired reserve bank governor, and a Zimbabwe Broadcasting Corporation employee.[10]

His thesis looks in most detail at Goromonzi district, Mashonaland East, which is close to Harare and thus is particularly attractive for Harare-based elites. There are 432 A2 farms in the district, and he gives a list of 20 "high profile land allocations in Goromonzi." The district is in Natural Region IIa, the maximum farm size should be 350 ha, and 8 of his 20 are over that. The largest farm went to the former Zanu-PF provincial chair of Mashonaland East (1,606 ha) and next went to the director of prisons (1,028 ha); neither of those are listed in the *A2 Land Audit* and seem to have been transferred as whole farms outside the fast track.

Others on the Marongwe list include a director in the Central Intelligence Organisation (432 ha), another cabinet minister, the governor of Harare Province, and the director general of the Central Intelligence Organisation. Other political figures who received medium or large A2 farms in Goromonzi, according to Marongwe, included the chair of the Mashonaland East Women's League, the former chair of the Education

Table 9.2 Size of A2 Farms in Mashonaland West Province, 2004

Farm size (ha)	Number of farms
1–19.9	326
20–49.9	2,750
50–99.9	910
100–199.9	437
200–499.9	283
500–1,499.9	48
1,500–2,999.9	4
3,000–4,999.9	3
Total	4,767

Source: Marongwe, "Interrogating," from various government documents, 2008.

committee, the deputy secretary of the Ministry of Health and Child Welfare, another cabinet minister, the deputy director in the Office of the President, and the district administrator of Goromonzi.[11]

More Productive, but Not Enough Yet

The decision to retain a large-scale farming sector remains controversial and must be justified in part on productivity. In chapter 3 we established the white farmers as a benchmark: using only one-third of the land, and only one-third of the farms being significantly profitable. We argue that is not good enough, and the new larger farmers can be considered a success only if they do significantly better than their white predecessors. But we also recognize that it takes a generation to make a farm successful, and we still have a long way to go.

Lack of data is a serious problem. The *A2 Land Audit* in 2006 surveyed 79% of allocated A2 farms. It gives a snapshot from early in land reform and those data are still widely cited. It ranked their A2 farming and found more than half to be "productive" and 4% to be "highly productive" (see Table 9.3). This was impressive in 2006, considering the slowness of the applications process and assigning land, plus the need to arrange financing, which delayed people taking on the farms. (Chapter 6 gives more details from the audit, including the self-identification of the beneficiaries.) But as Table 9.3 also makes clear, in 2006, nearly half of A2 farms were under-used or not used at all.

As the table also shows, Mashonaland West was the only province where less than half of the land was productive or highly productive, although Mashonaland East also scored poorly; at independence, white farmers in those two provinces only cropped 25% and 15% of the land, respectively, but the new farmers should have been doing much better than their white predecessors. Both provinces suffered political infighting that delayed land allocation and made people feel insecure and less willing to invest.

Six years have passed since the 2006 *A2 Land Audit,* and there is no comparable more recent survey. But we know that the 2006–8 hyperinflation made investment almost impossible, so there was probably little change over the next three years. However, dollarization made dramatic changes to the economy, and we saw new investment on A2 farms. We also saw empty and under-used A2 farms. In chapter 3, we cited the chairman of the Rhodesia rural land board flying over Mashonaland in

1965 and calling it "a national disgrace that so much land is lying idle."
The equivalent of flying is Google Earth, and the most recent images
(2009 and 2010) show extensive farming in Mashonaland, which suggests that much less land was under-used in 2010 than in 2006. Not a
"national disgrace" as in the white era, but still some way to go.

There is also debate about small versus large A2 farms, and granting
or leasing some entire former white farms. But the *A2 Land Audit* showed
large A2 farms to be more productive than average in 2006, with many
more "highly productive" and far fewer underused (see Table 9.4).[12]

Table 9.3 Productivity Levels of A2 Farms, 2006

	Highly productive	Productive	Under-utilized	Not used
Manicaland	5%	55%	28%	11%
Mashonaland Central	3%	54%	40%	2%
Mashonaland East	5%	48%	43%	4%
Mashonaland West	4%	43%	44%	9%
Masvingo	4%	72%	15%	10%
Matebeleland North	5%	64%	28%	4%
Matebeleland South	8%	51%	33%	9%
Midlands	5%	64%	28%	4%
Total	4%	51%	37%	7%

Source: A2 Land Audit Report.

Table 9.4 Productivity of Large A2 Farms Compared to All A2 Farms,
2006

	Highly productive	Productive	Under-utilized	Not used
Mashonaland Central				
All A2 farms	3%	54%	40%	2%
Large A2 farms	24%	52%	20%	4%
Mashonaland East				
All A2 farms	5%	48%	43%	4%
Large A2 farms	21%	53%	17%	9%
Mashonaland West				
All A2 farms	4%	43%	44%	9%
Large A2 farms	23%	44%	26%	7%

Source: A2 Land Audit Report.

Of Marongwe's 20 "high profile land allocations in Goromonzi," we can find 6 on the 2006 *A2 Land Audit*. Marongwe's third-largest farm is that of General Constantine Chiwenga, commander of Zimbabwe Defence Forces (1,020 ha), of whom the 2006 *A2 Land Audit* says, "highly productive farmer. The farmer has constructed tobacco barns and greenhouses where he is growing roses for export." Next is Zanu-PF Politburo member and Mashonaland East governor David Karimanzira (941 ha), who was rated "highly productive" by the *A2 Land Audit*. The four others who can be identified from the 2006 audit are all considered to be "productive." They are David Chapfika[13] (351 ha), MP for Mutoko (Mashonaland East) and later deputy minister of finance; Dr. Olivia Muchena (228 ha), who was deputy minister of lands and agriculture until 2001, and who was a senior lecturer in agriculture at the University of Zimbabwe before going into government; Herbert Murerwa (499 ha), minister of finance and later minister of lands; and Patterson Karimanzira (brother of David, 370 ha), whom the audit considered "a promising farmer with a good future in farming."[14]

Goromonzi highlights what has become a central debate in land reform. Once it has been decided that a large-scale, capital-intensive farming sector should continue, and that the demand for these big farms will be much larger than the supply, is it reasonable to give some of these farms to ministers who then use the land productively or highly productively? A 2006 joint statement by Zimbabwean churches said: "Most worrying is the seemingly unfair advantage captured by highly placed officials and those connected to them in land and water allocation over poor communal farmers and other disadvantaged groups."[15] But once it has been decided that there is to be an A2 sector where priority goes to people with money, how does one define *fair*? And there is another question: Are generals and ministers—even if highly productive—to be subject to the same maximum farm sizes as other land-reform farmers?

Bootstrap Investment

Large-scale farming is capital-intensive, and white farmers in the colonial and UDI eras received huge subsidies. The scale of investment needed was shown by a 2011 article in *African Affairs,* the journal of the Royal African Society in the United Kingdom, on 13 Zimbabwean farmers who went to Kwara state in Nigeria to set up farms of 1,000 ha each. Federal and state governments and Nigerian banks invested at least $37 million—nearly $3,000 per hectare—and in 2011, the farmers were in trouble and unable to repay their debts.[16] In the previous chapter we cited Scoones and colleagues' calculation that A1 farmers were investing less than that per farm, because they had to find the money themselves. In the mid-1970s, white farmers were being subsidized by the Rhodesian government at the equivalent of $10,000 per A2 farm per year (see chapter 8).

The *Baseline Survey* (see chapter 6) showed just how serious the under-capitalization is. In 2006, only 32% of A2 farmers owned a tractor; indeed, only 80% even owned a wheelbarrow. And 83% of A2 farmers were reliant on their own financial resources.[17] To be sure, this was a condition that A2 applicants were supposed to meet, but pulling yourself up by your bootstraps makes developing a farm much slower.

The *A2 Land Audit* confirms this picture, also showing that only 31% of A2 farmers owned a tractor. But the audit asked more detailed questions, and the results are shown in Table 9.5. In particular, 52% could afford to hire a tractor when they did not own one, which meant that only 17% depended entirely on cattle or hand digging.[18]

There is also some movement between A1 and A2. Farmers who are doing poorly on A2 move back to A1, while others move up the ladder. Alice Masuka graduated from an A1 farm to an A2 farm because of her

Table 9.5 How A2 Farmers Plowed in 2006

	Own tractor	Hired tractor (but do not own)	Own cattle (do not use tractor)	Own no cattle or tractor, & hire cattle or hand dig
Manicaland	22%	61%	12%	5%
Mashonaland East	35%	54%	11%	1%
Mashonaland Central	43%	47%	10%	0%
Mashonaland West	30%	50%	18%	1%
Masvingo	19%	70%	10%	1%
Matebeleland North	21%	68%	11%	0%
Matebeleland South	11%	43%	45%	1%
Midlands	21%	46%	30%	3%
Total	**31%**	**52%**	**16%**	**1%**

Note: Those who own a tractor may also hire one, or also use cattle, and some who hire tractors also use cattle.

Source: A2 Land Audit Report.

hard work and production record in Vungu, a region of relatively low agricultural potential. The A2 farm was virgin land and she sold her house in town to pay for clearing the land. "I made people realize that poverty can be alleviated through farming and their standards of living can improve through hard work and practice of good farming methods." She has become a role model inspiring and assisting other women farmers in the area. But we also met an A2 farmer in Spring Valley, Goromonzi, who had been so good as an A1 farmer that he bought a tractor and was given his 75-ha plot in 2008. But now the tractor is broken and he does not have enough money to hire one to plow his fields. "I am penniless," he admits. "In reality, we are not surviving."

Others, too, are in trouble. We visited an A2 farm of a woman who crossed the border to Mozambique to join the guerrillas in 1975 and also played a leading role in the *jambanja*. She finished her schooling after the war and was employed by the Ministry of Education, but now is full-time on her farm. She is using less than half her 100 arable hectares for maize and tobacco (using the tobacco barns of the old white farmer). She earns enough to pay school fees for her two sons at boarding school, but we arrived to find her tobacco workers on strike, because she did not have enough money to pay them. She is seriously under-capitalized and is having trouble making enough profit to reinvest. "I am struggling," she admits.

Any criteria of "fairness" would suggest that this woman war veteran deserves land, but without support, can she make a go of A2 commercial farming?

The Report of the Utete Committee noted, "Most of the beneficiaries indicated that they had basic farming skills and, at the same time, expressed the need to be trained in farm management, marketing and use of irrigation equipment."[19]

Many A2 farmers have realized that to be successful requires multiple income streams, as in the case of the former diplomat at the beginning of the chapter who marketed his own pigs. Lethinali Sidimeli is a war veteran who trained as a nurse and then set up a small chemical company selling cleaning and water chemicals. She has 190 ha arable; the former white farmer is still there, because he kept his rose greenhouses. She is using all of the land for maize, soya, and sugar beans but says, "This cannot be viable on its own." Using her chemical company experience, she bought a water-bottling system in South Africa for $25,000 and now sells Glendale Spring bottled water (which we later bought in a Goromonzi supermarket). Her next project is fish.

A2 farmers are required to bring their investment capital with them. Chiripanyanga Paradzai owns two supermarkets and was given an A2 tobacco farm on Springdale in 2006. He is using profits from the supermarkets to rehabilitate the farm and admits he is not making money yet. The farm had 16 derelict tobacco barns and he has rehabilitated four. He started with 5 ha of tobacco and is now up to 30 ha and will keep expanding as he rehabilitates more barns. Like others, he has other sources of income—in his case, beef—and is planning to expand to raise chickens.

In addition to the ordinary A2 farmers, there are about 1,000 black large-scale, commercial farmers who bought white farms or leased them from the government, plus 200 who have been given large A2 farms. Together they now account for about 3% of the farmland. In a study of Mazowe district, Prosper Matondi found that there were 49 indigenously owned farms on 34,000 ha, accounting for 10% of the farmland in the district; these were not taken under Fast Track, but there appears to have been some swapping, with farmers being given alternative land. They range in size from over 1,000 ha in dry parts of the district to as small as 20 ha.[20]

The White Cornucopia and Black Disaster Myth

Charles Tafts, head of the white Commercial Farmers Union, took BBC World Service journalist Martin Plaut along the road northwest of Harare toward Banket in November 2011. Plaut saw "derelict fields, with hardly anything here. It's a pretty depressing picture. . . . It seems completely dry." Plaut asked, "If I had been here ten years ago, what would I have seen?" Tafts replied, "You would have seen green fields throughout. . . . You are seeing an area where it has gone back to subsistence farming."[21] November is the end of the dry season. Driving along that road, you see tall brown grass that largely blocks the view of the fields behind. Even with some irrigation, you would never have seen "green fields throughout" at the end of the dry season, when most of the crop has been harvested and fields are bare. White farmers only used a small part of their land in the dry season, and contrary to what Tafts says, in November a decade ago it would have looked very similar. White farmers, like the new black farmers, had no magic powers to create green fields in November. But the Google Earth satellite pictures of Harare-Banket road show extensive farming.

Plaut interviewed consultant John Robertson, who said, "In most parts of the country, you will find that the land that has been allocated to all of these farmers has lain vacant," which we have seen was not true even in 2006, when A2 farmers were already using more land than their white predecessors had.

Meanwhile, the black disaster myth bumps into the stories of evil cronies. In 2009, there was a scandal in Europe because Nestlé Zimbabwe was buying a million liters of milk a year from Gushungo Dairy Estate, controlled by Grace Mugabe, wife of the President.[22] Grace Mugabe is subject to EU sanctions, but Nestlé is a Swiss company and Switzerland does not impose sanctions on Zimbabwe. Far from being vacant, idle, or just subsistence, the farm was producing so much high-quality milk that it could sell to one of the world's largest multi-national food companies. We also visited the farm of a sanctioned minister who was exporting oranges to Zambia and producing large quantities of potatoes.

White Farmers in the New Zimbabwe

Coincidences sometimes provide a reality check. We were at a *braai* (barbeque) where we met a black farmer who was not in fact a land-reform farmer, but the son of a purchase farmer. Like many other bright young men, he had turned his back on farming and had gone into tourism. But as his father was getting older, he paid more attention to the family farm. "I started getting into cattle" in the 1990s, he explained, and he started talking to the neighboring white farmer who was already well known in the community as a cattle breeder with a pedigree Brahman herd. But the white farmer stressed the value of traditional Shona cattle, which are slightly smaller but hardier and adapted to Zimbabwe; they are much more drought- and disease-resistant and survive on local grass. The white farmer promoted cross-breeding of Shona and Brahman cattle and lent his neighbor a breeding bull, and he started to build his herd. Through the white farmer, "I came to understand that I could make a good living from cattle. Now, I have a passion for cattle." We asked the name of the white farmer, and he said Keith Campbell, whom we had interviewed two weeks before.

Sitting in the living room of his well-worn farmhouse on Constantia Estates, with his dog curled up on a chair, Keith Campbell says land reform "had to happen. The communal lands were overcrowded; something had to be done. I regularly went into the communal areas trading cattle and I saw it. But a lot of the guys [white farmers] didn't, so they didn't understand [the occupations]." Keith also talks of his "passion" for cattle. And he is a practical man. As a farmer, he says, "There is nothing worse than living next to a poor neighbor." A good farmer will keep the fences mended, protect the trees, and not set snares (traps for wild animals that often also catch cattle). There were neighboring purchase farmers—black Zimbabweans who could buy land in the colonial era—with whom he already had links, but when some neighboring farms were divided up for resettlement in the early 1980s, he helped the new farmers with cattle, selling them heifers (virgin females) and assisting with spraying and vaccinating. Then, in 2000, "about 25 people led by the war veterans came and said, 'We want your farm.' So I invited them into this living room and passed around a bottle of brandy and we negotiated." He kept 2,250 ha of his 14,000 ha, and the occupiers agreed that they would resettle Keith's farmworkers as well. Well-known in the community, Shona-speaking, and willing to talk, he kept part of his farm. A white neighbor who was well-known locally for supporting the local school also kept part of his farm. Keith stresses, "There was no violence in this area, because we talked about it."[23] In 2011, representatives from Zanu-PF came and said they wanted his farm. Again he negotiated; new regulations meant a maximum of 500 ha per person, so he and his son, Craig, could keep half the farm. Initially the Zanu-PF group wanted the land next to the river, but after hours of talking, they negotiated boundaries that ensured both had access to the river and all of their cattle had water.[24]

Keith's son, Craig, had been farming tobacco and had helped some of the 1980s resettlement farmers to grow it as well. With the 2000 occupation, his own tobacco land was taken, and Craig went to Tanzania. But with dollarization, he has come back and established a contract farming company for resettlement tobacco farmers.

The Campbells illustrate the new role of white Zimbabwean farmers. Keith has kept some land and is still farming, as one of several hundred white farmers still on the land. Craig has moved up the value chain and is now a trader, supporting resettlement farmers.

This shift in the role of former white farmers was also noted in the study of Masvingo. Some former white ranchers were renting land from resettlement farmers, providing services (water pumps, veterinary drugs, transport, or fuel), or buying cattle in new resettlement areas. Former large-scale, commercial ranchers decided to stay and integrated into a new marketing system alongside smaller players.[25]

Sam Moyo notes that "former white farmers have moved up or downstream in the commercial farming chain by acting as contract financiers and marketers (even supervisors of the farming operations of the new farmers), and as such have retained financial interest and influence in areas such as poultry, tobacco, export beef, and horticulture."[26]

John Sole's Heyshott Farm in Glendale, Mazowe, has 21 ha of rose greenhouses and remains a major exporter, employing more than 1,000 people. In the 1990s, he owned three farms and released two of them for resettlement. One was Kiaora, where he kept a small area with a rose greenhouse, and where he is now responsible for the barley contract farming project mentioned in chapter 7. Delta, the brewery, will not buy from small farmers, so Sole acts as middleman, doing plowing and spraying and buying the crop from individual farmers and selling to Delta; he is expanding into soya contract farming with the A1 farmers on his former land.

Sole is also reported to have helped Vice President Joseph Msika (who died in 2009) develop his farm; Msika is said in 2007 to have opposed the eviction of white famers. A US embassy cable released through WikiLeaks said that white "farmers' fate depends to a large extent on whom they know. A connection to Msika, for example, . . . can result in cessation of an eviction process."[27] On the other hand, Sole unexpectedly sought a High Court order in 2009 to evict six land-reform farmers from land they had been allocated on Heyshott Farm.[28]

Scoones and colleagues, too, note that away from the limelight, the remaining white farmers in Masvingo have made arrangements with resettlement farmers, sharing grazing or marketing.[29] Prosper Matondi discovered that "in Mazowe district some white farmers regarded as good neighbours were also classified as 'indigenous' and had their farms spared, although in most cases on reduced land or one farm. In Mazowe, by 2004, 11 white individual farmers remained."[30]

Nelson Marongwe quotes a government document on white farmers giving reasons why some should remain: a farmer was "very forthcoming and straightforward, contributed to Zanu-PF party fund raising campaigns and also assists A1 and A2 farmers"; a farmer assisted in local area development, constructed a primary school, and was assisting A2 farmers; and farmers were assisting surrounding A1 settlers with tillage services. One farmer was said to support the surrounding community with transport, tillage, planting, and harvesting services; contributed to national events like the Independence celebrations; and was "cooperative and supported by local communities. Victory of Zanu-PF party in the last elections was attributed to him."[31]

But former white farmers are not necessarily sympathetic to the new farmers. In our research, we found that former white farmers working for nongovernmental organizations (NGOs) or contract farming companies were sometimes reluctant to work with land-reform farmers and would only work in communal areas. And sometimes it's personal and perhaps understandable. Davidson Nago was given land near Chiredzi, Masvingo. It was thick forest with huge trees that he had to clear by hand. He explained: "When we wanted to hire bulldozers, we couldn't, because the owners of these farms were the owners of the machinery. I went to talk to someone, saying I want you to clear my land, maybe 5–6 ha. And he agreed, and we agreed on a price, and when he asked me, where is your farm, and when I said Fair Range, he just walked away, and said, 'That's my uncle's farm,' and he just walked away from me."[32]

"A number of black large-scale or A2 farmers have hired white farm managers who were either former landowners or farm managers, and they are paid salaries and/or shares of the farm produce," notes Sam Moyo.[33] But our interviews showed that there are many problems with managers, black and white, and that it is essential for the owner to be present on the farm and not try to run it by cell phone. We often heard the aphorism, "It is the eye of the master that fattens the beast."

In his study of Concession, Mazowe district, Angus Selby found that of the 58 white farmers in the case-study area, 3 were still farming, 30 were in Harare, and 25 had left the country. This corresponded to other figures suggesting that more than half of the evicted farmers had stayed in Zimbabwe, at least initially. Selby stresses that it is simplistic to see white farmers as a homogeneous group: "White farmers, as a community, as an interest group, and as an economic sector, were always divided by their backgrounds, their geographical regions, their land uses and crop types. They were also divided by evolving planes of difference, such as affluence, political ideologies and farm structures."[34]

Estate Farms

"Substantial areas of large-scale foreign and state-owned agricultural estates were retained despite the extensive fast track land distribution process," reports Sam Moyo in the most detailed survey of that sector.[35] There are 247 large estate owners growing sugar, coffee, tea, timber, and beef and with wildlife conservancies; their area has been reduced from 2.6 mn ha in 2000 to 1.5 mn ha, with the rest occupied. Land not used for the main purpose, such as cattle land owned by a sugar estate, was taken, and white sugar and tea outgrowers have been partly replaced by black outgrowers. Main shareholders of these large estates are foreign or state companies.

Sugar, tea, and citrus production has returned to 1990s levels, although coffee has not. Sugar plantations had 47 white outgrowers, most of whose land was taken as part of land reform, and there are now 560 outgrowers (including one white outgrower).[36] Sugar is the main area of expansion. Triangle and Hippo Valley are run by Tongaat Hulett Sugar of South Africa. Triangle produced sugar-based ethanol to blend with petrol in the UDI period and this continued until 1992, when fuel prices were low. Production resumed in 2006 and is now being expanded rapidly. Development Trust of Zimbabwe (DTZ), founded by Joshua Nkomo (a founder of ZAPU and later vice president of Zimbabwe, who died in 1999) and a large and sometimes controversial landowner set aside 60,000 ha for resettlement and is developing a large sugar for ethanol project with white Zimbabwean businessman Billy Rautenbach's Zimbabwe Bio Energy. And the Agricultural Rural Development Authority (ARDA) is establishing 55,000 ha of sugarcane for ethanol, with three Zimbabwean companies.

Summing Up:
Large Farms and a Productive Elite

Maintaining a larger-scale commercial farming sector in which farmers are expected to provide their own capital automatically creates an elite sector. Some white farms have been maintained intact and many have been divided into three to six A2 farms, which are still quite large. In Zimbabwe, farming is seen as a means of accumulation, so there has been political infighting and favoritism in the allocation of A2 farms. The government set maximum farm sizes and a one-person, one-farm rule, but neither has been enforced consistently.

A2 farmers started more slowly, in part because the infighting delayed allocation, and then because hyperinflation made investment difficult. Some A2 farms remain empty or under-used. However, the new larger-scale farmers are proving to be as productive as their white predecessors, with a small group being highly productive. Both more "ordinary" new farmers and members of the political elite are proving successful. Investment remains an issue, and successful farmers need an off-farm source of money and will have to reinvest their farm income for the next decade to build up productivity.

Meanwhile, although many former white farmers left Zimbabwe, many others have stayed, some still with farms and others in agriculture-related businesses, and with links to the new farmers.

Larger farms are more politically charged and the Global Political Agreement calls for a land audit. Also, the rule of thumb that it takes a generation to develop a new farm applies to A2 as well as to A1. So the next decade will see many changes in the large commercial farming sector.

Notes

1. There were also peri-urban farms and a whole set of issues around urban expansion and taking over farmland for housing, which we do not consider in this book.

2. Charles Utete, *Report of the Presidential Land Review Committee on the Implementation of the Fast Track Land Reform Programme, 2000–2002* (Harare, Zimbabwe, 2003), 32 and 35 [known as the Report of the Utete Committee and cited here as the Utete Report], citing *The Herald,* July 31, 2003.

3. Ministry of Lands, Agriculture and Rural Resettlement, "Application for Land Under the Commercial Farm Settlement Scheme" (Harare, Zimbabwe: Author, 2000).

4. Utete Report, 38, 51.

5. Nelson Marongwe, "Interrogating Zimbabwe's Fast Track Land Reform and Resettlement Programme: A Focus on Beneficiary Selection" (PhD thesis, Institute for Poverty, Land and Agrarian Studies [PLAAS], University of the Western Cape, 2008), 154, 202–5 [Marongwe, "Interrogating"].

6. Utete Report, 47, 50, 54, 59.

7. Ibid., 47, 51, 55.

8. Ibid., 38, 51.

9. Marongwe, "Interrogating," 161–62.

10. Ibid., 149, 159.

11. Ibid., 235, 239.

12. Mashonaland Central (71 farms > 400 ha), Mashonaland East (47 farms > 500 ha), and Mashonaland West (61 farms > 500 ha).

13. David Karimanzira, Herbet Murerwa, and David Chapfika were on sanctions lists.

14. Marongwe, "Interrogating," 235, 239; Ministry of Lands, Land Reform and Resettlement & Informatics Institute, *A2 Land Audit Report* (Harare, Zimbabwe, 2006) [*A2 Land Audit Report*].

15. Zimbabwe Catholic Bishops Conference, Evangelical Fellowship of Zimbabwe, and Zimbabwe Council of Churches, "The Zimbabwe We Want:

Towards a National Vision for Zimbabwe" (Harare, Zimbabwe, 2006), available at http://zimjournalist1.blogspot.com/2006/11/section-5-national-economic-and-social.html (accessed December 15, 2011).

16. Abdul Raufu Mustapha, "Zimbabwean Farmers in Nigeria: Exceptional Farmers or Spectacular Support?" *African Affairs,* 110 (2011): 535–61.

17. Sam Moyo et al., *Fast Track Land Reform Baseline Survey in Zimbabwe* (Harare, Zimbabwe: African Institute for Agrarian Studies, 2009), Tables 2-24 and 4-25.

18. *A2 Land Audit Report.* The report was completed in eight volumes, one for each province, issued at different times during 2006.

19. Utete Report, 47.

20. Prosper Matondi, "Fast Tracking Land Reforms in Mazowe District in Zimbabwe" (Harare, Zimbabwe, 2011) [Matondi, "Fast Tracking"].

21. Martin Plaut, "Crossing Continents: Farming Zimbabwe," BBC Radio 4, December 1 and December 5, 2011 [Plaut, "Crossing Continents"], available at http://www.bbc.co.uk/programmes/b017mvx6#synopsis (December 7, 2011).

22. Sebastien Berger, "Nestlé to Stop Buying Grace Mugabe Dairy's Milk," *The Telegraph,* October 2, 2009, available at http://www.telegraph.co.uk/news/worldnews/africaandindianocean/zimbabwe/6252534/Nestle-to-stop-buying-Grace-Mugabe-dairys-milk.html (December 7, 2011).

23. The Utete Report (70) notes that in Midlands "most of the land acquisition in the province was carried out in consultation with the owners, which meant that most of it was acquired by consent."

24. Interview, April 11, 2011.

25. Blasio Mavedzenge et al., "The Dynamics of Real Markets: Cattle in Southern Zimbabwe Following Land Reform," *Development and Change,* 39, no. 4 (2008): 623.

26. Sam Moyo, "Three Decades of Agrarian Reform in Zimbabwe," *Journal of Peasant Studies,* 38, no. 3 (2011): 507 [Moyo, "Three Decades"].

27. WikiLeaks US Embassy Harare cable 07HARARE942, FINAL PUSH ON LAND SEIZURES, October 18, 2007, available at http://www.insiderzim.com/stories/2420-mujuru-and-mutasa-clash-over-farm-evictions.html (December 6, 2011).

28. "White Farmer Seeks to Evict Six Beneficiaries," *Herald,* August 25, 2009; see also Matondi, "Fast Tracking."

29. Ian Scoones et al., *Zimbabwe's Land Reform: Myths & Realities* (Woodbridge, Suffolk, UK: James Currey, 2010), 34.

30. Matondi, "Fast Tracking."

31. Marongwe, "Interrogating," 162–64, citing "Schedule A: Summary of Number of White Farmers to Remain and Number of White Farmers Before the Land Reform by Province."

32. Plaut, "Crossing Continents."

33. Moyo, "Three Decades," 507.

34. Angus Selby, "Commercial Farmers and the State: Interest Group Politics and Land Reform in Zimbabwe" (PhD thesis, University of Oxford, 2006), 10, 319.

35. Sam Moyo, "Land Concentration and Accumulation After Redistributive Reform in Post-settler Zimbabwe," *Review of African Political Economy,* 38, no. 128 (2011): 257–76.

36. Sam Moyo, "Changing Agrarian Relations After Redistributive Land Reform in Zimbabwe," draft, April 27, 2011.

10

Women Take Their Land

SITTING IN HER KITCHEN, YOU KNOW THIS IS THE CENTER OF TABETH GOROVO'S WORLD.
It is the standard round brick Shona kitchen with a thatched roof and fire
and cooking area in the middle, and a bench running around the wall,
but it is larger than usual and bright and airy. She has a solar panel outside, linked to the radio, which is on. Tabeth was a second wife and she
had to share just 1 ha of land with the other wife. So during *jambanja*
she came here and occupied the land. She built her house in 2002 and
this kitchen in 2003. She grows maize and groundnuts, some of which
she sells, and makes peanut butter and her own cooking oil from her sunflower seeds. With a gross cash income of perhaps $2,000, she is in the
upper part of the middle range of farmers whom we defined in chapter
8. She has two full-time workers, has built her house and kitchen, and is
slowly expanding her numbers of chickens and cattle. But she explains
that what is important to her is "peace of mind." She has her independence and her own land; she is living much better than she was in the
communal area.

Rosemary Mhiripiri's parents were part of the 1980s resettlement,
but there was no land for her, so she joined the occupation in 2000. She
met her future husband as part of the occupation, but insisted on keeping her own land on Springdale Farm, while her husband's land is on
another farm. "I produce enough to feed the family—no problem!" she
says.

The first phase of Zimbabwe's land-reform process, from 1980 to
1998, while alleviating poverty to some extent,[1] also continued the customary land policies that favored men over women. Permits were issued

157

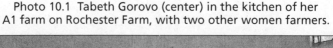

Photo 10.1 Tabeth Gorovo (center) in the kitchen of her
A1 farm on Rochester Farm, with two other women farmers.

to household heads, usually male. In the early stages of land reform, government policy was that a settler had to be either married or widowed, thereby discriminating against married women (since permits were issued in the name of the husband) and especially unmarried women.[2] Women were at the forefront of *jambanja*, participating alongside men in the struggle to gain access to land.[3] To a large extent, obtaining A1 land was self-determined, as those who really wanted it persevered until they were allocated, either individually or as part of the family. As these women show, having access to better and more land has transformed the lives of many of them. Their enthusiasm and joy, as well as sheer hard work and determination, are inspirational. Women are far from reaching equality, but the fast track land reform has been a major change, created by women themselves who have been pushing for quotas, credit, and their names on land documents. And the process has continued; women gained more land and power as the decade moved on.

Women have been organizing around land. Women and Land in Zimbabwe (WLZ) was established in 1998[4] by activists and academics who have had some success in improving women's formal rights to land. Then in 2006, a group of women land-reform farmers realized they

Photo 10.2 Rosemary Mhiripiri on Springdale Farm, shelling groundnuts.

needed different kinds of support and formed the Women Farmers Land and Agriculture (WFLA) Trust.[5] It now has more than 2,000 members. Some are women farming with their husbands but with the women being the managers and running the farm; others are single women farmers who are divorced, widowed, or never married. This chapter draws on action research by WFLA Trust that directly involved women farmers in Goromonzi and Vungu in 2009[6] and Goromonzi, Mazowe, and Murehwa districts in 2011. Phides Mazhawidza, WFLA Trust executive president and herself a farmer, and Fadzai Chiware, WFLA program officer, coordinated the research. The group in Goromonzi in the first photo in chapter 2 is part of WFLA.

In this chapter we look at how women fared, focusing on their experiences in the land-reform process, not just in accessing and securing land, but how they are using the land and how doing so has changed their lives. While working with the women farmers we found them well-organized and highly efficient. They would mobilize themselves quickly, agree on a leader, and organize the research schedules. During our research visits, the women farmers would proudly show us their production, insisting that we tour all of their fields. On our journeys home, our vehicle was loaded down with sweet potatoes and pumpkins of all shapes and sizes, given to us by the women farmers.

Traditional patriarchal systems in Africa were reconstructed under colonialism in ways that benefited men, disadvantaged women, and strengthened male control over female labor.[7] As Mwalimu Julius Nyerere, lamented: "Women in Africa toil all their lives on land that they do not own, to produce what they do not control, and at the end of the marriage, through divorce or death, they can be sent away empty-handed."[8] Too often, this did not change after independence, and in Zimbabwe, the land-reform program focused on racial imbalances of highly skewed landholdings and discriminatory land tenure systems, rather than addressing gender disparities, and some researchers maintain that land reform in Zimbabwe discriminated against women. For example Goodhope Ruswa argues that very few women benefited from the land-reform process,[9] while Allison Goebel argues that the Fast Track Land Reform program continues to privilege men as primary recipients of resettlement land, and the involvement of traditional authorities in the land-reform process continues to marginalize women.[10] Even at the global level, reviews show that no land-access project has had unqualified success in allocating land to women and men at equitable levels.[11]

Zimbabwe's process was "gender neutral," but in a male-dominated society, neutrality results in gender gaps in land ownership, control, management, and productivity. At the onset of the resettlement, the policy framework did not provide an enabling environment to redress gender imbalances of land and inheritance issues, especially those pertaining to widows. This resulted in ad hoc practices based on prevailing customs. The existence of the dual legal system, with both customary law and statutory law in issues of inheritance and marriage, has resulted in discrimination against women in terms of accessing land in their own right or as equal citizens.[12]

However, no process is static; 11 years down the line there have been fundamental changes in both policy and practice. Women still do not receive their fair share of land, but they have made significant gains, first as active participants in the *jambanja,* and now increasingly inheriting land, which follows directly from campaigns to ensure that married couples had both names on the letters granting them their farms. Gertrude Chimbwanda is an A1 farmer who had just received $4,200 from the sale of her tobacco when we talked to her in 2011. "As a widow and woman farmer, I think I have done well for myself because I managed to build a homestead, I own a few goats and road runners [chickens]. This farming season I planted tobacco, barley and maize. I am honoured to be a woman land owner and it has helped to look after my family after my husband passed away."

Numerous policy statements recognize the need for women to have fair access to land and for the land-reform process to be gender-sensitive. The September 2008 Global Political Agreement (GPA), which created the unity government, has a clause (5.8) "recognising the need for women's access and control over land in their own right and as equal citizens."

Allocations to Women Under Fast Track

Overall, 34% of households in Zimbabwe are female-headed, with a higher percentage, 38%, in rural areas.[13] The number of de facto female heads is higher as men often migrate to towns and mines in search of work, leaving their wives to care for their families in rural villages. This led women's groups, notably WLZ, to lobby for a 20% quota for women. The document prepared for the ill-fated 1998 donors' conference on land reform mentions women as a "special group" and talks specifically of working with WLZ, but it set no quota.[14]

The Utete Committee in 2003 found that more than 23,500 women had received land, but "that the number of females allocated land under the Fast Track was very low country wide." Women-headed households received only 18% of A1 farms and 12% of A2[15] (see Table 10.1). Sam Moyo and his team found a slightly higher figure in their 2006 *Baseline Survey:* 21% women in A1 and 15% women in A2.[16] This compares to 4% of white farms owned by women, and 5% of 1980s land-reform farms given to women.[17]

Patterns vary greatly throughout the country; women received over 20% of farms in only two provinces: Mashonaland East A1 and Matabeleland South A2. "Given the historically diverse and pivotal role of women in all aspects of agriculture in the communal lands and the need to strike an overall gender balance in this crucial sector of the economy," the Utete Committee recommended that "a quota of at least 40% of the land allocations should be made to women especially in A1 areas."[18]

It does appear that more women have been obtaining land as time passes. In research in 2007 in Zvimba district (Mashonaland West), in an area not far from Harare, Tendai Murisa found that 25% of the A1 beneficiaries were women, while 22% of the A2 beneficiaries were women.[19]

Table 10.1 Land Allocation Under the Fast Track Land Reform
Programme by Gender and Province

Province	A 1 Model				A 2 Model			
	Male beneficiaries		Female beneficiaries		Male beneficiaries		Female beneficiaries	
	%	Number	%	Number	%	Number	%	Number
Midlands	82	14,800	18	3,198	95	338	5	17
Masvingo	84	19,026	16	3,644	92	709	8	64
Mash. Central	88	12,986	12	1,770	87	1,469	13	215
Mash. West	81	12,782	19	5,270	89	1,777	11	226
Mash. East	76	12,967	24	3,992	No data	No data	No data	No data
Mat. South	87	7,754	13	1,169	79	215	21	56
Mat. North	84	7,919	16	1,490	83	574	17	121
Manicaland	82	9,572	18	2,190	91	961	9	97
Total	82	106,986	18	22,723	88	6,043	12	796

Note: Mash. = Mashonaland; Mat. = Matebeleland.
Source: Utete Report, 25.

Ian Scoones and colleagues found that in their study in Masvingo, relatively few women received land initially (14% of A1 and 12% of A2),
but that a much larger number gained access when land was transferred,
through either inheritance or reallocation (30% of A1 and 50% of A2).[20]
In the three resettlement farms we looked at more closely, with 102 farmers, at Kiaora Farm (Mazowe), women constituted 33% of beneficiaries. At Springdale (Murehwa) and Brookmead (Goromonzi), women
accounted for only 16% of formal beneficiaries, but at Springdale 23%
of women were the key decision maker and 16% at Brookmead, even
though the farm was in the name of a husband or son.

Women in *Jambanja*

A determined woman farmer and war veteran in Concession area of
Mazowe, Chipo Chimurenga, describes *jambanja* as being "well coordinated with organised structures, dominated by war veterans. Both men
and women—and all were treated as equals." Our research confirms
this. Some women, such as Agnes (who lost her leg in the war and is

interviewed in chapter 1), led and organized invasions and drew on their experience in the liberation war. Wilbert Sadomba notes that during the invasions in Goromonzi, the War Veterans Committee was led by three powerful women, more active and senior than the men on the committee.[21] Joseph Chaumba and colleagues noted that in Chiredzi district farm invasions men and women were segregated at night and that some settlers were visited regularly by their wives, who would bring food and do their washing.[22] *Jambanja* was often a family event, with family members assisting and supporting those who were occupying and taking turns to sustain the occupation.

Chipo, who was eventually resettled on an A2 farm, tells one story: "At the beginning of 2000, together with about 25 others, more women than men, we invaded a farm and occupied it for between three and four months. There was no violence. The objective was to frustrate the white farmer until he could no longer operate effectively and left, by such annoying activities as drumming, singing, whistling, dancing and lighting cooking fires in odd places like in front of the farmhouse. Eventually the commercial farmer left and the farm was divided into plots for resettlement. In our case, all of the invaders were allocated land, but not necessarily on the farm we invaded."

Fabby Shangwa, a white-haired woman with a big laugh and a farmer on Belmont Farm, Goromonzi, describes the often tenuous process and various problems she encountered, and how she was determined to overcome these problems: "On June 15, 2002, as a group we invaded a farm and on June 20, 2002, government orders were read and orders were given for us to be allocated land. We were made to pick pieces of paper from a hat. The papers had numbers on them. The number that one picked was the number of the plot we would be allocated. After settling on my plot the white farmer would sometimes come and threaten us to leave the farm. The white farmer was conniving with the then District Administrator who, in some way which we did not understand, gave the land back to the white farmer. The District Administrator told us if we did not want to leave we were going to be arrested. I was so angry that day I messed my pants. The white farmer did not stop there—he let his cattle destroy our maize crops. I thought enough was enough and I confronted the farmer and told him I wanted my maize that his cattle had eaten. The white farmers ended up buying me 10 kg of fertilizer and 10 kg of maize seed as compensation."

Driven by the opportunity for better and more land, some women farmers from nearby congested communal areas initiated the invasions, while their husbands stayed at home. However, as things got tougher and conditions more difficult, many of the women who participated at first eventually gave up. Lack of infrastructure such as sanitation, schools, and markets in these farms affected women, who are the child caregivers and food providers, more seriously than men. Furthermore, there were several instances where married couples successfully fought together during *jambanja* for the land, but afterward they divorced, and the women lost their access to the plot.

We found a link between women who had participated in the liberation war and those who accessed land. Women war veterans, together with women from communal areas, displayed singular determination and perseverance to acquire and secure land for themselves and others. Women war veterans, such as Alice and Agnes, were catalysts for mobilizing other women. This link is remarkable in that the occupations occurred 20 years after independence. Although these women became mothers, wives, and homemakers,[23] our research indicates that they never lost the initial passion for land that drove them to join the liberation struggle.

Family structures in rural Zimbabwe are often complex. Men and women often have former partners and children from other relationships. Women's and men's interests within the family and with respect to land are both joint and separate. For women, land can be important to support their children. Some women, like Gorovo at the beginning of the chapter, used *jambanja* to create personal independence and to get away from polygamous marriages. Others were escaping disputes with neighbors or accusations of witchcraft. "Women were able to join the land occupations freely and were warmly welcomed," and independent women were allocated land alongside men, notes Ian Scoones. "Some, and particularly women, point to the emancipatory potentials of joining a new community, away from abusive husbands or families and escaping accusations and marginalisation. Others looked to a future offering the potential of handing down land to the next generation."[24]

Women as Partners

Although some women accessed land in their own right, most obtained it indirectly through their husbands, or as daughters and sisters. The *A2 Land Audit Report* noted that only 1,315 women were given A2 farms, but 8,032 gained access through their husbands. Similarly, 9,167 men received land in their name, but an additional 577 gained access to land because their wives had been given an A2 farm.[25]

Within the household, women and men both participate in farming activities, but in Zimbabwe there is some gendered division of labor where men plow and women weed, and both take part in harvesting. Women concentrate more on vegetables and gardens; men tend to be responsible for cattle, and women for chickens and goats.

But wives and husbands accessed and use the land together; rather than taking a backseat, our research showed women taking a lead in managing the farms and making decisions. All married women we talked to had a real sense of ownership and involvement in the farming operations. Decisions about farming, unlike family issues, appear to be more democratic, with more room for women to negotiate on an equal footing with men. Women are regarded as equal partners, with their role in farming operations acknowledged.

Ottilia Muguti, in her early 40s and mother of three, left her teaching job in Harare to join her husband, who had been allocated an A2 farm. She finds farming more rewarding, although it is hard work and she has to get up in the middle of the night to attend to the dairy. Without any formal training, she had to learn on the job, often making discouraging mistakes, and now manages most of the farm activities with her husband. Despite setbacks, she would not like to go back to teaching. Ottilia explains that discussions and decisions about farm management are separate from discussions about family issues. These discussions used to take place in the bedroom, but since not all farming deliberations could be agreed upon easily or amicably, and sometimes were left unresolved, Ottilia decided to convert an unused room into the "boardroom" to be used exclusively for discussing farm business.

Often we saw men deferring to their wives regarding farming, especially where men have kept a job in the city. When we interviewed Fidalis Mhonda, a senior military police officer, he said, "Talk to my wife—she's the one who runs the farm. She has the strategic plan and even drives the tractor." This decision-making role of wives is corroborated by Prisca Mugabe, who found that in a study in Chimanimani, some women had influence on land use in their households, despite the fact that the land was not registered in their names. Some women make decisions because the household is female-managed while others make decisions even when the husband is present.[26]

Women's Solidarity

Esther Makwara (introduced in chapter 7) and Teresa Mawadza are both A1 farmers in Mazowe district. Both of their husbands died recently, but at the time of land reform the husbands kept their jobs, stayed in the background, and supported their wives and were proud of their farming achievements. They even admitted that their wives' farming was more lucrative than their jobs in town. Teresa, a former teacher, gave up her job and put all her resources into farming, including buying cattle; she is the village head of the A1 settlement of Kiaora. With her A1 farm profits she is able to send her children to university in South Africa. On the other hand, Esther reinvested her profits back into the farm and has bought a tractor and other farm equipment. But Esther and Teresa show how solidarity between women can play an important role—Esther lends her tractor to Teresa because she sees the importance of Teresa's children going to university.

We found that the major constraint women faced in accessing land was the bureaucratic process. Women succeeded by persevering, women helping other women, and, often, just being in the right place at the right time. A civil servant with a sound agricultural background, including a diploma and degree in agriculture, first applied for land in 2000 when the advertisement appeared in the national newspapers. It took her nearly four years to acquire her A2 plot on Goromonzi, during which time she had gone to the Ministry of Lands almost every month to remind it about her application. "It depends on who you know in the offices and you have to practice a lot of patience!" But she attributes her eventual success to the assistance of the provincial chief lands officer, who was a woman. "She helped me because I am a woman, and she also helped other women to get land."

And a woman war veteran in Mazowe said she was helped in the application process by the presence of another woman war veteran on the Provincial Land Committee for Mashonaland Central, in Bindura.

These experiences reflect what Sam Moyo[27] sums up as the difficulties women face in applying for land, namely bureaucratic constraints, gender biases among selection structures made up mainly of men, the lack of information about the process, and poor mobilization of women's activist organizations around the issue of applications. Even though the government selection procedure for A2 applicants gives more score points to women, the proportion of access for women did not increase adequately. However, we have seen that when women were determined to get land, and were prepared to push for it, they were successful.

Inheritance Still a Source of Insecurity

Land reform has made much clearer a woman's right to land, irrespective of her marital circumstances. However, women's security of tenure is not automatic and often has to be fought for. "Traditional" male power remains an issue, for names on offer letters and for subsequent inheritance and transfer.

A current case in Concession, Mazowe district, typifies the issues. A woman battled to secure an A1 farm in her own name, but out of respect for her husband and in observance of customary norms, she had the lease changed to her husband's name. However, several years later, the husband took another wife, and not only divorced the first wife, but took the children and tried to evict her from the farm. Because she refused to move, it became a court case and an eviction order was issued. However, the community and local leadership who regard the husband's behavior as cruel and unwarranted are supporting the woman's wish to stay on the farm.

When Mr. Mwashita, a war veteran who had been allocated a section of Harmony Farm in Mazowe, died, it took several years for his widow to acquire the necessary documentation for the farm. Since she was married according to customary law, she had to obtain affidavits from her husband's relatives. Other war veterans in the area assisted her so she and her children could benefit from her husband's efforts.

Inheritance is a continuing source of insecurity for women. Nelson Marongwe[28] relates this incident in Goromonzi in 2002: "A woman beneficiary lost her husband at Lot 2 of Buena Vista. The husband was buried at their communal home in Uzumba Maramba Pfungwe District, Mashonaland East Province. The woman spent several months absent from her plot. While she was away, a member of the Committee of Seven reallocated the plot to a local businessman, allegedly after receiving a bribe. The 'new beneficiary' had already planted crops when the woman returned. The Committee of Seven,[29] and the District Administrator's office failed to resolve the situation. The case was brought to the Provincial Land Committee which ordered the businessman to vacate the plot and make way for the woman."

Some women had registered farms in their sons' names, probably to keep the farm in the patriline, for security against other claimants. Women usually pass land through inheritance to male rather than female children, who could "lose" the farm to their husbands or children through marriage. The son preference in relation to inheritance was dominant even among women.[30] A woman civil servant in Gweru acquired land in her own name through a fast track application but faced family pressure. "There was no peace in the home and my husband complained all the time about me having land in my own name and even threatened to divorce me. So in the end, for the sake of peace and my marriage, I gave in and put the land in the name of my son." Kwanele Ona Jirira and Charles Mangosuthu Halimana[31] noted that in some cases sons were heads of households when plots had been allocated to women, thus reflecting the continued pervasiveness of patriarchy.

Although initially the offer letter or permit was only in the name of the applicant, irrespective of marital status or gender, it is now official national policy that the offer letter or lease, for married couples, reflect both the husband's and wife's names. In many areas the policy is already being implemented. For example, at a 2009 stakeholder meeting, facilitated by the WFLA Trust, held at Alice Masuka's farm in Vungu, among women A1 farmers from Lancashire Farm resettlement and provincial and district officials, the provincial lands officer stated that the policy was to have joint names of spouses on leases and permits.

In some areas, documents are being recalled to add the other spouse's name. Nevertheless, Sam Moyo points out, the policy does not allow government officials to force applicants to register jointly, as this would be regarded as an intrusion into matrimonial affairs and is not enforceable by law. Thus, while officials are expected to and do tend to encourage joint registration, those who are gender-biased may not do so, leading to practice varying across provinces.[32]

District and Provincial Land Committees have discretionary powers in solving land disputes and inheritance issues. We found these offices were gender-sensitive and generally sympathetic to women. In the case of a husband dying, on both A1 and A2 resettlement schemes, even though the permit or offer letter is in the name of the man, the general practice in both Goromonzi and Vungu districts is that the widow is allowed to stay on the farm. In such cases, the permit or offer letter is transferred to the widow's name.

This sort of local intervention may indicate changing attitudes. In one case, a married woman farmed together with her husband but he had been allocated the land. When they got divorced, the husband remained on that farm, but the ex-wife was allocated land elsewhere, as the Land Committee was sympathetic and recognized that she was the one who was doing most of the farming.

Increasingly, official numbers of beneficiaries may mask reality on the ground. Even when allocated, women do not always remain in control of the land, but in other cases, women control land that is in the man's name. Farming is usually a family affair, and in most cases, the name on the permit does not seem to matter, as long as there is an understanding that the land is "family land." Attitudes are changing, propelled by the land-reform process, but equality has not been reached yet.

Producing and Selling More

Chapters 7 through 9 have shown that many land-reform farmers are producing more and some are becoming more commercial. A significant number of women have become land-reform farmers, and some are becoming successful commercial farmers.

Most of the complaints we heard from women farmers were common to all farmers. One of the biggest problems on the ground is lack of traction. Few farmers have tractors and many do not have cattle, so most borrow or hire tractors or oxen or donkey-drawn plows. Esnath Moyo, a woman farmer in Vungu, pointed out, "It takes five days with an animal-drawn plow to plow a field, which would take only a few hours with a tractor. The donkeys that we have are slow and very stubborn; this is a major challenge to our farming activities." And, like all farmers, women lament the lack of access to farming inputs: seed, fertilizer, and pesticides. In the hyperinflation period they were difficult to procure; now they are available, but at prohibitive prices. And women—and all farmers—complain of low producer prices and high input costs. Precious Zikhali[33] in 2008 found gender discrimination in access to fertilizers, with male-headed households using more fertilizers than female-headed ones. Older research indicates that women are generally discriminated against in access to productive inputs.[34] And women also accused the government of discriminating against them in the 2007 mechanization program. Furthermore, it is more difficult for women than for men to obtain loans from financial institutions, which demand collateral in the form of a house or shares, which most women do not have. However, interviews with Agritex officers in 2011 found no difference in access to fertilizer and other inputs by men and women except that widows appear to be in an advantageous position in acquiring free or subsidized inputs, from relatives, the community, and the Grain Marketing Board (GMB).

Success for women, similar to that for men farmers, is linked to access to outside resources, either a salary or mortgageable assets, which are used as start-up capital and invested in the farming business. Phides

Mazhawidza was able to mortgage her house in Harare to buy essential equipment for her A2 farm, but for most women, even if they have a house, it is in their husband's name.

A feature of continued success is reinvestments of profits into farming, but this is more difficult for women; Teresa in Mazowe, for example, is working to send her children to university. Besides reinvesting profits into the farm business, Ottilia and her husband have to use some of their profits to pay school fees. Women have myriad family responsibilities, from putting food on the table to sending children to school.

On one farm we were greeted by a woman in a pink hat who had been part of *jambanja*, has the land in her name, and is caring for a severely disabled daughter. She tries everything, tobacco one year, groundnuts another, roundnuts another, but never seems to build up the skills in any crop. Now she is caught in the downward spiral and can no longer afford fertilizer for her maize. It is hard to see how she can survive on her A1 farm.

In the middle we see women like Tabeth Gorovo (pictured at the beginning of this chapter) who are comfortable and doing well by their own standards. And then there is the commercial group, spurred on by dollarization and crops like tobacco. In Goromonzi, Violet Nyakwenha gained only $500 from 1 ha of tobacco in the 2008/9 season and just $600 in the 2009/10 season, but in 2010/11 she increased her income to $1,200—slow progress, but a steady rise in income. On Springdale Farm, we met Gertrude Chimbwanda and Tatenda Gombe, who had been growing tobacco for two seasons. In the 2009/10 season, Gertrude grew tobacco on 1 ha, selling 1.2 tonnes for $3,600, and in the next season she was up to 1.5 tonnes for $4,200. Tatenda Gombe only harvested 0.6 tonnes in 2009/10, but the quality was good and she sold it for $1,800; in the 2010/11 season, Tatenda sold 0.90 tonnes for $2,250. Neither of these women is wealthy, but they are graduating into the class of serious commercial farmers.

Norea Manyika (known to everyone as Councillor Gutu) has an A2 farm as part of Howick Ridge Farm in Concession, Mazowe. Her father was a purchase farmer, and had been a communal farmer growing cotton in Gokwe, then became a teacher and was teaching in Mazowe when she applied for the land. After she received the land, she took a horticulture course (which she paid for—new farmers have none of the training offered to white soldiers in the 1950s) at the Women's University of Africa. Her first season of export horticulture was 2010/11, when she exported 530 tonnes of baby corn, cauliflower, broccoli, carrots, and sweet corn.

She knows there are many years to go, and substantial investment is still required, but when she takes you around her farm, there is no question about her drive and commitment. Her husband is now retired and lives with her on the farm—but there is no doubt that it is her farm. She has paid for her son to do agricultural training, and he will take over the farm one day.

Summing Up: Women Moving Up

Patriarchy has not gone away; land reform is still male-dominated and women are still disadvantaged. But the decade after the occupations saw dramatic changes in ensuring that women receive land in their own right and have their names on offer letters and leases of joint farms. And with that has come a real change in attitudes, within families and communities, as women take the right to be seen as farmers. Women have benefited significantly from the Fast Track Land Reform. It has been a real struggle for women, perhaps more than for men; as one woman farmer put it: "You have to be aggressive and strong—you have to act like a man and not give up." Some did not succeed and dropped out or are now failing. But a decade on, many women have come out the other end as successful farmers and have transformed their lives—politically, socially, and economically.

Notes

1. Bill Kinsey, "The Implication of Land Reform for Rural Welfare," in *Land Reform in Zimbabwe: Constraints and Prospects,* ed. Tanya Bowyer-Bower and Colin Stoneman (London, UK: Ashgate, 2000).

2. Goodhope Ruswa, "The Golden Era? Reflections on the First Phase of the Land Reform Programme in Zimbabwe," Occasional Research Paper Series, Number 01/2007 (Harare, Zimbabwe: African Institute for Agrarian Studies, 2007) [Ruswa, "Golden Era"].

3. Women and Land Lobby Group, "Consultative Planning Workshop Report," report of June 1998 workshop, Harare, Zimbabwe, 6; Tanya Lyons, *Guns and Guerrilla Girls: Women in the Zimbabwean Liberation Struggle* (Trenton, NJ: World Africa Press, 2004) [Lyons, *Guns and Guerrilla Girls*].

4. Initially as the Women and Land Lobby Group.

5. The mandate for the Trust is to ensure women farmers' contribution to national food security and economic empowerment of women through land use

through capacity building; lobbying and advocacy; and facilitation of women's access to farming resources such as equipment, irrigation, and inputs.

6. Phides Mazhawidza and Jeanette Manjengwa, "The Social, Political and Economic Transformative Impact of the Fast Track Land Reform Programme on the Lives of Women Farmers in Goromonzi and Vungu-Gweru Districts of Zimbabwe" (Rome: International Land Coalition, 2011), available at http://landportal.info/sites/default/files/wlr_8_zimbabwe.pdf (November 27, 2011).

7. Robin Palmer, "Challenges in Asserting Women's Land Rights in Southern Africa," presentation at "Decentralising Land, Dispossessing Women? Recovering Gender Voices and Experiences of Decentralised Land Reform in Africa," Maputo, Mozambique, May 2009, 4.

8. UN Food and Agriculture Organization (FAO), "Gender, Property Rights and Livelihoods in the Era of AIDS," Proceedings Report of FAO Technical Consultation, November 28–30, 2007 (Rome: FAO, 2008), 10.

9. Ruswa, "Golden Era."

10. Allison Goebel, "Zimbabwe's 'Fast Track' Land Reform: What About Women?" *Gender, Place and Culture,* 12, no. 2 (2005): 145.

11. World Bank, *Gender in Agriculture Sourcebook* (Washington, DC: World Bank, 2008), available at http://siteresources.worldbank.org/INTGENAGRLIV SOUBOOK/Resources/CompleteBook.pdf (accessed January 3, 2012).

12. Kwanele Ona Jirira and Charles Mangosuthu Halimana, "A Gender Audit of Women and Land Rights in Zimbabwe," paper prepared for the Zimbabwe Women's Resource Centre and Network (ZWRCN), Harare, Zimbabwe, 2008, 14 [Jirira and Halimana, "Gender Audit"].

13. Government of Zimbabwe, *Zimbabwe: 2003 Poverty Assessment Study Survey, Main Report* (Harare, Zimbabwe: Ministry of Public Service, Labour and Social Welfare, 2006), 25, 26.

14. Sam Moyo et al., *Inception Phase Framework Plan 1999 to 2000* (Harare, Zimbabwe: Technical Committee of the Inter-Ministerial Committee on Resettlement and Rural Development and National Economic Consultative Forum Land Reform Task Force, n.d. [but surely 1998]), 11, 23, 43.

15. Charles Utete, "Report of the Presidential Land Review Committee on the Implementation of the Fast Track Land Reform Programme, 2000–2002" (Harare, Zimbabwe, 2003), 25 [Utete Report].

16. Sam Moyo et al., *Fast Track Land Reform Baseline Survey in Zimbabwe* (Harare, Zimbabwe: African Institute for Agrarian Studies, 2009), 26 [Moyo et al., *Baseline Survey*].

17. Sam Moyo, "Three Decades of Agrarian Reform in Zimbabwe," *Journal of Peasant Studies,* 38, no. 3 (2011): 504.

18. Utete Report, 6, 84.

19. Tendai Murisa, "Social Organisation and Agency in the Newly Resettled Areas of Zimbabwe: The Case of Zvimba District," Monograph Series, Issue No. 1/07 (Harare, Zimbabwe: African Institute for Agrarian Studies, 2007).

20. Ian Scoones et al., *Zimbabwe's Land Reform* (Woodbridge, Suffolk, UK: James Currey, 2010), 55–56 [Scoones et al., *Land Reform*].

21. Zvakanyorwa Wilbert Sadomba, *War Veterans in Zimbabwe's Revolution* (Woodbridge, Suffolk, UK: James Currey, 2011), 126.

22. Joseph Chaumba, Ian Scoones, and William Wolmer, "From *Jambanja* to Planning: The Reassertion of Technocracy in Land Reform in South-eastern Zimbabwe," Sustainable Livelihoods in Southern Africa Research Paper 2 (Brighton, UK: Institute of Development Studies, 2003), 10, available at http://www.ids.ac.uk/download.cfm?objectid=F964600F-5056-8171-7B27BE59A953D7B4 (November 27, 2003).

23. Lyons, *Guns and Guerrilla Girls,* chap. 9.

24. Scoones et al., *Land Reform,* 52, 55.

25. Ministry of Lands, Land Reform and Resettlement & Informatics Institute, *A2 Land Audit Report* (Harare, Zimbabwe, 2006); the report was completed in eight volumes, one for each province, issued at different times during 2006.

26. Prisca Mugabe, "Impacts of Land Reform Migrations on Forest Resources Management in Model A1 Resettlement Areas of Chimanimani District in Zimbabwe" (Harare, Zimbabwe: Institute of Environmental Studies, 2011), 10.

27. Sam Moyo, "Emerging Land Tenure Issues in Zimbabwe," Monograph Series, Issue No. 2/07 (Harare, Zimbabwe: African Institute for Agrarian Studies, 2007), 24.

28. Nelson Marongwe, "Interrogating Zimbabwe's Fast Track Land Reform and Resettlement Programme: A Focus on Beneficiary Selection" (PhD thesis, Institute for Poverty, Land and Agrarian Studies [PLAAS], University of the Western Cape, 2008), ¶7.5.

29. Under fast track, seven-member committees were established in each resettlement scheme to oversee administration and management.

30. Sunungurai Chingarande, Prisca Mugabe, Krasposy Kujinga, and Esteri Magaisa, "Agrarian Reforms in Zimbabwe: Are Women Beneficiaries or Mere Agents?" (Harare, Zimbabwe: Institute of Environmental Studies, 2011); summary at http://hdl.handle.net/10625/47628 and http://web.idrc.ca/uploads/user-S/12850776031Agrarian_land_reforms_in_Zimbabwe-_are_women_beneficiaries_or_mere_agents.pdf (November 28, 2011).

31. Jirira and Halimana, "Gender Audit," 22.

32. Moyo et al., *Baseline Survey,* 40.

33. Precious Zikhali, "Fast Track Land Reform and Agricultural Productivity in Zimbabwe," Environment for Development Discussion Paper Series (EfD DP 08-3), October 2008, 20.

34. See, for example, C. R. Doss, "Twenty-Five Years of Research on Women Farmers in Africa: Lessons and Implications for Agricultural Research Institutions," CIMMYT Economics Program Paper, no. 99-02 (Mexico DF, Mexico: CIMMYT, 1999).

11

Cutting Down Trees

When Phides Mazhawidza was shown her newly allocated A2 farm in Goromonzi, she was dismayed to find that it was covered with trees. While she admired the miombo woodland[1] with its beautiful musasa and munondo trees, her heart sank when she realized that she would have to clear much of it to farm. Phides's farm was a subdivision of a large commercial farm in a region of high agricultural potential, and her section had not been used for crops. Clearing was expensive and time-consuming, although Phides bartered her cut wood with neighboring tobacco farmers in exchange for use of their tractor to plow her field. Fanuel Mutandiro, the tomato farmer interviewed in chapter 7, was allocated a plot covered with gum trees (eucalyptus), which he had to clear.

Zimbabwe's biggest environmental concern remains the communal areas and issues linked to colonialism and population growth.

But land reform poses a new set of environmental issues. It involves not simply change in ownership, but significant change in land use, as the new occupants farm more of the land than their white predecessors. Trees, as Phides and the new tobacco farmers know, are a central issue. There is much debate and contradictory data, and it remains impossible to know whether the bulk of the new land-reform farmers are causing significant deforestation. However, the warning flags are up and there is increasing research.

But land reform and hyperinflation have caused two very serious problems—major damage to timber plantations in the Manicaland highlands, where change of use is having dramatic impacts, and gold panning, where an important livelihood and source of government earnings is leading to confrontations with new farmers.

An Inherited Ecological Crisis

Pushing most of the people onto the poorest half of the land was inevitably going to cause problems. As far back as 1920, the Native Department reported: "Deterioration in the Reserves assumed such proportions that even laymen can note it and present methods of agriculture cannot continue. . . . The soil is being exhausted."[2] The Danziger Committee was set up in 1948 to look at the question of "native" land occupation and concluded that each family needed 2.4 ha of arable land plus grazing land for six beasts, or 40 ha per family. Even then, the African reserves needed 40% more land, Danziger concluded, and future population growth would have to take place in urban areas.[3]

Instead, the government introduced the Native Land Husbandry Act in 1951. One of its objectives was "to require natives to perform labour conserving natural resources and for promoting good husbandry."[4] Fines were imposed on those who did not comply. In introducing the act, Minister of Native Affairs Patrick Fletcher said that "grave problems flow from crowded and stagnant communities scraping a bare existence from the exhausted countryside."[5]

The act proved to be a disaster. Barry Floyd, who wrote his PhD thesis in 1959 after working as a land development officer in the Department of Native Agriculture, concluded, "The advancement of individual farms in the reserves can only presume a large scale exodus of surplus population from African rural areas," but that seemed unlikely because in 1958, government had rejected a proposal to allow more urban migration, in part to prevent African competition with semi-skilled white workers. The Land Husbandry Act was "attempting to deal with one-half of a problem that is really indivisible; agricultural schemes cannot be divorced from urban expansion."[6] In 1960, the *Second Report of the Select Committee on the Resettlement of Natives* concluded that if the Land Husbandry Act were really to be enforced, 30% of African families would have to be thrown off the land.[7] In particular, it was caught in the Rhodesian contradiction of wanting African labor but not wanting that labor to live in the cities. This ended up with a migrant labor system, with men "temporarily" in towns and farming increasingly done by women. Barry Floyd found that "attempts by demonstrators to introduce new skills requiring longer hours in the fields were faced with a shortage of man power," because men and boys had been driven to the towns by poverty and "the women and children were left to fend for themselves."[8]

Some people attribute land degradation in communal areas to mis-management and inappropriate farming methods,[9] but it was colonial policy that inevitably created over-crowding, over-cultivation, and over-grazing. Malcolm Rifkind in his 1968 thesis said that keeping most of the people on half the land was "untenable." He continues: "Because of political considerations, the government attempted to modernize the Reserves but at the same time to maintain land segregation. These two objectives were, in the Rhodesian context, irreconcilable, and in the end the attempt at good husbandry had to be abandoned."[10]

The official response to environmental degradation was a set of technical solutions such as plowing along contours, constructing con-tour ridges, filling in gullies, not cultivating wetlands, and limiting stock numbers. Zephaniah Phiri, now an 85-year-old farmer in Zvishavane, southern Zimbabwe, is known as the "Water Harvester" because of his innovative techniques in using every drop of water to transform his resource-starved subsistence plot into a green productive farmstead. He relates: "The settler government we had before independence did not like us to use our own ideas. The agriculture ministry forced us to do things to protect our natural resources. Only now it turns out that some of these were wrong for our environment. . . . But if any of us African farmers tried to do something different, something for ourselves, we had a heavy price to pay. Fines. Jail."[11]

Phiri continues, "The most dangerous thing . . . we all had to do . . . was the contour ridge. We all had to dig them or go to jail," Phiri continued. "Contour ridges were supposed to prevent erosion, but really they were the cause of erosion in dry parts of our country" because they diverted rain from the fields, increasing runoff, and also carried off top-soil. If the water was directed instead into infiltration pits, it recharged the groundwater and trapped the topsoil. He explains that he was us-ing the methods developed by his ancestors, and that the settlers did not understand how to farm these fragile lands and they farmed "in a wrong way." But they also imposed these wrong methods on African farmers.[12]

Phiri's experience shows the politicization of "environment" by the settler government and its links to the liberation war. He was first detained and then sacked in the 1960s for being in the railway workers union. Later he was arrested and fined several times for his water-harvesting methods, even though they obviously worked. He was arrested again in

1976, suspected of supporting the freedom fighters, and this time tortured and had his hip broken (he still walks with a cane) and kept in leg irons until the end of the war.[13]

During the Liberation War, from the mid-1960s to 1980, many farmers purposely neglected contour ridges and other government-prescribed conservation measures as a token of resistance to the oppressive UDI regime. This association of contour ridges with repression continues today, and in some areas, small-scale farmers resist constructing ridges. Nevertheless, the Environmental Management Agency still insists on them and maintains that it is the responsibility of the resettled farmer to construct the contours and failure to construct would be an offense.[14]

Thus, Zimbabwe came to independence with an environmental crisis in its communal areas. Colonial authorities had packed in far more people than the land would support and worsened the problem by misunderstanding the ecology. Even sensible environmental methods were politicized, and thus rejected by local people. More than 30 years after independence, the communal areas remain Zimbabwe's biggest environmental problem.

As in many other areas, the Zimbabwe government is following colonial models. It continues to see the problem of communal areas as one of overcrowding. It had been hoped that land reform would allow people to move out of the communal areas, but fewer people have been resettled than the population has increased since independence. Thus, reducing the population density of communal areas in the long term depends on creating urban jobs—a central development issue for Zimbabwe. But urbanization creates its own environmental problems: as farm and forest land is taken over, demand for food, water, and energy increases and more pollution and waste are produced.

And clearly the communal areas are overcrowded, using present farming methods on relatively poor soils. But so far there has been little lateral thinking about how to raise the carrying capacity of communal lands—imaginatively rather than through coercive controls.

Zimbabwe has contradictory attitudes toward natural resource management. On the one hand, as in so many ways, it follows colonial models of top-down technicist prescriptions, imposed forcibly, to effect what is seen as sustainability, which marginalize local inputs and participation. However, Zimbabwe is also a world leader in community-based natural resource management epitomized by the Communal Areas Management Programme for Indigenous Resources (Campfire). Under Campfire, local people manage, and more important, benefit from, wildlife such as elephants and other large mammals and from other natural resources in their areas. It does not always work, but at its best, Campfire presents an alternative model for land-reform resource management.

Can Resettlement Solve the Environmental Crisis?

If resettlement is to be successful, new farmers will have to use the former white farms more intensively and more extensively. These land use changes will have environmental implications that will need to be managed. Three issues are on the table but have not yet become serious problems: irrigation (discussed in more detail in chapter 12), using marginal lands, and veld fires.

As more marginal lands are farmed, including rangelands or wildlife areas in the dry Natural Regions IV and V that may not be suitable for rain-fed agriculture, soil erosion and environmental degradation can occur, and more attention may need to be paid to forms of conservation farming that are not yet common in Zimbabwe.

One of the most difficult environmental problems is veld fires, which neither colonial nor independence governments have been able to deal with. Low-intensity bush or veld fires keep the undergrowth clear and are part of the ecology of these miombo grasslands, savannas, and shrublands.[15] But there are indications of an increase in their frequency and intensity in recent years; they are becoming much more damaging due to increasing population and farm density and are causing massive damage to vegetation and also property, not to mention the tonnes of carbon dioxide being spewed into the atmosphere. Much of Zimbabwe is covered in tall grass, which burns intensely when dry, and uncontrolled veld fires can destroy property as well as grazing land, crops, and woodland. But fires are part of the conventional agricultural management practices in Zimbabwe. Cotton farmers are required by law to burn their fields by a certain date after harvest, and cattle farmers burn the dry grass to improve grazing land. Sometimes fires are caused by poachers or during hunting of small mammals such as mice and rabbits or during land clearance. In 2010, the Environmental Management Agency (EMA) reported over 9,000 fires on more than 1 mn ha; 25 human lives were lost, as were 29 elephants. In a veld fire at the Xanadu Farm resettlement, Mazowe district, an elderly woman and two children were burned to death.

Are More Trees Being Cut?

Forests are essential to control erosion and to protect watersheds and catchment areas. Trees also provide energy, building materials, fencing, fodder, and fuel for firing bricks and curing tobacco; fuelwood is the main source of energy for almost 70% of the population;[16] and dry wood and dead branches are regularly collected for firewood.

Woodlands and forests cover 21 mn ha, 54% of Zimbabwe. The EMA points to increased deforestation, with an estimated loss of 100,000–320,000 ha per year (0.5% to 1.5% of forest).[17] But what is the cause of the increased deforestation? It is clear that at the peak of hyperinflation in 2007–8, many people returned to communal areas and there was increased cutting of timber for fuel and to barter. Resettlement farmers are definitely clearing land (further evidence of how little land was used by white farmers), selling timber, and using wood to cure tobacco.

Two recent studies in Mazowe district indicate an increase in tree cover during the Fast Track Land Reform. Kelman Taruwinga used satellite imagery of miombo woodland on resettled A2 farms in the Christonbank farming area of Mazowe and found a 15% increase in tree canopy cover between 2003 and 2010.[18] Veronica Gundu found a decline in woodland between 1986 and 2003, but then an increase in woodland cover between 2003 and 2009.[19] There are two possible explanations for the increase. Resource constraints mean A2 farmers are still not using all of their land, and trees are growing on some of the unused land. And the increase in canopy cover may be attributed to selective cutting, targeting small trees and leaving the bigger ones whose canopies continue to grow and increase in size and consequently their crowns cover a large area.

A 2005 survey in Mazowe by Nelson Marongwe found that 38% of the new farmers had woodlots on their resettlement schemes.[20] At the time, 90% saw the trees as a common property resource, and timber was harvested haphazardly, with most of the wood sold as firewood in Harare and nearby towns and townships. More recently, there is anecdotal evidence of regeneration, regrowth, and coppicing of trees, as well as tree planting by farmers. Fruit and other useful trees are also being maintained and planted.

Recently, tobacco growing has sharply increased, particularly among resource-poor smallholders who treat trees as common property and do not include the cost of woodfuel in their calculations for profit margins. The EMA reports tobacco farmers are denuding whole hillsides of woodland at an alarming rate. Two of the A1 farms we surveyed (see chapter 8) grow tobacco. Both Brookmead (Goromonzi) and Springdale (Macheke) used wood from miombo woodland, either on their farm or in nearby woodland. However, on Springdale Farm, 61% of these farmers had woodlots as well. And in Goromonzi as well as other areas, the tobacco companies are distributing gum tree seedlings. This is encouraged by the Forestry Commission, which wants to make woodlots compulsory for tobacco farmers. Gum trees take five years to mature, so new farmers will need a source of wood until then, and not all A1 farmers have sufficient land for woodlots.

So we do not know the implications of land reform on trees on farms and in surrounding areas. It appears that in some places they are well managed and in others not. But there also appears to be growing recognition that this could become an issue.

Dollars Allow Enforcement

The government sees inequitable access to land as being at the heart of poverty, food insecurity, lack of development, and environmental damage in Zimbabwe, and it has been argued that sustainable development is not possible without agrarian reform.[21] Indeed, one of the objectives of land reform was to "promote environmentally sustainable utilisation of land."[22]

A1 fast track settlers were given permits that specify the holder's right to erect a house and engage in farming activities, but also mandate them to abide by the natural resources conservation legislation. A2 applicants for a 99-year lease must obtain approval by both district and provincial EMA officers, who have to inspect and give their opinion on the level of environmental management and any degradation occurring on the farm.

Between 2000 and 2005, there was a series of conferences, plans, and policy statements aimed at preventing resettlement from being environmentally damaging and promoting more diversified incomes,[23] but they have been largely forgotten and sidelined. District, ward, and even farm environmental committees have been created, but their effectiveness is inhibited by a lack of resources and training. Dollarization is making a difference, however, and allowing a more serious attitude toward monitoring environmental management and protection during resettlement. Since 2010, fines for environmental crimes have to be paid in US dollars (regarded as "real" money after years of hyperinflation of the Zimbabwean dollar), and this has empowered the EMA to be more efficient and better-resourced, especially in terms of vehicles and equipment. Cars marked "EMA patrol" are now a common sight on the roads.

The Forestry Commission and EMA are undertaking fire awareness and other environmental campaigns. But an EMA officer expressed skepticism: "Settlers seem very receptive to what we say, but taking action is another thing. For example, they will say, 'Poaching is very bad,' but check their granaries and they are full of biltong [dried game meat]!"[24] Recent surveys show that the majority of Zimbabweans are aware that randomly cutting down trees is illegal, and that there are both statutory and traditional rules governing tree cutting.[25] But piles of firewood for sale on the roadsides are frequently seen.

To some extent, the EMA is caught up in colonial strategies of top-down plans and policies imposed through enforcement and fines. Colonial-style prescriptive protection measures will not be any more effective now than they were 50 years ago. Indeed, there is no evidence of significant environmental damage being caused by most resettlement farmers, and our interviews show that land-reform farmers are thinking long term and do not want to destroy their own resource base. Agritex extension officers show that farmers act on good advice when they see the benefit. Zephaniah Phiri shows just how important it is to work with farmers, rather than against them. Instead of fines and lectures, the EMA will have to develop practices that assist farmers to enhance their production while maintaining their natural resource base. And there is a danger that, as in the colonial era, environmental threats will be exaggerated for political ends and to maintain environmental management jobs.

But if the bulk of land-reform farmers are being environmentally sensitive, two serious environmental problems have been caused by fast track land reform—destruction of plantation trees in Manicaland and increased gold panning. Neither is a simple enforcement issue. It is not clear that plantation trees are the best use of that land, and gold provides important income for both gold panners and the government. But both are presently causing significant damage.

Manicaland Timber Plantations

One-third of trees in the timber plantations of the high-rainfall areas of the Eastern Highlands of Manicaland, near the border with Mozambique, have been lost in the past decade to fires and resettlement.

Established in the early 1950s to meet Rhodesia's commercial timber requirements, by 2000 there were well-established exotic (non-native species) timber plantations covering 155,853 ha.[26] Of these, 90% were in the Eastern Highlands: 71% softwoods (pines), 13% hardwoods (eucalyptus), and 16% wattle (acacia, used for tanning).

This was an area of spontaneous resettlement immediately after the war, as people moved to retake land from which they had been expelled, and that had often been abandoned during the war because of the closeness to the border (see chapter 4). Two-thirds of plantations were listed for acquisition under the Fast Track Land Reform. Some were formally taken by A1 and A2 settlers selected by District and Provincial Land Committees, and some were occupied by informal settlers. Border Timbers, sold by Anglo-American to the Zimbabwe Stock Exchange–listed Radar Group in 2000, took a hard line, did not originally cede any of its land following the occupations, and had all of its plantations designated for resettlement. Some were occupied informally by settlers led by traditional leaders claiming ancestral lands; seven hundred families from the nearby overcrowded communal lands in Chief Chikukwa's area settled on Border Timbers' Charter Estate in Chimanimani.

Formally assigned plots ranged from 18.5 ha to 272 ha despite the Forestry Commission's recommending not to sub-divide timber plantations, considering the long rotation time timber crops require. The plots are too small and not viable for forestry business and most settlers switched to other short rotation crops such as potatoes and maize. Trees were cut down and some were sold as fuelwood. Both mature and young trees were harvested. In some cases, after the standing trees were cut down and the timber was sold, the settlers moved off the land.

Since the majority of plantations are on steep slopes, deforestation has led to widespread sheet erosion, causing loss of fertile topsoil and siltation of streams. For example, the Tanganda valley, Chimanimani, is an environmentally sensitive area where 50 households settled and are practicing subsistence agriculture. Trees were cut down and there is already erosion, causing siltation of the Tanganda River.

Plantation soils are of varying fertility. Those under pines and eucalyptus are acidic, infertile, and inappropriate for farming; eucalyptus, in particular, makes the soil more acidic. On the other hand, soils on wattle plantations are more fertile because wattle trees are leguminous and therefore add nitrates to the soil.

Table 11.1 shows that resettlement in plantations began in 2000 and continues. There were two peaks of resettlement, the first during fast track in 2001, while the second, of over 9,000 ha, occurred in 2008/9

Table 11.1 Resettlement on Commercial Timber Plantation Areas

Year	Resettlement losses (ha)
2000/1	1,318
2001/2	7,808
2002/3	1,208
2003/4	1,107
2004/5	2,120
2005/6	1,249
2006/7	755
2007/8	587
2008/9	9,373
2010	101
Total	**25,626**

Source: Timber Producers Federation's Commercial Plantation Annual Statistics, Timber Producers Federation, Mutare, Zimbabwe.

during the hyperinflation crisis—a period of political instability and uncertainty during which large areas of plantations were systematically destroyed.

Fires are particularly destructive in forests. Before the occupations, fire damage to plantations was negligible, because the timber companies managed the forests, cleared undergrowth, and maintained 9-meter-wide cleared strips as firebreaks; often this was not continued after land reform. Over 35,000 ha of forests were negatively affected by fires between 2002 and 2010, with 2008/9 being the worst year on record, with over 18,000 ha destroyed (see Table 11.2). Forests that are not adequately managed and protected are susceptible to runaway fires that can result in total destruction of plantations. Anglo's estates were clearly a target. Of a national total of 2,048 ha of forest affected by fire in 2003/4, half was on Charter Estate. And again, in 2008/9, most of the 18,049 ha destroyed by fire were Border Timbers pine plantations in Chimanimani.

Gold Panning

Zimbabwe is richly endowed with minerals, including substantial alluvial gold reserves. The gold price was around $300 per ounce from 1998 through 2002 and rose to $400 per ounce in 2005, $800 in 2008, and

Photo 11.1 Gold panning in Tarka Forest, Chimanimani, Manicaland.

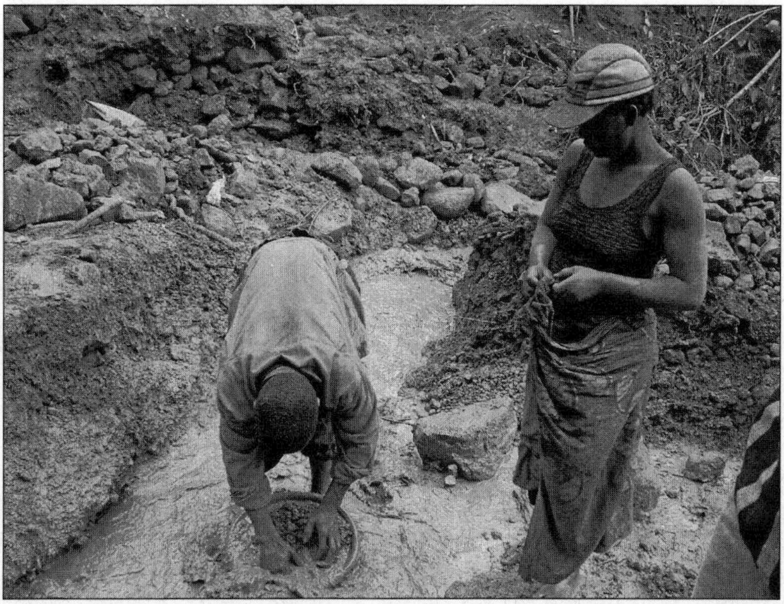

Photo: Allied Timber Holdings.

Table 11.2 Fire Losses on Timber Plantations

Year	Fire losses (ha)
2002/3	1,025
2003/4	2,048
2004/5	—
2005/6	9,732
2006/7	1,924
2007/8	2,265
2008/9	18,049
2010	500
Total	**35,543**

Source: Timber Producers Federation's Commercial Plantation Annual Statistics, Timber Producers Federation, Mutare, Zimbabwe.

more than $1,700 in 2011, which made gold increasingly attractive for individual miners. Many farmworkers who had lost their jobs took up gold panning; in Kadoma district in 2003, gold panning was the major source of income for 46% of former farmworker households.[27] Rising gold prices, which made gold panning more profitable than farming, plus the hyperinflation of 2007/8, meant many other people joined them. In a recent case at Netherfields Farm, Mazowe, ex–commercial farmworkers are occupying the workers' houses in the compound but not working for the new farmers. Instead they are engaged in gold panning. Many resettlement farms have streams and rivers with alluvial gold and panning is largely uncontrolled.

Panning is carried out unsystematically, usually in riverbeds, banks, and floodplains with no concern for the environment. Trees are cut down haphazardly, pits several meters deep are dug, and alluvial soil is removed, resulting in erosion and siltation as the soil and rocks are washed into the streams. No rehabilitation is carried out and the proliferation of deep pits, which are a hazard to cattle and game, becomes a source of conflict with farmers. Panners and small-scale miners have no environmental management plans and do not even know about the Environmental Management Act regulations. Under both the Mines and Minerals Act and the Environmental Management Act, prospective miners are required to obtain permission from farmers before prospecting or mining on farms. However, the miners go ahead regardless of any permission from the farmer, claiming their certificates from the Ministry of Mines supersede everything else. Although the EMA is energetic in issuing tickets and stop orders, gold panning continues unabated and is actually increasing, because it is so profitable. Uncontrolled panning and small-scale mining are damaging the environment and, furthermore, local communities are not benefiting from the mineral resources. Middlemen and gold buyers profit most, with little contribution to communities or national reserves.

Gold is a valuable resource that, if managed carefully, can give economic benefits while maintaining environmental quality. The Campfire approach could be applied to alluvial gold and other mineral resources to ensure that farming communities benefit directly from their natural resources. Communities would monitor and police themselves and ensure that pits were filled and streams rehabilitated.

Summing Up:
Gold and Timber Mar a More Positive Picture

Environmental degradation in Zimbabwe is being driven by poverty, which has its roots in the economic and conservation dualism of colonial policies, manifested in the unequal racial distribution of land resulting in overpopulation in the communal areas, most of which have low agro-ecological potential. The communal lands remain the country's biggest environmental challenge, and ways must be found to make them more sustainably productive.

Managing natural resources will require a shift from the colonial-style, top-down plans, lectures, enforcement, and fines to more collaborative methods, in both communal and land-reform areas.

Land reform means unused land is being cleared and land is being used more intensively, which makes trees a key issue. There is an increased demand for wood for fuel, in particular for curing tobacco and to sell to urban dwellers. So far land-reform farmers seem to be managing their trees, but they will need to be monitored.

Fast track land reform and the economic crisis caused by hyperinflation have created two serious environmental problems that will not be solved by simple enforcement. In the forest plantations of the Manicaland highlands, one-third of trees have been lost to fires or settlers, and there is a serious battle over how forested plantation land should be used. High gold prices mean gold panning has become a vital source of income for many Zimbabweans as well as for the country. Done badly, gold panning causes substantial damage to streambeds and farms. While gold prices remain high, panning will continue—legal or not. Can more environmentally sound methods be found?

Notes

1. Miombo, or *Brachystegia,* is the most extensive woodland type in Zimbabwe. It is dominated by musasa (*Brachystegia spiciformis*), munondo (*Julbernardia globiflora*), and mupfuti (*Brachystegia boehmii*). Characteristically the trees shed their leaves for a short period in the dry season and produce a flush of new leaves, with rich gold and red colors masking the underlying chlorophyll, reminiscent of temperate autumn colors, just before the onset of the rainy season.

2. Bruce Campbell and P. N. Bradley, "Trees, Wood and the Small-Scale Farmer: Rethinking Woodfuel Development in Zimbabwe," draft paper, Department of Biological Sciences, University of Zimbabwe and the Stockholm Environment Institute, November 1993, 11, citing Michael Drinkwater, *The State and Agrarian Change in Zimbabwe's Communal Areas: An Application of Critical Theory* (London, UK: Macmillan, 1991).

3. Malcolm Rifkind, "The Politics of Land in Rhodesia" (MSc thesis, Edinburgh University, 1968), 82–84 [Rifkind, "Politics of Land"], citing Max Danziger, *Report of the Committee to Enquire into the Question of Additional Land*

for Native Occupation (Salisbury, Rhodesia, 1948), available at http://www.open ac.uk/zimbabwe (June 20, 2012).

4. Barry Floyd, "Changing Patterns of African Land Use in Southern Rhodesia" (PhD thesis, Syracuse University, 1959), Lusaka, Zambia: Rhodes-Livingstone Institute, 134 [Floyd, "Changing"], citing Native Land Husbandry Act, Act No. 52, 1951.

5. Floyd, "Changing," 114, citing Patrick Fletcher, foreword to *What the Native Land Husbandry Act Means to the Rural African and to Southern Rhodesia* (Salisbury, Rhodesia: Southern Rhodesia Native Affairs Department, 1955).

6. Floyd, "Changing," 272, 274, 279, 353.

7. Rifkind, "Politics of Land," 141, citing Jack Quinton, *Second Report of the Select Committee on the Resettlement of Natives,* 216, 217.

8. Floyd, "Changing," 129.

9. See, for example, D. Nkala, "Tackling Agricultural Development With Land Dearth," in *Balancing Rocks: Environment and Development,* ed. C. Lopes, A UNDP Zimbabwe Staff Research Project (Harare, Zimbabwe: SAPES and Uppsala, Sweden: Nordiska Afrikainstitutet, 1996).

10. Rifkind, "Politics of Land," 172.

11. Mary Witoshynsky, *The Water Harvester* (Harare, Zimbabwe: Weaver, 2000), 12. Most of the book is based on interviews with Zephaniah Phiri.

12. Ibid., 13–16.

13. Ibid., 10, 16, 28.

14. Jeanette Manjengwa, "Local Environmental Action Planning in Zimbabwe: An Analysis of Its Contribution to Sustainable Development" (PhD thesis, Institute for Development Policy and Management, University of Manchester, 2004), 164 [Manjengwa, "Local Environmental"].

15. See note 1.

16. Ministry of Public Service, Labour and Social Welfare, *Zimbabwe 2003 Poverty Assessment Study Survey Main Report* (Harare, Zimbabwe, 2006), 726.

17. Mutsa Chasi, "The State of the Environment and the Challenges in the Face of Increasing Poverty," presentation at the Moving Zimbabwe Forward conference, December 7–8, 2010, Harare, Zimbabwe. These figures are also given in the 2010 Zimbabwe Millennium Development Goals Status Report.

18. Kelman Taruwinga, "Remote Sensing and GIS Based Spatial and Temporal Change of Woodland Canopy Cover and Tree Density in Miombo Woodland, Mazowe District, Zimbabwe" (MSc Thesis, Department of Geography and Environmental Science, University of Zimbabwe, Harare, 2011).

19. Veronica Gundu, "The Impact of Land Reform on Natural Resources: A Case Study of Land Use Changes in Mazowe District" (MA dissertation, Department of Geography and Environmental Science, University of Zimbabwe, Harare, 2011).

20. Nelson Marongwe, "Environmental Concerns in Fast Track Schemes in Mashonaland Central: Mazowe District" (draft document), Harare, 2005.

21. Charles Utete, *Report of the Presidential Land Review Committee on the Implementation of the Fast Track Land Reform Programme, 2000–2002* (Harare, Zimbabwe, 2003).

22. Sam Moyo et al., *Inception Phase Framework Plan, 1999–2000: An Implementation Plan of the Land Reform and Resettlement Programme–Phase II* (Harare, Zimbabwe: Technical Committee of the Inter-Ministerial Committee on Resettlement and Rural Development and National Economic Consultative Forum Land Reform Task Force, n.d. [but actually 1998]), 2–3.

23. Government of Zimbabwe, *Zimbabwe's Fourth National Report to the Convention on Biological Diversity* (Harare, Zimbabwe: Ministry of Environment and Natural Resources Management, 2010), 31–32 [GoZ, *Fourth National Report*].

24. Manjengwa, "Local Environmental," 168.

25. See recent surveys, such as "Moving Zimbabwe Forward: Well-being and Poverty Assessment," carried out by the Institute of Environmental Studies, University of Zimbabwe, 2011, and research by Veronica Gundu, 2011 (see note 19).

26. GoZ, *Fourth National Report*, 9.

27. Zimbabwe Community Development Trust (ZCDT), "Report on Internally Displaced Farm Workers Survey: Kadoma, Chegutu and Kwekwe Districts" (Harare, Zimbabwe: Author, 2003).

12

Workers, Water, and Widows

Fast track land reform really was fast—and the haste and structure of an occupation-based land reform means that organization has been done after the fact and is continuing. Resettlement takes a generation, and we have seen that, especially post-dollarization, new farmers have become productive and are stepping up their production. However, serious problems remain in three areas: displaced farmworkers and new labor relations; irrigation; and tenure and the broader issue of how land is transferred to widows, more productive farmers, and the next generation.

Farm Labor

Farmworkers from the former white farms remain one of the most difficult issues. Amnesty International and the General Agricultural and Plantation Workers Union of Zimbabwe (GAPWUZ) have run a widely noticed (if also very exaggerated) campaign to highlight their plight. In 2011, Amnesty said, "Today mountains of food are rotting in fields and storerooms. The farm workers who once cultivated the fields and harvested the crops have been driven from the farms." This is, of course, opposite to what Charles Tafts, head of the white Commercial Farmers Union, told the BBC (see chapter 9), that the land had "gone back to subsistence farming" and nothing was being produced. Amnesty also says, "Hundreds of thousands of farm workers have been forced out of their homes—many of them having been savagely beaten."[1]

Despite the exaggerations, tens of thousands of workers did lose jobs and homes—perhaps even more than were displaced by structural adjustment in the 1990s. Agriculture was Zimbabwe's largest employment sector, with 26% of the wage labor force in 1999.[2] Throughout the first two post-independence decades, the number of permanent, full-time farmworkers remained steady at 167,000, 30% of whom were women.[3] GAPWUZ had 65,000 members, one-third of all permanent workers.[4] There were 146,000 casual and seasonal workers in 2000, 55% of whom were women. Two-thirds of farmworkers were in the three Mashonaland provinces.

The position of workers on white farms varied considerably. Casual workers tended to be linked to nearby communal areas. Permanent workers tended to live on farm compounds, although 40% of male permanent workers maintained a communal area home.[5] Another survey showed that of the permanent workers, 98,000 were still employed on plantation estates and the remaining big farms in 2006.[6] Up to 15% of former farmworkers obtained land under the Fast Track Land Reform, some directly as farmworkers and others who identified themselves as being from their communal areas and did not disclose their farmworker status.[7] A 2002 survey by Lloyd Sachikonye for the Farm Community Trust of Zimbabwe found that one-third of male farmworkers (both permanent and casual) and half of women farmworkers (again both permanent and casual) lost their jobs. Many farmworkers lived on the farm, and of those who lost their jobs but lived on the farm, about half remained in farm housing;[8] some with links in the communal areas moved there, but others were forced to move to temporary roadside squatter camps. "Because most workers lived with their families, the total number affected by the evictions was considerable," Sachikonye notes.

Sam Moyo of the African Institute for Agrarian Studies (AIAS) estimated in 2011 that "about 100,000 former farm workers, 30 percent of whom are alleged to be of 'foreign migrant origin' remain as residents on insecure labour tenancies within the redistributed lands, in A2 and A1 areas," and "around 45,000 former farm workers are known to have been physically displaced and living as 'squatters.'"[9] The *A2 Land Audit Report* in 2006 found a much smaller number and identified 14,400 former farmworkers still living on A2 farms but not employed by those farms.[10] A 2006 survey of six districts in six provinces by AIAS found that 36% of occupants of resettled farms were former or retired farmworkers (8,813 farmworker families compared to 13,159 resettlement families).[11] Some have small plots, but all have to earn additional money—gold panning, trying to work in towns, or increasingly working for resettlement farmers.

The new land-reform farmers arrived with little capital and equipment and had none of the support given to new white farmers in the 1950s or to resettlement farmers in the 1980s. It took several years before significant production levels were restored. Thus, in addition to a real fall in food production, the new farmers were not in a position to hire. However, this changed over time. The AIAS carried out its *Baseline Survey* of 2,100 resettlement households (A1 and A2) in 2006. It found 31% of A1 farmers hired permanent labor (averaging 5 workers) and 57% hired casual labor.[12] Overall, resettlement households (A1 and A2) hired on average 2 full-time workers and 8 part-time workers and used 4 family members[13]—much more labor-intensive than the old white farms. In the Masvingo study, Ian Scoones's team found that 11% of A1 farmers hired full-time labor for cropping (averaging 3 workers) and most hired part-time workers, while 72% of A2 farmers hired full-time workers (average 4) as well as part-time workers, particularly for weeding and harvesting.[14]

By 2011, the total number of people working full-time on resettlement land had increased fivefold, from 167,000 to over 1 million, according to Walter Chambati of AIAS.[15] He estimated in 2011 that 240,000 people were full-time employed on A1 farms and 115,000 on A2 farms. But equally important, 510,000 people from the A1 farmers' families were "self-employed" full-time and 55,000 from extended families on A2 farms. With nearly 100,000 still employed on corporate and other large-scale commercial farms, this means more than 1 million people are now working full-time on this land, compared to 167,000 before land reform.

Chambati points to the tendency of some analysts to dismiss self-employed farmers as "peasants" who are somehow more backward than wage laborers and thus do not count, but as we have seen, many are small-scale commercial farmers and not simply subsistence producers, and this is a huge gain in livelihoods. This is because small farms tend to be much more labor-intensive, partly due to less mechanization. Chambati notes that in the 1990s, large-scale commercial farms had only 0.7 workers per cropped hectare, while 1980s resettlement farms had 3.5.[16]

The number of full-time farmworkers has increased substantially, but many old farmworkers remain unemployed. Our interviews indicated that although some former farm laborers work on different farms from the ones in the past (due to mutual distrust), most new farmworkers come from communal areas and extended families. Chambati also reports that on the resettlement farms "work relations are defined by kinship ties" and social links. He adds that resettlement farmers are tending to build housing for their farmworkers within the family compound, which "is quantitatively different from the overcrowded compound which was located far away from the white farmers' luxurious mansions."[17] In our interviews we also noted farmers building houses for workers next to their own.

So there has been a huge increase in the number of people working on the land, but two issues remain outstanding: tens of thousands of people have lost jobs, and the working conditions and wages of farmworkers appear to have deteriorated. Both issues are partly related to history. In the colonial era, workers were recruited from Zambia, Malawi, and Mozambique and lived for generations on farm compounds without rights and as neither Zimbabweans nor foreigners. This was because Zimbabweans would not work for the very low wages, and was also an explicit attempt to recruit farmworkers who did not have local links, to make them totally dependent on their employers, as indeed happened. More than half were foreign in the 1950s, but after independence this fell to below 30%.[18] The AIAS surveyed former farmworkers in 2006 and found that 26% were descendants of migrant workers, but only 10% had been born outside Zimbabwe.[19]

Farmworkers have always been the lowest paid, with the worst working and living conditions. The Riddell Commission in 1981 noted that "it is clear that some fundamental changes are necessary to improve the pay, working and living conditions on commercial farms," and that "social conditions on some commercial farms are below an acceptable standard of human decency."[20] In a survey in Mashonaland Central in 1981–83, René Loewenson found that "the health status of children was poorest in the commercial farm areas. Poor health status was associated with other unfavourable factors including overcrowding, poor housing, poor access to water supplies and insanitary conditions."[21] But little was done to improve conditions, and structural adjustment introduced "flexible" labor regulations, which reduced protection for workers, so new farm jobs were casual, temporary, or seasonal; horticulture farmers, in particular, preferred to hire female labor only in peak periods. Wages fell dramatically during the 1990s Economic and Structural Adjustment Programme (ESAP), both in real terms and in proportion to the minimum wage for other sectors. In 1997, there was an unprecedented nationwide strike by the farmworkers, joining with many other strikers, and there was some violence. Yash Tandon reports that "taking whatever farm instruments came to hand, they ran amok in small groups, slashing fields, burning down tobacco barns, blocking rural roads, setting alight cars belonging to (white) commercial farmers, and looting shops, most of them farm stores."[22] Workers won a temporary wage increase,[23] but it was soon eaten up by inflation. In both 1996 and 2001, the minimum farm wage was $33 a month, but in 1996, it was 44% of the minimum wage for other sectors, while in 2001 it was down to 32% of other sector wages. Timothy Neill, director of the Zimbabwe Community Development Trust, found that "many farm workers were barely surviving and were worse off economically than they were twenty years ago."[24]

Permanent workers on white farms did have job security, but low wages meant they were totally dependent on their employer for a range of "benefits."[25] Only 3% of farmworkers received more than the minimum wage, but many white farmers provided housing and subsidized maize meal, fuel, and sometimes small plots of land—although Rene Loewenson in her Mashonaland Central survey in 1981/82 found that most farmers did not provide food, and farmworkers were expected to buy from the farm shops, which were more expensive than those off the farm, with workers spending up to two-thirds of their income on food. She also found that many farmworkers were expected to build their own housing when there was no farm work, and two-thirds of her sample lived in mud and thatch houses.[26] By the time of fast track, housing was still overcrowded and poorly built and there was a lack of clean water.[27] Some farm owners paid school fees for workers' children; nevertheless, school attendance rates for children of farmworkers were low—in 1997, only 57% of farmworker children went to school, compared to 79% in communal areas.[28]

For many farmworkers, the white farm was home. They were totally dependent on white farmers for housing, food, and often schooling and health care—and for older people, the right to remain living there when they could no longer work. Many lacked links with local communities and some workers had been born on the farm. Many farms were sold in the two decades after independence, and some individual farmers had six or more farms, so farmworkers rarely saw the white owners. The 1997 violence showed the ambivalent relationship these farmworkers had with their employers, but their homes and livelihoods were completely tied to the farm. Thus, during the occupations, some farmworkers joined to try to obtain their own land, but most resisted and fought against the occupiers. And the violence was real; 13% of farmworkers experienced violent confrontation with the new land occupants.[29]

But the politics were very complex and local. Prosper Matondi's study of Mazowe district concludes that "farmworkers were not essentially victims, but were at times willing participants in assisting land occupiers."

But this was not unproblematic; he cites two farms where war veterans pegged out land for farmworkers, and the district administrator took the land away and gave it to other people.[30]

Former farmworkers were caught, and are still trapped, in an unfortunate political split between workers and peasants. At the time of *jambanja,* workers tended to support their employers and oppose the occupations. The trade unions, including the farmworkers' union, were seen as part of the formation of the MDC, founded by the secretary-general of the Zimbabwe Congress of Trade Unions, Morgan Tsvangirai, which received strong and public backing from white farmers in its opposition to the new constitution, including land reform. GAPWUZ opposed the land occupations.[31] Thus, farmworkers were seen as opposed to land reform—and still are. In 2011, the BBC World Service went to GAPWUZ in Harare, and the farmworker the BBC interviewed said, "Before land reform we didn't have any problems with our employers. It was very nice. . . . This land reform must be reversed, and maybe our life can change."[32] He seems to have forgotten the 1997 strikes.

In chapter 1, we said there are countless questions about what would have happened *if.* If more farmworkers had joined with the occupiers and taken land. If GAPWUZ, instead of opposing occupations, had backed them in exchange for land. If more white farmers had been like Keith Campbell and had negotiated with occupiers to ensure that workers received land. Or if land reform had not taken place. But we also said in chapter 1 that this is not a book about what might have been, could have been, or should have been. Land reform will not be reversed—the Global Political Agreement (¶5.5) includes the phrase, "accepting the irreversibility of said land acquisitions and redistribution," and 2 million new occupants would not allow any change now. But in a highly polarized political atmosphere, the farmworkers' union has chosen to align itself with opposition politics and with international agencies who are seen as wanting to reverse land reform. It is hard to say whether this is still a sensible long-term strategy, especially when a survey showed that more than half of former farmworkers would like land and only one-third want to be reemployed.[33] But in the short term within Zimbabwe, it makes it much harder to negotiate some better treatment for displaced farmworkers. Whatever the political position of the union and the exaggerations of campaigners, there are tens of thousands of former farmworkers. The position of those expelled from the former white farms, and even those still living in the compounds, is worse than it was before 2000.

Fast track land reform has vastly increased the number of people working on the land, and even the number of full-time employed farmworkers has increased, but it appears that pay and working conditions remain poor. The official minimum wage is $2 per day, almost double the minimum wage on the old white farms. But even middle A1 farmers cannot afford that. We found that $1 a day plus food is very common on A1 farms, similar to that previously on the white farms.[34] And there is substantial seasonal and casual labor. Workers do not have the benefits and job security they had on the white farms. An AIAS report concluded, "Wages are usually below the stipulated minimum and former farm workers re-engaged to work on new farms are earning less than their previous establishments with a diminished set of benefits."[35] Indeed, wages are so low that in some places there are labor shortages, because farmworkers can find other livelihoods such as gold panning.[36] A serious problem is that land-reform farmers, both A1 and A2, received little support from government and cannot obtain credit for expenses like wages; even contract farming only supplies inputs. They are accumulating from below and reinvesting their own money. In particular, they receive money only when they sell a crop, which means that even successful farmers are squeezed and have trouble meeting a wage bill before the harvest.

And many of the new farmers are not making pension payments for their workers. In 2011, the National Social Security Authority (NSSA) took former Mashonaland West Governor Nelson Samkange to court over unpaid $3,173 pension contributions for his workers on his Rukoba Farm in Banket. On July 5, 2011, NSSA "noted with concern the low compliance rate in the commercial farming sector with many farmers failing to register their enterprises and their workers and remitting contributions and premiums of the Pensions and Other Benefits Schemes and Accident Prevention and Workers Compensation Insurance Fund."[37]

There is clearly a need for GAPWUZ to organize the new generation of farmworkers. Also, it might still be possible for GAPWUZ, NGOs, and donors to try to obtain land for former farmworkers, especially if A2 farms are being reallocated or downsized, releasing more land. Gold panning has become an important activity for former farmworkers, and again there could be a role for GAPWUZ and NGOs to organize them into more environmentally sustainable groups, as noted in chapter 11.

Irrigation

Irrigation is central to Zimbabwean agriculture, for winter crops and to supplement irregular rains in the summer (see Figure 4.1). This was recognized by both the Rhodesian and Zimbabwe governments, which subsidized irrigation, mainly for large-scale commercial farms. In 1997, 187,000 ha was irrigated, but only 12,000 ha was in communal or re-settlement areas.[38] Wheat and sugarcane were the main irrigated crops, followed by soya beans, tobacco, winter maize, and barley.

But irrigation is proving to be very difficult for resettlement farmers, who are finding it almost impossible to run inherited irrigation schemes collectively or cooperatively. By 2004, there had been a "near collapse of the irrigation sector during the fast track land reform period," and to-tal irrigated land had fallen by 66,000 ha.[39] A 2006 government survey found nearly 500 irrigation systems not in use.[40] Management is made even more difficult by erratic electricity, which makes it hard to plan ir-rigation rotations. The new farmers lack both technical and managerial skills—technical in the sense of distributing water efficiently and appro-priately for the crops, and managerially in terms of water allocation and coping with irregular electricity supplies, equipment maintenance, and cost recovery.

On Springdale Farm some people had grown wheat and an irriga-tion system with pipes and a pump was set up in 2003 with a loan. It had been intended to serve 31 A1 farms, but now serves only 8 that can afford to pay for electricity (about $200 per farm per season) and repairs, and some farmers are excluded because they owed from previous years.

When white farms were broken up into both A1 and A2 farms, irri-gation was rarely taken into account, so groups of new farmers received land irrigated by a central system of pipes, pumps, and a dam. No man-agement systems were set up. Also, in the initial confusion, pumps, pipes, and electricity transformers were stolen and sold by the white farmers[41] and the new settlers. Again, at the height of hyperinflation, there was a problem of equipment theft.

We saw a successful A1 irrigation program at Kiaora Farm in which farmers took turns using irrigation pipes, and in Mashonaland Central, a 2006 survey found that most inherited irrigation systems were in use.[42] But we saw many failures in which new farmers were not able to form working irrigation committees. Resettlement farmers, unlike those in communal areas, do not come from the same clans or lineage; neighbors arrive as strangers and have to build social links. This takes time, although studies show that local farmer and other groups are being formed and land-reform farmers are more likely to be in formal groups than com-munal farmers because the former have more need of such groups.[43] Nevertheless, these ad hoc local groups are not proving robust enough to manage irrigation systems. Farmers have no experience with this type of organization or with stakeholder management of a relatively complex system, and they received no training.

There is a high level of distrust that the lazy will take advantage of the hardworking, that officeholders will abuse their positions, or that people will take petty advantage of having pipes stored on their land or being nearer the dam. And there are enough examples to reinforce the distrust. One study of Lot 3 of Buena Vista Farm in Goromonzi found that a group was formed in 2007 to hire a contractor to prepare land collectively, but somehow, although all paid, only the land of the 14 committee members was prepared.[44] A study of Athlone Farm, Murehwa, Mashonaland East, found that "since pipes are carried from one field to the other, responsibility and accountability has reportedly been difficult to enforce."[45] A particular problem was ensuring that all members paid for electricity, pump maintenance, and replacement pipe. Building mutual trust and solidarity takes time—and support. But studies show that private and state management of smallholder irrigation has not been effective,[46] so solving the collective action problem and building stakeholder management seems the only option.

Hyperinflation also caused problems, because community groups were often organized around savings clubs or systems of payment over time, and hyperinflation destroyed those savings. Similarly, when loans were obtained, by the time the money was available it was no longer enough to buy the equipment. On Lot 3 of Buena Vista, A1 farmers inherited a system that had irrigated 350 ha and obtained two pumps from the government; but by the time of a 2008 study, they were irrigating only 18 ha close to the dam, in part because they had been unable to buy sprinklers and valves in the era of hyperinflation, which demoralized the new farmers. On nearby Dalkeith Farm, irrigation of winter wheat did not go ahead due to non-availability of electricity.[47]

White farmers received substantial subsidies and extensive training for irrigation. Collective management, particularly by A1 farmers, will require similar long-term support and training. It was unrealistic to assume the new farmers could simply take over, rehabilitate, and manage the existing irrigation systems without support. In the long term, resettlement farmers will be productive, commercial, and profitable only if they can produce two crops per year, so an irrigation program will be essential for a winter crop.

Nationally, the potential for increased irrigation is substantial. Most irrigation is based on rainfall captured in ponds and lakes behind dams, with some water taken directly from rivers and some from boreholes.

It is estimated that another 200,000 ha have suitable soil and could be irrigated, and the amount of rainfall captured for irrigation could be doubled; there also appears to be significant untapped groundwater.[48] However, there are growing concerns that global warming is making rainfall more irregular.

Thus, irrigation is going to be a central social and technical issue for land-reform farmers in the coming decade and is going to require substantial technical, financial, and organizational support. So far, irrigation has largely used inefficient sprinkler or canal systems, but the rising costs of electricity and infrastructure and the desire to irrigate more land will force a move to more efficient systems—potentially increasing investment costs and management demands.

What Tenure Is Secure?

How can land-reform farms be passed on to others? An issue raised in chapter 10 is whether widows like Mrs. Mwashita or children will inherit. Can farms be leased or sold? This remains largely unresolved. A few land-reform farmers have 99-year leases, most only have a permit or letter (usually called an "offer letter") allocating land to them, and many have nothing and officially are still "squatting" on their land. There has been a huge debate about tenure and security around the question: Will people invest if they are afraid they might be thrown off the land? Some fear their land might be grabbed by powerful people, and there have been cases of people being pushed off their land. In particular, there are cases of women who had accessed land being elbowed out by men. The Global Political Agreement (¶5.5 and 5.9) accepts the land reform and present land distribution, but also cites the need to "ensure security of tenure to all land holders."

Nevertheless, in our research, we heard very little about concerns of titles or security of tenure. Whereas the intellectual debate is usually presented in terms of "people will not invest without security," what we saw on the ground was just the opposite. Both A1 and A2 farmers felt that investment and production was the way to develop security—that it is harder to remove a productive farmer than one who is not. Ian Scoones and colleagues confirm that they found that "most settlers feel that tenure is secure enough and the likelihood of land being taken away is small."[49]

Fabby Shangwa, a 60-year-old woman farmer who has an A1 permit in her own name, told us that when she was allocated a plot number "that same day I took an axe and went and built a shelter from tree branches [*kutema musasa*] on my plot. I went back home and brought a cooking pot, a hoe and a blanket, from that day I have never left the farm." A widow in Goromonzi was so desperate for land that she identified and occupied a plot of District Council land and started farming. After three years without an offer letter, and effectively as a "squatter," she is increasing her security through investments in plowing and inputs. The social importance of using the land is demonstrated by the case of a woman ex-combatant who had a farm and an offer letter, but was moved out because a senior army officer wanted the land. She fought and was eventually allocated another farm in 2007, which was larger than the original one.

In a study of Goromonzi and Zvimba districts of Mashonaland East Tendai Murisa reported two cases in 2006 where a local politician and someone with political influence were able to arrange for A1 farms to be rezoned as A2 and the A1 farmers were told they had to move. In both cases, they were able to resist, with the help of provincial officials and a local MP, and have the rezoning reversed.[50]

Although politicians at various levels want to maintain the power to evict farmers, many recognize that some form of improved security and clearer tenure must be established. There has been a big push for freehold tenure, allowing land to be bought and sold freely, although there are also strong arguments against this policy. In particular, Lionel Cliffe, an expert on land reform in Africa, and others note, "Individual tenure has not facilitated agricultural credit nor provided security of tenure through the market, and does not even operate in practice. A cautionary tale for Zimbabweans."[51]

The biggest advocates of freehold tend to be US diplomats and some in the World Bank, who often promote Hernando de Soto's 2000 book, *The Mystery of Capital*. This line is also supported by people who want to speculate in land, particularly those who want to obtain farms in the land reform and later sell them. De Soto argues for a formal property system with titles that are easily tradable and transferable. Formal titles allow poor property owners to mobilize the "sleeping capital" embodied in their land because titles allow "contracts with strangers," in particular as a way to obtain credit. De Soto argues that formal titles are the fundamental explanation of "why capitalism triumphs in the West and fails everywhere else."[52]

But he continues, "What made this stake meaningful was that it could be lost. A great part of the potential value of legal property is derived from the possibility of forfeiture." If people "have no property to

lose, they are taken seriously as contracting parties only by their immediate family and neighbours."[53] Thus, the risk that people will be thrown
off their land is fundamental to de Soto's system of bringing capitalism
to the poor.

De Soto remains a controversial figure. He was a governor of Peru's
central bank and a backer of the 1992 "auto-coup" by Alberto Fujimori
and his CIA-linked security head, Vladimiro Montesinos.[54] As Fujimori's
principal advisor, he initiated the economic reforms that brought such
hardship to Peru that Fujimori and Montesinos were eventually over-
thrown. Yet de Soto also warns that "most economic reform programmes
in poor economies may be falling into the trap that Karl Marx foresaw:
the great contradiction of the capitalist system is that it creates its own
demise because it cannot avoid concentrating capital in a few hands.
. . . At present, capitalist globalization is concerned with interconnect-
ing only the elites."[55]

De Soto has a two-part prescription for expanding capitalism to developing countries. The first is clear and tradable property titles. But those
who oppose Zimbabwe's land reform tend to ignore the second part,
squatting, which he sees as ending what he calls "property apartheid" and
instead accommodating what he calls "extra-legal property rights" where
the poor have taken control of land.[56] Indeed, the pioneers who settled
the United States were "nothing but squatters." Much of the expansion
of the United States in the 18th and 19th centuries was fueled by squatters occupying unused land owned by someone else—often challenging
a "propertied elite." De Soto points to the US Congress in 1830, 1832,
1838, 1840, and 1841 giving rights to squatters, and that the Homestead
Act of 1862 just legalized squatters[57]—not very different from the Fast
Track Land Reform law in Zimbabwe. And then in the nineteenth century, the United States developed "occupancy laws" giving rights to land
based on improvements made to it. Finally, de Soto notes that the US
Congress used land to pay soldiers, giving 26 mn ha to veterans of the
revolution, War of 1812, "Indian" war, and wars with Mexico.[58] De Soto
argues that "there is much to learn" from the US nineteenth-century experience.[59] Zimbabwe seems to be following the US model quite closely.

But once the occupation is recognized, as is done with an offer letter
or 99-year lease, there is a whole series of questions relating to use and
transfer of the land. So far this is being done on an ad hoc basis. Inheritance rights are recognized and land is passed on to spouses or children.
There is also a growing move to withdraw offers on land that is not used,
and for several years Provincial Land Committees have been reallocating

unused land. Where only a small part of an A2 farm is being used, it is sometimes "re-dimensioned," with part given to someone else. One rule is not enforced: farmers are clearly not allowed to lease land, either for money or for a share of the crop, yet this is very common; many of the better farmers we met were "borrowing" additional land. Two rules are largely, but not completely, enforced: land cannot be sold or transferred outside a family, and a person cannot have more than one farm. Thus, a form of custom and practice is evolving, but its very unofficial nature makes it subject to political manipulation—land committees are not prepared to challenge big men who do not use their land or who have multiple farms.

Freehold is not the only titling system, and in many countries and cultures there is a belief that people cannot "own" land—that land is part of common resources and is lent to people to use in their lifetimes or for a period. And it could be argued that land is a natural resource for all people, and that its use should be under the authority of a democratic state. But any tenure system must deal with four issues:

1. **Sale and Transfer:** Can land be sold or transferred outside the family? Should there be restrictions on buyers (such as no one can own more than one farm)? Are mortgages allowed? If a person defaults on a mortgage or loan, can the bank or lender evict the family and sell the land and buildings? Are companies allowed to own A1 and A2 farms? Can farms be divided or merged? Should some agency approve (or at least have the right to reject) any transfers?
2. **Other Users:** Can land be leased, shared, sharecropped, or otherwise farmed by someone who is not the title holder?
3. **Inheritance:** Is land heritable? What rules apply? What happens in the event of divorce?
4. **Use:** Should occupancy or title be conditional on use? What conditions should be set (such as percentage use or years of failing to use)? Should there be social exemptions (such as veterans or older people)? Who would decide whether land was not adequately used?

An alternative to freehold is leasehold, which is common throughout the world. Indeed, all three authors live in properties that are on long leases, and the Zimbabwe government has given some 99-year leases for A2 farms. Leases can be transferred, but leases also can include conditions; for example, a lease on a house can say it cannot be used for business. One of us owned a house in London and the lease, dating back to the beginning of the twentieth century, said that cattle could not be grazed on the land. The point of such conditions is that they can be enforced, usually by court action, the lease canceled, and property taken away.

Leases can be mortgaged and transfers restricted. For example, the regulations might say that a bank could repossess a farm, but could only sell it to an individual who does not already own a farm. Key points here are transparency and justice—everyone needs to know the rules, and there must be some court or tribunal to which someone can appeal about the loss of a lease.

De Soto and others often argue for leasehold or freehold because they see land mortgages as the only way farmers can obtain credit. But Zimbabwe, and Rhodesia before it, has a long history of providing credit with the crop used as collateral—tobacco or maize must be sold to the company that provided the inputs, and the company gives the farmer the money after deducting its costs. Often this is linked to some form of insurance, so that if the rains fail, the insurer (often the government) pays the debt. There are a number of issues around this, especially the worry that the farmer will sell the crop secretly to someone else (known as side-selling) and not pay that bill and might run up a string of bad debts. This problem can be resolved by simply having a land register and setting up a clear list of unpaid debts—farmers would be allowed only one unpaid debt. They would no longer be able to get credit, but they would not lose their land.

The choice of leasehold, freehold, offer letters, or some other tenure system is less important than that it satisfy a few basic conditions: it provides security of tenure, the rules must be clear, inheritance is defined, and there is a public record of landholdings. And with Zimbabwe's long history of squatting and the importance of land as a national asset, there probably need to be some conditions to ensure that land is used.

Summing Up: Difficult Outstanding Problems

A decade after land reform, three difficult problems remain:

1. More than 1 million people are now working full-time on re-settlement farms, compared to 167,000 before land reform. But their salaries are low and working conditions are often poor, so a problem from the 1970s and 1990s remains—how to raise the living standards of these very poor workers. Meanwhile, tens of

thousands of people lost their jobs to structural adjustment in the 1990s and other tens of thousands lost their jobs, and sometimes their homes, to fast track land reform. These tend not to be the same people who are newly employed on land-reform farms, and many remain in poverty. Thus, it becomes urgent to create jobs or find land for those displaced by these two major economic upheavals.

2. Boosting agricultural production and raising the living standards of A1 farmers requires a major increase in the use of irrigation, both for a second winter crop and to ensure the summer crop under Zimbabwe's variable rainfall. That requires substantial investment in dams, boreholes, pumps, and other irrigation equipment. But it also requires a long process of training and support for farmers on water management—how to participate in committees, about rights and responsibilities, and building trust. NGOs and agricultural extension workers will need to spend a decade of hand-holding and capacity building to ensure that stakeholder management works.

3. There is no single answer to the question of tenure and security. Rather, what is needed is a more open discussion of goals, and how to balance often-conflicting goals of fairness, equity, security, and productivity.

There is no "fast track" to addressing these problems. Instead there is a need for a less polarized and more fundamental discussion, balancing goals and options.

Notes

1. Amnesty International, "Trade Unions in Zimbabwe," available at http://www.amnesty.org.uk/content.asp?CategoryID=12094 (accessed December 8, 2011).

2. Walter Chambati, "Restructuring of Agrarian Labour Relations After Fast Track Land Reform in Zimbabwe," *Journal of Peasant Studies,* 38, no. 5 (2011): 1028, citing Central Statistical Office data [Chambati, "Restructuring"].

3. Walter Chamabati and Sam Moyo, "Land Reform and the Political Economy of Agricultural Labour in Zimbabwe," occasional paper 4/2007 (Harare, Zimbabwe: African Institute for Agrarian Studies, 2007), 10–11 [Chamabati and Moyo, 2007]. Note the spelling of the first author was changed to Chambati in subsequent publications.

4. Sam Moyo et al., *Fast Track Land Reform Baseline Survey in Zimbabwe* (Harare, Zimbabwe: African Institute for Agrarian Studies, 2009): 157 [Moyo et al., *Baseline Survey*].

5. Chamabati and Moyo, 2007, 14.

6. Chambati, "Restructuring," 1028, Table 5, and Ian Scoones et al., *Zimbabwe's Land Reform* (Woodbridge, Suffolk, UK: James Currey, 2010), 127 [Scoones et al., *Land Reform*].

7. GAPWUZ estimates that only 5% of former farmworkers have received land. Shingayi Jena, "Displaced Farm Workers Wallow in Poverty," *Financial Gazette,* June 29, 2011, available at http://allafrica.com/stories/201107040077.html (accessed December 8, 2011). International Organisation on Migration estimated that 15% of former farmworkers obtained land, cited in Moyo et al., *Baseline Survey,* 33. Looking at it from the other end, Moyo's survey suggests at least 8% of beneficiaries were former agricultural workers, and Scoones et al., *Land Reform,* 127, estimates that between 7% and 10% of new beneficiaries were former farmworkers, perhaps 15,000 families.

8. Lloyd Sachikonye, "The Situation of Commercial Farm Workers After Land Reform in Zimbabwe" (Harare, Zimbabwe: Farm Community Trust of Zimbabwe, 2003), available at http://www.zimbabwesituation.com/farmworkers.html (April 28, 2012) [Sachikonye, "Situation"].

9. Sam Moyo, "Three Decades of Agrarian Reform in Zimbabwe," *Journal of Peasant Studies,* 38, no. 3 (2011), 207–8 [Moyo, "Three Decades"].

10. Ministry of Lands, Land Reform and Resettlement & Informatics Institute, *A2 Land Audit Report* (Harare, Zimbabwe, 2006); the report was completed in eight volumes, one for each province, issued at different times during 2006.

11. Moyo et al., *Baseline Survey,* 11, 31.

12. Ibid., Table 6.4.

13. Ibid., 513.

14. Scoones et al., *Land Reform,* 134.

15. Chambati, "Restructuring," 1016, 1028.

16. Ibid., 1025.

17. Ibid., 1025, 1030.

18. Chamabati and Moyo, 2007, 7.

19. Chambati, "Restructuring," 1032. Under a 2004 law, people born in Zimbabwe to parents from neighboring countries are entitled to Zimbabwean citizenship.

20. Roger Riddell, *Report of the Commission of Inquiry into Incomes, Prices and Conditions of Service,* 1981, 42.

21. René Loewenson, "Farm Labour in Zimbabwe: A Comparative Study in Health Status," *Health Policy and Planning,* 1, no. 1 (1986): 48 [Loewenson, "Farm Labour"].

22. Timothy Neill, "Labour and Union Issues in the Zimbabwean Agricultural Sector in 2004" (Harare, Zimbabwe: Zimbabwe Community Development

Trust, 2004), 11 [Neill, "Labour"], citing Yash Tandon, "Trade Unions and Labour in the Agricultural Sector," in *Zimbabwe Striking Back: The Labour Movement and the Post-Colonial State in Zimbabwe 1980–2000,* ed. Brian Raftopoulos and Lloyd Sachikonye (Harare, Zimbabwe: Weaver, 2001).

23. Sachikonye, "Situation."

24. Neill, "Labour," 11.

25. Chamabati and Moyo, 2007, 10–13, 19, 39.

26. Loewenson, "Farm Labour," 54, 55.

27. Neill, "Labour," 11.

28. Chamabati and Moyo, 2007, 25.

29. Moyo, "Three Decades," 511.

30. Prosper Matondi, "Fast Tracking Land Reforms in Mazowe District in Zimbabwe" (Harare, Zimbabwe, 2011).

31. Moyo et al., *Baseline Survey,* 158.

32. Martin Plaut, "Crossing Continents: Farming Zimbabwe," BBC Radio 4, December 1 and 5, 2011, available at http://www.bbc.co.uk/programmes/b017mvx6#synopsis (December 7, 2011)

33. Moyo et al., *Baseline Survey,* 33.

34. Chambati, "Restructuring," 1029, reports that the 2011 prevailing wage was $30 to $50 per month.

35. Chamabati and Moyo, 2007, 28.

36. Chambati, "Restructuring," 1027.

37. The farm and the new governor had already been subject to court action in 2005, when William Nyabonda, secretary general of the Indigenous Commercial Farmers Union, sued then-governor Nelson Samkange, claiming the then-governor had let him use the farm to grow tobacco because Samkange admitted he did not have any skills or resources to use the farm and wanted to avoid the embarrassment of leaving the farm unused. But then Samkange took the crop at the end of the season. "Governor Samkange in $4 bn Tobacco Row," *Daily Mirror,* May 25, 2005, available at http://www.zimbabwesituation.com/may26a_2005.html; Feluna Nleya, "Samkange Hauled to Court Over Pensions," *Newsday,* June 26, 2011, available at http://www.newsday.co.zw/article/2011-06-26-samkange-hauled-to-court-over-pensions; Clarkson Mambo, "Deadline for NSSA Defaulters," *The Mail,* July 6, 2011, available at http://www.mailonline.co.zw/index.php?option=com_content&view=article&id=1168:deadline-for-nssa-defaulters&catid=77:other&Itemid=1080 (all accessed December 26, 2011).

38. Johannes Makadho, Prosper Matondi, and Mabel Munyuki-Hungwe, "Irrigation Development and Water Resource Management," in *Zimbabwe's Agricultural Revolution Revisited,* ed. Mandivambi Rukuni et al. (Harare, Zimbabwe: University of Zimbabwe, 2006), Tables 11.1 and 11.2 [Makadho, "Irrigation"].

39. Makadho, "Irrigation."

40. Nelson Marongwe, "Redistributive Land Reform and Poverty Reduction in Zimbabwe," n.d. (probably 2008), available at http://lalr.org.za/zimbabwe/

redistributive-land-reform-and-poverty-reduction-in-zimbabwe (December 26, 2011) [Marongwe, "Redistributive"].

41. Ibid.

42. Ibid.

43. Tendai Murisa, "Local Farmer Groups and Collective Action Within Fast Track Land Reform in Zimbabwe," *Journal of Peasant Studies,* 38, no. 5 (2011): 1113–34 [Murisa, "Local Farmer Groups"].

44. Tendai Murisa, "Farmer Groups, Collective Action and Production Constraints: Cases From A1 Settlements in Goromonzi and Zvimba," Livelihoods After Land Reform in Zimbabwe, Working Paper 10, 2010, http://www.lalr.org.za/zimbabwe/zimbabwe-working-papers-1 (April 28, 2012).

45. Shingirai Mandizadza, "The Fast Track Land Reform Programme and Livelihoods in Zimbabwe: A Case Study of Households at Athlone Farm in Murehwa District," Livelihoods After Land Reform in Zimbabwe, Working Paper 2, 2010, http://www.lalr.org.za/zimbabwe/zimbabwe-working-papers-1 (April 28, 2012).

46. Marongwe, "Redistributive."

47. Murisa, "Local Farmer Groups," 1113–34.

48. Makadho, "Irrigation."

49. Scoones et al., *Land Reform,* 68.

50. Murisa, "Local Farmer Groups."

51. Lionel Cliffe, Jocelyn Alexander, Ben Cousins, and Rudo Gaidzanwa, "An Overview of Fast Track Land Reform in Zimbabwe: Editorial Introduction," *Journal of Peasant Studies,* 38, no. 5 (2011): 26.

52. Hernando de Soto, *The Mystery of Capital* (London, UK: Black Swan, Transworld, 2001), 55, 108ff, 219ff, 241 [de Soto, *Mystery*].

53. Ibid., 54–55.

54. *El Comercio,* Lima, Peru, March 31, 2002.

55. de Soto, *Mystery,* 224, 242.

56. Ibid., 27, 225, 242.

57. Ibid., 16, 110, 134, 155, chap. 5.

58. Ibid., 130, 136.

59. Ibid., 158.

13

Conclusion
Occupied and Productive

"THERE IS LITTLE DOUBT THAT AS LONG AS LAND IS RESERVED ON A RACIAL BASIS THERE will be ready arguments available to the agitator. . . . It is well recognised that the word 'land' is very often one of the slogans in revolutionary movements and it has a popular emotional appeal,"[1] warned the *Second Report of the Select Committee on the Resettlement of Natives in 1960.*

And so it came to pass.

"Were there to be an African government in this country—and indeed that seems inevitable, and very soon—and if the present laws which have been enacted and applied to create and preserve privilege—if these were retained and applied in reverse against the European, what a protest there would be! . . . Thousands of whites could be driven from their homes and farms without compensation," warned Catholic Bishop Donal Lamont in his speech from the dock in 1976 when he was convicted of treating guerrillas in church hospitals.[2]

And so it came to pass. Lamont hoped "Europeans might possibly be treated better than Africans were." But the new leaders had learned their lessons well and evicted white farmers without compensation. And as the bishop predicted, what a protest there has been!

In the biggest land reform in Africa, 6,000 white farmers have been replaced by 245,000 Zimbabwean farmers. Some settled in the 1980s, but most since 2000. These are primarily ordinary poor people who have become more productive farmers. The change was inevitably disruptive at first, but production is increasing rapidly. Agricultural production is now returning to the 1990s level, and resettlement farmers already grow 40% of the country's tobacco and 49% of its maize. As Barry Floyd noted in his PhD thesis more than 50 years ago, "Tobacco in its growth pays scant attention to the pigment of the plowman's skin."[3]

As we've said earlier, it takes a generation for farmers to master their new land. White farmers, especially war veterans, had extensive support in the 1950s—and, as we saw, only a third became successful. Zimbabwe's first land reform, in the 1980s under willing seller, willing buyer, where the former colonizers kept the best land but there was some initial support, the new farmers, on average, did well, increasing production and reducing poverty. "Resettled farmers were found to be more productive, on average, than communal farmers," according to long-term research by Bill Kinsey, and there is "enormous scope for many farmers to catch-up to the best farmers in the sample."[4]

The fast track land reform in 2000 was largely self-funded with little support, but fast track farmers had the enthusiasm of occupiers and they had finally taken the best land. On average, the fast track farmers are doing well, raising their living standards and increasing production, and over the next decade can be expected to continue growing—the best are doing very well, and a middle group is still catching up.

Not All the Same

The British colonizers developed a dual agriculture system, with most people on smallholdings and a privileged group having larger farms. And they racialized the land, defining some land as "European" and some land as "African." On the surface, the dual system and racial land definitions have continued since independence. But beneath the language of "white farmers" and "large-scale farms," there have been changes. In terms of farm size, Zimbabweans improved on their teachers—the small farms are bigger, and the large farms are smaller—leading to better land use and increased commercial production.

Similarly, the colonial shorthand of white and black farmers is still used, but in reality neither group is homogeneous. White farmers became famous because some were highly profitable and productive. Yet, as a group, at independence, white farmers were using less than one-third of their land, and most were not doing very well—one-third were insolvent and one-third were only breaking even. The white minority fought a brutal war to maintain its privilege and power, yet after independence, many in the white community took places in the new Zimbabwe. There are still white farmers like Keith Campbell who have built good relationships with land-reform farmers and other white Zimbabweans are involved in agri-business.

On the side of the land-reform farmers, there are the hugely success-ful farmers like Fanuel Mutandiro and Esther Makwara, who use every corner of their land. There are vacant plots and farmers who are doing very poorly. And there are many in between, struggling to invest and grow, sometimes supported by contract farming. The decision to main-tain a large-scale farming sector accessible only to the better-off remains controversial, and some of those farms have been given to influential people. Yet even the so-called "cronies" are not homogeneous—some are sitting on the land hoping to sell or lease it, while others are highly productive and hope to get rich from farming.

Pumpkins and Getting On With Farming

Land reform can never be neat or simple anywhere in the world. Land is a finite resource that is taken away from one group and given to another. And land reform usually takes place at times of economic and social stress

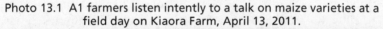

Photo 13.1 A1 farmers listen intently to a talk on maize varieties at a field day on Kiaora Farm, April 13, 2011.

or transition. Intense political and social conflicts are inevitable—from the level of setting goals and priorities down to the distribution of bags of fertilizer. These debates will continue in Zimbabwe, and many issues remain unresolved. But it is essential to step back from the loud, angry, and continuing media and political confrontations to talk to the people who have land—the actual farmers.

The most striking memory of the research for this book is how proud the fast track farmers are of their new farms. They were anxious to take us around, insisting that we see every field and hear in detail about the new tobacco barn. They were pleased with their production. A1 farmers insisted on giving us something, and each day we returned home with a carload of pumpkins.

Land reform has taken place under often inauspicious conditions, and with waxing and waning political support. Resettlement was driven in both the early 1980s and the late 1990s by occupations, which government leaders vociferously opposed. The 1980s land reform never had full political backing and lost most of that limited support after four years. It was done under the cloud of apartheid destabilization, lack of international assistance, serious droughts, and structural adjustment. Fast track started with occupations by war veterans in opposition to Zanu-PF and took place under the cloud of political conflict and sanctions. The 2005–8 hyperinflation, one of the worst in history, affected the new farmers as much as everyone else. What is most remarkable is that, despite the problems, farmers have made both land reforms work—creating successes on the ground despite the continuing confusion over their heads. And despite confused and changing instructions from the top, the government extension agency Agritex has provided important support to the new farmers.

The Global Political Agreement (GPA) in late 2008 and unity government in 2009 have proved vital in creating the stability needed to move forward. Dollarization in January 2009 prompted a remarkably rapid economic turnaround and has been central in allowing small farmers to obtain inputs and sell their produce.

Political tensions remain and international hostility, represented by sanctions, continues. Problems remain, particularly around environment and former farmworkers. And a huge amount of reconstruction is still required—to finish redressing the heritage of minority rule, re-create the 60,000 or more jobs lost under structural adjustment, and repair the damage hyperinflation did to the economy.

In a thoughtful 2010 essay, Sam Moyo pointed to the polarization in Zimbabwean society and "the pervasiveness of conflict-generating

behaviour across the divide," by both domestic and international actors. He argues that the "domestic crisis over Zimbabwe's external isola-
tion, fueled by confrontational strategies on both sides of the divide, . . .
led, since 2002, to legal restrictions on the media, NGOs and public
assembly in general, foreign financing of civil society and the increased
use of force (including arrest and torture)."[5] What is needed is "normalization." This started with the Utete and other commissions on land,
governance reforms, and the GPA and economic changes such as dollarization and price decontrol. Moyo warns that "normalization, however,
faces critical internal and external resistance, given the entrenchment of
some 'conflict entrepreneurs' on both sides of the divide. These include
those who seek a rapid, radical and comprehensive overhaul of the existing political power structure, leadership and policy process, and those in
power bent on suppressing dissent."[6]

Similarly, researcher Tendai Murisa, who studied farmer groups,
warns that fast track resettlement areas not "receiving support from development and relief NGOs is convenient for both civil society and the
state." International civil society "can continue to dismiss the land reform
process as largely benefiting politically connected elites. In the meantime
the Zanu-PF dominated state remains the only active external agent in
providing support."[7]

The GPA and public opinion now recognize there is no going back
on land reform. It may have been chaotic and ad hoc, but it will not be
reversed. So it is now possible to look forward to how agriculture can be
supported and all farmers promoted to produce more. Getting out of
the hole caused by political tensions and hyperinflation has required so
much attention that few people have been able to look at the longer-term
implications of land reform. And as the liberation generation retires, the
process will be steered by new people thinking about economic and social development.

Two linked issues stand out as priorities—putting the land to the
best possible use and promoting investment in farming.

Generations

Building up a farm does not happen in a week or a year; it takes a generation. But then what happens? As Kinsey notes: "The major gains
from small-scale resettlement are exhausted within a single generation.
Five hectares make an economically viable farm for a nuclear, not an extended family. One adult son—or daughter—can succeed the patriarch,

but the other siblings will have to move on."[8] Land-reform farmers are using more of the land—compared to white farmers who only used one-third—and the intensity of use will continue to increase for another decade or more. The gains of land reform are far from exhausted. But land reform is a once-and-for-all process; there is little land left to redistribute. In addition, resettlement has not reduced land pressure in the communal areas and has only kept up with population growth—communal areas did not become more crowded, but they did not become less congested. So what happens next?

In our interviews, we saw two processes happening. In one group, one or more children were taking agricultural courses and were expecting to take over the farm and make the next productivity leap; already some were involved in running the farm—particularly with their mothers. On the other side, some war veterans and others see land reform as ensuring enough money to send their children to school and often university, but these children expect to live in the city and have no interest in farming. There is no discussion yet about how these farms are to be kept in production over the longer term.

In the short term, land reform has served a mix of social and economic objectives. For the next generation, land-reform farms cannot remain simply the survival base of a single family—they will have to be a source of jobs, both on the farm itself and in agriculture-related industries. The GPA (¶5.7, 5.9) recognizes "the need to ensure that all land is used productively," and that there is a need for a "non-partisan land audit" partly to eliminate multiple farm ownerships. Together that means resolving the land tenure issue in a way that ensures that people feel secure and invest, and that spouses and children can inherit, but that also allows unused land to be rented or reallocated.

This raises a broader issue about Zimbabwe's future economic development. Resettlement has caused a big change in who is employed, but low-paid farm jobs are hardly appropriate for a well-educated workforce. For the next decade, resettlement farmers can probably depend on cheap labor, but that is unlikely to continue in the long term, as more suitable jobs are created elsewhere.

Investment

"With no outside investment and few resources, the achievements of these new farmers were remarkable," said Martin Plaut, Africa editor of the BBC World Service, in a report on resettlement farmers in Masvingo.[9] New white farmers in the 1950s received major government support— credit, training, subsidies, and financial and technical support for new investments such as irrigation. Bill Kinsey points to the support received by the resettlement farmers in the 1980s. Yet the fast track farmers have received virtually nothing; the government has provided little money, and donors and NGOs refuse to help new farmers on formerly white land. As Ian Scoones and colleagues note, the new farmers are accumulating from below—investing their own money from salaries and off-farm activities and reinvesting farm profits. With little support and in only a decade, about one-third of the new farmers have become commercial— the same ratio as the white farmers after 30 years and the 1980s resettlement farmers after 15 years.

But new farmers are still constrained by cash, power, and markets. Dollarization meant that by 2011 inputs and equipment were available, but with no support and little credit, seriously undercapitalized new farmers cannot afford to buy what they know they need. The most successful farmers could do better, while the potential of the farmers in the middle is huge.

Another problem is electricity. Profitability requires two crops a year, which demands irrigation, and electricity supplies are too unstable. This has blocked the revival of wheat, for example. The problem is lack of investment in electricity supplies over two decades caused by both adjustment and hyperinflation.

The third problem is marketing. Tobacco, cotton, and some other crops have assured markets—through contracts and auctions—while the huge demand for feed guarantees a market for soya. But staples, particularly maize, depend on the Grain Marketing Board, which is still the most important buyer for small producers and a major supplier of inputs. It, too, is under-capitalized and is often late in making payments.

New farmers have done remarkably well on their own. Whether it has been mortgaging houses in Harare or bringing cattle from communal areas, they have found the resources to get started. Giving support to resettlement farmers would give them the capital needed to propel many of them into being successful small and medium commercial farmers.

In chapter 3, we noted that during the UDI era, each white farm had a subsidy and loans, in current money, of about $40,000 per year—in addition to huge extension support and guaranteed markets, tightly controlled by the state. In chapter 8, we estimated that that was equivalent to $80–$130 per arable hectare. Also in chapter 8, we saw that necessary annual investment for an A1 farmer was $100 to $790 per arable hectare for seed, fertilizer, plowing, and so on, depending on the crop. So the UDI subsidy and loans were close to the minimum investment needed for an A1 farm. Thus, the Ian Smith UDI government was right—to build a group of successful farmers, basic annual investment costs had to be subsidized, credit had to be cheap, and inputs had to be backed up by extension and markets.

Another way to project the investment need is to use the chapter 8 estimate that the UDI subsidy was equivalent to $500–$800 per A1 farm and $10,000 per A2 farm. Given to all 245,000 resettlement farmers, that would be $340–$400 mn per year; some of this could be low-interest loans for capital investments.

"The few examples of large-scale land reform (such as those in Japan, the Republic of Korea, and Taiwan, China) were implemented under strong pressure from the international community and with its financial support," notes a 2010 World Bank study on Zimbabwe land reform.[10] "Clearly the national interests that the government of Zimbabwe sought to address with the Fast Track program did not coincide with the interests of the dominant international agenda. Therefore the programme could not be underwritten ideologically and financially." But the report also stresses that the government "should allocate more resources to the agricultural sector," and that credit and investment, particularly in irrigation, are essential. Nevertheless, even the World Bank thinks Zimbabwe is on its own.

But Zimbabwe does have extensive mineral resources, which could be invested. *Economist* estimates Zimbabwe could earn $1–$2 bn per year from diamonds.[11] In a parliamentary statement in August 2011, Finance Minister Tendai Biti said that diamonds that recently sold for $167 mn actually had a value of $1.5 bn, and thus more than $1.3 bn in diamond money had gone missing.[12] If the unity government can capture the mineral revenue, then there will be sufficient money to invest in land-reform farmers—and in linked agro-industry.

Impressions

It is the images that stick in the mind—walking into living rooms of both A1 farmers and elite A2 farmers to find the furniture has been moved out and the room filled with sacks of maize and groundnuts, or noting that money has been used to buy machinery rather than new furniture or a fancy car.

These are educated, high-tech farmers. A1 farmers have mobile phones even if they have no electricity, they know the varieties of hybrid maize and which fertilizers and pesticides go with them, and they plow with oxen and tractors—these are not hoe farmers as one would see across the border in Mozambique. A2 farmers are using the Internet to check on animal feed and crops and to arrange export contracts. And we heard two things repeatedly at both A1 and A2 levels—"farming is a business" and "you must have a plan." Farming is difficult anywhere, facing the vagaries of markets and weather, but the good farmers—small and large—are doing their sums and thinking long term. They know they have had these farms for a decade or less, and there is still a lot to do.

For Zimbabweans, it is not the land itself that is important, but farming. Agriculture is seen as a means of betterment and accumulation, and people are prepared to work at it and get their hands dirty. For ordinary A1 farmers, increased production provides a better house and better life for themselves and their children. For the best A1 farmers, maize or tobacco or soya gives them higher profits than the salary of a teacher or civil servant. And for A2 farmers, there is the potential for serious money that will come, not from land speculation, but from growing crops and cattle. And farmers were angry when they pointed out the unused and underused plots—A1 plotholders who still lived in Harare and A2 cell phone farmers or cronies speculating in land—because the empty land stood out like sore thumbs amid the other productive farms.

The farmers' attitudes were matched by the approach of researchers. Zimbabwe is the most literate country in Africa, and the University of Zimbabwe has a high standard of research. But more than that, we were struck by the willingness of researchers to go out to rural areas and spend long days there, sometimes interviewing hundreds of farmers. Research is not something they do just sitting at a desk; researchers, too, are willing to get their hands dirty. This book would have been impossible without the high-quality research already done by Zimbabweans—and their willingness to share. We came away not just with pumpkins, but with many papers and research reports as well.

The final impression is just how quickly Zimbabweans are recovering from the hyperinflation era, and how outsiders (even Zimbabweans abroad) have missed that change. The introduction of the US dollar as currency in January 2009 brought an end to one of the world's worst hyperinflations and brought a return of economic life much more quickly than many expected. In May 2011, when we did much of our fieldwork, the Harare supermarkets were packed with goods and shoppers, and farmers were selling their maize and tobacco to pay school fees and buy seed. Of course, there are not enough dollars—physically, in the sense that the dollar bills handed over at the toll booths on the roads out of Harare are tattered and dirty, and economically, in that most people remain poor and farmers are under-capitalized. Nevertheless, in a remarkable way Zimbabweans have moved on—the economy seems "normal" and people talk about the hyperinflation time only if you ask.

Thus, outside commentators tend to underestimate two aspects of Zimbabwe. The first is the tie to the land and farming, even for academics and elites. The other is the speed of the recovery under dollarization, itself a testament to the resilience and creativity of Zimbabweans, but also showing that the economic crisis of 2005–8 was caused by hyperinflation and not land reform.

Zimbabwe's land reform has not been neat, and huge problems remain. But 245,000 new farmers have received land, and most of them are farming it. They have raised their own standard of living; have already reached production levels of the former white farmers; and, with a bit of support, are ready to substantially increase that production.

In 1952, Godfrey Huggins, prime minister of Southern Rhodesia, said, "The ultimate possessors of the land will be the people who can make the best use of it."[13] Sixty years later, this has come to pass.

Notes

1. Malcolm Rifkind, "The Politics of Land in Rhodesia" (MSc thesis, Edinburgh University, 1968), 141 [Rifkind, "Politics of Land"], citing Jack Quinton, *Second Report of the Select Committee on the Resettlement of Natives,* 1960, ¶216, 217, available at http://www.met.open.ac.uk/zimbabwe (June 20, 2012).

2. Donal Lamont, *Speech From the Dock* (Leigh-on-Sea, Essex, UK: Keven Mayhew, 1997), 65.

3. Barry Floyd, "Changing Patterns of African Land Use in Southern Rhodesia" (PhD thesis, Syracuse University, 1959) (Lusaka, Zambia: Rhodes-Livingstone Institute), 345.

4. Bill Kinsey, "Zimbabwe's Land Reform Program: Underinvestment in Post-conflict Transformation," *World Development,* 32, no. 10 (2004): 1,684 [Kinsey, 2004].

5. Sam Moyo, "The Zimbabwe Crisis, Land Reform, and Normalization," in *The Struggle Over Land in Africa,* ed. Ward Anseeuw and Chris Alden (Cape Town, South Africa: Human Sciences Research Council, 2010), 246, 249.

6. Ibid., 257, 261.

7. Tendai Murisa, "Farmer Groups, Collective Action and Production Constraints: Cases From A1 Settlements in Goromonzi and Zvimba," Livelihoods After Land Reform in Zimbabwe, Working Paper 10, 2010, http://www.lalr.org.za/zimbabwe/zimbabwe-working-papers-1 (April 28, 2012).

8. Kinsey, 2004, 1689.

9. Martin Plaut, "Crossing Continents: Farming Zimbabwe," BBC Radio 4, December 1 and 5, 2011, available at http://www.bbc.co.uk/programmes/b017mvx6#synopsis (accessed December 6, 2011).

10. Simon Pazvakavambwa and Vincent Hungwe, "Land Redistribution in Zimbabwe," in *Agricultural Land Redistribution: Toward Greater Consensus,* ed. Hans Binswanger-Mkhize, Camille Bourguignon, and Rogerius van den Brink (Washington, DC: World Bank Publications, 2009), 160–61.

11. "Zimbabwe and Its Diamonds: Forever Dirty," *Economist,* June 30, 2011, available at http://www.economist.com/node/18898238 (January 5, 2012).

12. Clemence Manyukwe, "Diamonds Worth US$1bn Missing," *Financial Gazette,* August 12, 2011, available at http://eu.financialgazette.co.zw/national-report/9417-diamonds-worth-us1bn-missing.html (January 5, 2012).

13. Rifkind, "Politics of Land," 106, citing *Rhodesia Herald,* May 22, 1952.

Bibliography

Books, Articles, and Other Published Material

Alexander, Jocelyn. *The Unsettled Land.* Oxford, UK: James Currey, 2006 [Alexander, *Unsettled*].

Bailey, Martin. *Oilgate.* London, UK: Hodder & Stoughton, 1979.

Binswanger-Mkhize, Hans, Camille Bourguignon, and Rogerius van den Brink. *Agricultural Land Redistribution: Toward Greater Consensus.* Washington, DC: World Bank Publications, 2009.

Bond, Patrick. *Uneven Zimbabwe.* Trenton, NJ: Africa World Press, 1998.

Bourne, Richard. *Catastrophe: What Went Wrong in Zimbabwe?* London, UK: Zed, 2011.

Bowyer-Bower, Tayna, and Colin Stoneman, eds. *Land Reform in Zimbabwe: Constraints and Prospects.* London, UK: Ashgate, 2000.

Catholic Commission for Justice and Peace in Zimbabwe. "Breaking the Silence—Building True Peace: A Report Into the Disturbances in Matabeleland and the Midlands," 1999.

Centro de Estudos Africanos de Universidade do Maputo. *A Questão Rodesiana.* Lisboa, Portugal: Initiativas Editoriais, 1978.

Chamabati, Walter, and Sam Moyo. "Land Reform and the Political Economy of Agricultural Labour in Zimbabwe." Occasional paper 4/2007. Harare, Zimbabwe: African Institute for Agrarian Studies, 2007.

Chambati, Walter. "Restructuring of Agrarian Labour Relations After Fast Track Land Reform in Zimbabwe." *Journal of Peasant Studies,* 38, no. 5 (2011).

Chaumba, Joseph, Ian Scoones, and William Wolmer. "From Jambanja to Planning: The Reassertion of Technocracy in Land Reform in South-eastern Zimbabwe?" *Journal of Modern African Studies,* 41, no. 4 (2003).

———. "From *Jambanja* to Planning: The Reassertion of Technocracy in Land Reform in South-eastern Zimbabwe." Sustainable Livelihoods in Southern

Africa Research Paper 2. Brighton, UK: Institute of Development Studies, 2003.

Chimhowu, Admos, and David Hulme. "Livelihood Dynamics in Planned and Spontaneous Resettlement in Zimbabwe." *World Development,* 34, no. 4 (2006).

Chimhowu, Admos, Jeanette Manjengwa, and Sara Feresu, eds. *Moving Forward in Zimbabwe: Reducing Poverty and Promoting Growth.* 2nd ed. Harare, Zimbabwe: Institute of Environmental Studies, 2010.

Chingarande, Sunungurai, Prisca Mugabe, Krasposy Kujinga, and Esteri Magaisa. "Agrarian Reforms in Zimbabwe: Are Women Beneficiaries or Mere Agents?" Harare, Zimbabwe: Institute of Environmental Studies, 2011.

Cliffe, Lionel. "The Prospects for Agricultural Transformation in Zimbabwe." In *Zimbabwe's Prospects,* edited by Colin Stoneman. London, UK: Macmillan, 1988.

———. "The Politics of Land Reform in Zimbabwe." In *Land Reform in Zimbabwe: Constraints and Prospects,* edited by Tanya Bowyer-Bower and Colin Stoneman. Aldershot, UK: Ashgate, 2000.

Cliffe, Lionel, Jocelyn Alexander, Ben Cousins, and Rudo Gaidzanwa. "An Overview of Fast Track Land Reform in Zimbabwe: Editorial Introduction." *Journal of Peasant Studies,* 38, no. 5 (2011).

Deininger, Klaus, Hans Hoogeveen, and Bill Kinsey. "Economic Benefits and Costs of Land Redistribution in Zimbabwe in the Early 1980s." *World Development,* 32, no. 10 (2004) [Deininger, Hoogeveen, and Kinsey, 2004].

Dekker, Marleen, and Bill Kinsey. "Contextualizing Zimbabwe's Land Reform: Long-Term Observations From the First Generation." *Journal of Peasant Studies,* 38, no. 5 (2011).

de Soto, Hernando. *The Mystery of Capital.* London, UK: Black Swan, Transworld, 2001.

Doré, Dale, Tony Hawkins, Godfrey Kanyenze, Daniel Makina, and Daniel Ndlela. "Comprehensive Economic Recovery in Zimbabwe." Harare, Zimbabwe: UNDP, 2008.

Evans, Ifor Leslie. *Native Policy in Southern Africa.* Cambridge, UK: Cambridge University Press, 1934.

Flower, Ken. *Serving Secretly.* London, UK: John Murray, 1987.

Floyd, Barry. "Land Apportionment in Southern Rhodesia." *Geographical Review,* 52, no. 4 (1962).

Friis-Hansen, Esbern. *Seeds for African Peasants: Peasants' Needs and Agricultural Research, the Case of Zimbabwe.* Uppsala, Sweden: Nordic Africa Institute, 1995.

Gjerstad, Ole. *The Organizer.* Richmond, BC, Canada: LSN Information Center, 1974.

Goebel, Allison. "Zimbabwe's 'Fast Track' Land Reform: What About Women?" *Gender, Place and Culture,* 12, no. 2 (2005).

Golub, Stephen, and Jeffery McManus. "Horticulture Exports and African Development." Paper for the Expert Meeting of LDCs in preparation for the 4th United Nations Conference on Least Developed Countries, Kampala, Uganda, October 28–30, 2009.

Gunning, Jan Willem, John Hoddinott, Bill Kinsey, and Trudy Owens. "Revisiting Forever Gained: Income Dynamics in the Resettlement Areas of Zimbabwe, 1983–1997." Working paper WPS/99-14, Centre for the Study of African Economies (CSAE), Oxford University, May 1999 version [Gunning, Hoddinott, Kinsey, and Owens, CSAE].

———. "Revisiting Forever Gained: Income Dynamics in the Resettlement Areas of Zimbabwe, 1983–97." *Journal of Development Studies,* 36, no. 6 (2000) [Gunning, Hoddinott, Kinsey, and Owens, 2000].

Hammar, Amanda, Brian Raftopoulos, and Stig Jensen. *Zimbabwe's Unfinished Business.* Harare, Zimbabwe: Weaver, 2003.

Hanlon, Joseph. *Beggar Your Neighbours.* London, UK: James Currey, 1986 [Hanlon, *Beggar*].

———. "Paying for Apartheid Twice." London, UK: Action for Southern Africa, 1998.

Hanlon, Joseph, and Roger Omond. *The Sanctions Handbook.* Harmondsworth, UK: Penguin, 1987.

Horne, Gerald. *From the Barrel of a Gun: The United States and the War Against Zimbabwe, 1965–1980.* Chapel Hill, NC: University of North Carolina Press, 2001 [Horne, *From the Barrel*].

Huggins, Godfrey, foreword to A. C. Jennings, "Land Apportionment in Southern Rhodesia." *African Affairs* (1935), XXXIV (CXXXVI).

Hurungo, James. "An Inquiry Into How Rhodesia Managed to Survive Under Economic Sanctions: Lessons for the Zimbabwe Government." Harare, Zimbabwe: Trade and Development Studies Centre, TRADES Centre, 2011.

Jenkins, Carolyn. "Economic Objectives, Public-Sector Deficits and Macroeconomic Stability in Zimbabwe." Working paper 97-14, Centre for the Study of African Economies (CSAE). Oxford, UK: CSAE, 1997.

Jennings, A. C. "Land Apportionment in Southern Rhodesia," *African Affairs* (1935) XXXIV (CXXXVI) [Jennings, "Land"].

Jirira, Kwanele Ona, and Charles Mangosuthu Halimana. "A Gender Audit of Women and Land Rights in Zimbabwe." Paper prepared for the Zimbabwe Women's Resource Centre and Network (ZWRCN), Harare, Zimbabwe, 2008.

Jones, Tim. *Uncovering Zimbabwe's Debt.* London, UK: Jubilee Debt Campaign, 2011.

Kanji, Nazneen. "Gender, Poverty and Economic Adjustment in Harare, Zimbabwe." *Environment and Urbanization,* 7, no. 1 (1995).

Kanyenze, Godfrey. "Economic Structural Adjustment Programme." In *Post-independence Land Reform in Zimbabwe,* edited by Medicine Masiiwa.

Harare, Zimbabwe: Friedrich Ebert Stiftung, 2004 [Kanyenze, "Economic Structural"].

Kinsey, Bill. "Forever Gained: Resettlement and Land Policy in the Context of National Development in Zimbabwe." *Africa,* 52, no. 3 (1982) [Kinsey, "Forever Gained"].

———. "Land Reform, Growth and Equity: Emerging Evidence From Zimbabwe's Resettlement Programme." *Journal of Southern African Studies,* 25, no. 2 (1999) [Kinsey, 1999].

———. "The Implication of Land Reform for Rural Welfare." In *Land Reform in Zimbabwe: Constraints and Prospects,* edited by Tanya Bowyer-Bower and Colin Stoneman. London, UK: Ashgate, 2000.

———. "Zimbabwe's Land Reform Program: Underinvestment in Post-Conflict Transformation." *World Development,* 32, no. 10 (2004) [Kinsey, 2004].

Lamont, Donal. *Speech From the Dock.* Leigh-on-Sea, Essex, UK: Keven Mayhew, 1977.

Loewenson, René. "Farm Labour in Zimbabwe: A Comparative Study in Health Status." *Health Policy and Planning,* 1, no. 1 (1986).

Loewenson, René, and David Saunders. "The Political Economy of Health and Nutrition." In *Zimbabwe's Prospects,* edited by Colin Stoneman. London, UK: Macmillan, 1988.

Losman, Donald. *International Economic Sanctions.* Albuquerque, NM: University of New Mexico Press, 1979.

Lyons, Tanya. *Guns and Guerrilla Girls: Women in the Zimbabwean Liberation Struggle.* Trenton, NJ: World Africa Press, 2004.

Makadho, Johannes, Prosper Matondi, and Mabel Munyuki-Hungwe. "Irrigation Development and Water Resource Management." In *Zimbabwe's Agricultural Revolution Revisited,* edited by Mandivamba Rukuni, Patrick Tawonezvi, and Carl Eicher [Rukuni, Tamonezvi, and Eicher]. Harare, Zimbabwe: University of Zimbabwe Publications, 2006.

Mandaza, Ibbo, ed. *Zimbabwe: The Political Economy of Transition 1980–1986.* Dakar, Senegal: Codesria, 1986.

Mandizadza, Shingirai. "The Fast Track Land Reform Programme and Livelihoods in Zimbabwe: A Case Study of Households at Athlone Farm in Murehwa District." Livelihoods after Land Reform in Zimbabwe, Working paper 2. Cape Town, South Africa: Institute for Poverty for Land and Agrarian Studies (PLAAS), University of the Western Cape, 2010.

Marongwe, Nelson. "Redistributive Land Reform and Poverty Reduction in Zimbabwe." Working paper for research project on "Livelihoods after Land Reform," n.d. (probably 2008).

Mashingaidze, Kingstone. "Maize Research and Development." In Rukuni, Tamonezvi, and Eicher.

Masiiwa, Medicine. *Post-independence Land Reform in Zimbabwe.* Harare, Zimbabwe: Friedrich Ebert Stiftung, 2004.

Mavedzenge, Blasio, et al. "The Dynamics of Real Markets: Cattle in Southern Zimbabwe Following Land Reform." *Development and Change,* 39,
no. 4 (2008).

Mazhawidza, Phides, and Jeanette Manjengwa. "The Social, Political and Economic Transformative Impact of the Fast Track Land Reform Programme
on the Lives of Women Farmers in Goromonzi and Vungu-Gweru Districts
of Zimbabwe." Rome: International Land Coalition, 2011.

Media Monitoring Project Zimbabwe. *The Language of Hate.* Harare, Zimbabwe: Author, 2009.

Mlambo, Alois. *The Economic Structural Adjustment Programme—The Case of
Zimbabwe 1990–95.* Harare, Zimbabwe: University of Zimbabwe, 1997
[Mlambo, *Adjustment*].

———. *White Immigration Into Rhodesia.* Harare, Zimbabwe: University of
Zimbabwe, 2002.

Moyana, Henry. *The Political Economy of Land in Zimbabwe.* Gweru, Zimbabwe: Mambo Press, 1984.

Moyo, Sam. "The Land Question." In *Zimbabwe: The Political Economy of Transition 1980–1986,* edited by Ibbo Mandaza. Dakar, Senegal: Codesria, 1986.

———. *Land Reform Under Structural Adjustment in Zimbabwe.* Uppsala, Sweden: Nordiska Afrikainstitutet, 2000 [Moyo, *Land Reform,* 2000].

———. "Land Movements and the Democratisation Process in Zimbabwe."
In *Post-independence Land Reform in Zimbabwe,* edited by Medicine
Masiiwa. Harare, Zimbabwe: Friedrich Ebert Stiftung, 2004 [Moyo, "Land
Movements"].

———. "The Evolution of Zimbabwe's Land Acquisition." In Rukuni, Tawonezvi, and Eicher, 146.

———. "Emerging Land Tenure Issues in Zimbabwe." Monograph Series, Issue
No. 2/07. Harare, Zimbabwe: African Institute for Agrarian Studies, 2007.

———. "The Zimbabwe Crisis, Land Reform, and Normalization." In *The
Struggle Over Land in Africa,* edited by Ward Anseeuw and Chris Alden.
Cape Town, South Africa: Human Sciences Research Council, 2010.

———. "Land Concentration and Accumulation After Redistributive Reform
in Post-settler Zimbabwe." *Review of African Political Economy,* 38, no. 128
(2011).

———. "Three Decades of Agrarian Reform in Zimbabwe." *Journal of Peasant
Studies,* 38, no. 3 (2011) [Moyo, "Three Decades"].

Moyo, Sam, and Paris Yeros, eds. *Reclaiming the Land.* London, UK: Zed, 2005.

Moyo, Sam, et al. *Fast Track Land Reform Baseline Survey in Zimbabwe.* Harare, Zimbabwe: African Institute for Agrarian Studies, 2009 [Moyo et al.,
Baseline Survey].

Mugabe, Prisca. "Impacts of Land Reform Migrations on Forest Resources Management in Model A1 Resettlement Areas of Chimanimani District in Zimbabwe." Harare, Zimbabwe: Institute of Environmental Studies, 2011.

Muir-Leresche, Kay. "Agriculture in Zimbabwe." In Rukuni, Tawonezvi, and Eicher.

Mujeyi, Kingstone. "Emerging Agricultural Markets and Marketing Channels Within Newly Resettled Areas of Zimbabwe." Livelihoods after Land Reform in Zimbabwe, Working Paper 1. Cape Town, South Africa: Institute for Poverty for Land and Agrarian Studies (PLAAS), University of the Western Cape, 2010.

Mumbengegwi, Clever. "Continuity and Change in Agricultural Policy." In *Zimbabwe: The Political Economy of Transition 1980–1986,* edited by Ibo Mandaza. Dakar, Senegal: Codesria, 1986.

Murisa, Tendai. "Social Organisation and Agency in the Newly Resettled Areas of Zimbabwe: The Case of Zvimba District." Monograph Series, Issue No. 1/07. Harare, Zimbabwe: African Institute for Agrarian Studies, 2007.

———. "Farmer Groups, Collective Action and Production Constraints: Cases from A1 Settlements in Goromonzi and Zvimba." Livelihoods after Land Reform in Zimbabwe, Working Paper 10. Cape Town, South Africa: Institute for Poverty for Land and Agrarian Studies (PLAAS), University of the Western Cape, 2010.

———. "Local Farmer Groups and Collective Action Within Fast Track Land Reform in Zimbabwe." *Journal of Peasant Studies,* 38, no. 5 (2011).

Mustapha, Abdul Raufu. "Zimbabwean Farmers in Nigeria: Exceptional Farmers or Spectacular Support?" *African Affairs,* 110 (2011).

Mutisi, Martha. "Beyond the Signature: Appraisal of the Zimbabwe Global Political Agreement (GPA) and Implications for Intervention." *Policy & Practice Brief* 4. Umhlanga Rocks, South Africa: African Centre for the Constructive Resolution of Disputes, 2011.

Neill, Timothy. "Labour and Union Issues in the Zimbabwean Agricultural Sector in 2004." Harare, Zimbabwe: Zimbabwe Community Development Trust, 2004.

Nkala, D. "Tackling Agricultural Development With Land Dearth." In *Balancing Rocks: Environment and Development,* edited by C. Lopes. A UNDP Zimbabwe Staff Research Project. Harare, Zimbabwe: SAPES, and Uppsala, Sweden: Nordiska Afrikainstitutet, 1996.

Nziramasanga, Mudziviri. "Agriculture Sector in Zimbabwe." In *Zimbabwe: Towards a New Order,* Working Papers Vol 1. New York: United Nations, 1980.

Owens, Trudy, John Hoddinott, and Bill Kinsey. "The Impact of Agricultural Extension on Farm Production in Resettlement Areas of Zimbabwe." *Economic Development and Cultural Change,* 51, no. 2 (2003) [Owens, Hoddinott, and Kinsey, 2003].

Palmer, Robin. *Land and Racial Domination in Rhodesia.* Berkeley: University of California Press, 1977. [Palmer, *Land and Racial*].

Pazvakavambwa, Simon, and Vincent Hungwe. "Land Redistribution in Zimbabwe." In *Agricultural Land Redistribution: Toward Greater Consensus,* edited by Hans Binswanger-Mkhize, Camille Bourguignon, and Rogerius van den Brink. Washington, DC: World Bank Publications, 2009.

Phimister, Ian. "The Combined and Contradictory Inheritance of the Struggle Against Colonialism." In *Zimbabwe's Prospects,* edited by Colin Stoneman. London, UK: Macmillan, 1998.

Pwiti, Gilbert. "Trade and Economics in Southern Africa: The Archaeological Evidence." *Zambezia,* 18, no. 2 (1991).

Raftopoulos, Brian, and Alois Mlambo, eds. *Becoming Zimbabwe.* Harare, Zimbabwe: Weaver, 2009.

Raftopoulos, Brian, and Lloyd Sachikonye, eds. *Zimbabwe Striking Back: The Labour Movement and the Post-Colonial State in Zimbabwe 1980–2000.* Harare, Zimbabwe: Weaver, 2004.

Ranger, Terence. *Peasant Consciousness and Guerrilla War in Zimbabwe.* London, UK: James Currey, 1985.

Richardson, Craig J. "The Loss of Property Rights and the Collapse of Zimbabwe." *Cato Journal,* 25, no. 3 (2005).

Riddell, Roger. "The Land Question." *From Rhodesia to Zimbabwe,* pamphlet 2. Gwelo, Zimbabwe: Mambo, 1978 [Riddell, "Land Question"].

———. "Some Lessons From the Past and From Global Experiences to Help Move Zimbabwe Forward out of Poverty and Towards Sustainable Development." Speech at the Moving Zimbabwe Forward Conference: Pathways out of Poverty for Zimbabwe, Harare, Zimbabwe, November 30, 2011.

Roth, Michael, and Francis Gonese. *Delivering Land and Securing Rural Livelihoods.* Harare, Zimbabwe: Centre for Applied Social Sciences, and Madison, WI: Land Tenure Centre, 2003.

Rukuni, Mandivamba. "Revisiting Zimbabwe's Agricultural Revolution." In Rukuni, Tawonezvi, and Eicher.

———. "The Evolution of Agriculture Policy: 1890–1990." In Rukuni, Tawonezvi, and Eicher.

Rukuni, Mandivamba, et al. "Policy Options for Optimisation of the Use of Land for Agricultural Productivity and Production in Zimbabwe." Report submitted to the World Bank Agrarian Sector Technical Review Group (AS-TRG) by a Study Team, 2009 [Rukuni, "Policy Options"].

Rukuni, Mandivamba, Patrick Tawonezvi, and Carl Eicher, eds. *Zimbabwe's Agricultural Revolution Revisited.* Harare, Zimbabwe: University of Zimbabwe Publications, 2006 [Rukuni, Tawonezvi, and Eicher].

Ruswa, Goodhope. "The Golden Era? Reflections on the First Phase of the Land Reform Programme in Zimbabwe." Occasional Research Paper Series, Number 01/2007. Harare, Zimbabwe: African Institute for Agrarian Studies, 2007 [Ruswa, "Golden Era?"].

Sachikonye, Lloyd. "The Situation of Commercial Farm Workers After Land Reform in Zimbabwe." Harare, Zimbabwe: Farm Community Trust of Zimbabwe, 2003.

————. *When a State Turns on Its Citizens.* Pretoria, South Africa: Jacana, 2011.

Sadomba, Zvakanyorwa Wilbert. *War Veterans in Zimbabwe's Revolution.* Woodbridge, Suffolk, UK: James Currey, 2011 [Sadomba, *War Veterans*].

Scones, Ian, et al. *Zimbabwe's Land Reform.* Woodbridge, Suffolk, UK: James Currey, 2010.

Shillington, Kevin, ed. *Encyclopedia of African History.* New York: Fitzroy Dearborn, 2005.

Smart, Teresa. "Zimbabwe: South African Military Intervention." In Hanlon, *Beggar.*

Smith, Ian Douglas. *The Great Betrayal: The Memoirs of Ian Douglas Smith.* London, UK: Blake, 1997.

Stiff, Peter. *Cry Zimbabwe.* Alberton, South Africa: Galago, 2000.

————. *War by Other Means.* Alberton, South Africa: Galago, 2001.

Stoneman, Colin, ed. *Zimbabwe's Inheritance.* London, UK: Macmillan, 1981.

Stoneman, Colin. "Zimbabwe: The Private Sector and South Africa." In Hanlon, *Beggar.*

Stoneman, Colin, ed. *Zimbabwe's Prospects.* London, UK: Macmillan, 1998.

Stoneman, Colin, and Lionel Cliffe. *Zimbabwe: Politics, Economics and Society.* London, UK: Pinter, 1989 [Stoneman and Cliffe, *Politics*].

Tandon, Yash. "Trade Unions and Labour in the Agricultural Sector." In *Zimbabwe Striking Back: The Labour Movement and the Post-Colonial State in Zimbabwe 1980–2000,* edited by Brian Raftopoulos and Lloyd Sachikonye. Harare, Zimbabwe: Weaver, 2004.

Tawonezvi, Patrick, and Danisile Hikwa. "Agricultural Research Policy." In Rukuni, Tawonezvi, and Eicher.

Tekere, Moses. "Zimbabwe." In *WTO Agreement on Agriculture: The Implementation Experience,* edited by Harmon C. Thomas. Rome: FAO, 2003.

Unganai, Leonard. "Climate Change and Its Effects on Agricultural Productivity and Food Security: A Case of Chiredzi District." Paper presented at the National Climate Change Workshop, November 23, 2011, Harare, Zimbabwe.

Weiner, Daniel. "Land and Agricultural Development." In *Zimbabwe's Prospects,* edited by Colin Stoneman. London, UK: Macmillan, 1988.

————. "Agricultural Restructuring in Zimbabwe and South Africa." *Development and Change,* 20, no. 3 (1989) [Weiner, "Restructuring"].

Weiner, Dan, Sam Moyo, Barry Munslow, and Phil O'Keefe. "Land Use and Agricultural Productivity in Zimbabwe." *Journal of Modern African Studies,* 23, no. 2 (1985).

Whitsun Foundation. *Land Reform in Zimbabwe.* Project 3.23. Harare, Zimbabwe: Author, 1983.

Witoshynsky, Mary. *The Water Harvester.* Harare, Zimbabwe: Weaver, 2000.

Zamchiya, Phillan. "A Synopsis of Land and Agrarian Change in Chipinge District, Zimbabwe." *Journal of Peasant Studies,* 38, no. 5 (2011).

Zikhali, Precious. "Fast Track Land Reform and Agricultural Productivity in Zimbabwe." EfD Discussion Paper 08-30. Washington, DC: Environment for Development Initiative, 2008.

Zimbabwe Catholic Bishops Conference, Evangelical Fellowship of Zimbabwe, and Zimbabwe Council of Churches. "The Zimbabwe We Want: Towards a National Vision for Zimbabwe." Harare, Zimbabwe: Authors, 2006.

Zimbabwe Community Development Trust. "Report on Internally Displaced Farm Workers Survey: Kadoma, Chegutu and Kwekwe Districts." Harare, Zimbabwe: Author, 2003.

Zwizwai, Benson, Admore Kambudzi, and Bonface Mauwa. "Zimbabwe: Economic Policy-Making and Implementation: A Study of Strategic Trade and Selective Industrial Policies." In *The politics of trade and industrial policy in Africa,* edited by Charles Soludo, Osita Ogbu, and Ha-Joon Chang. Trenton, NJ: Africa World Press/IDRC, 2004.

Theses and Other Unpublished Material

Campbell, Bruce, and P. N. Bradley. "Trees, Wood and the Small-Scale Farmer: Rethinking Woodfuel Development in Zimbabwe." Draft paper, Department of Biological Sciences, University of Zimbabwe and the Stockholm Environment Institute, 1993.

Chigumira, Easther. "An Appraisal of the Impact of the Fast Track Land Reform Programme on Land Use Practices, Livelihoods and the Natural Environment at Three Study Areas in Kadoma District, Zimbabwe." MSc thesis, Rhodes University, 2006.

Dongo list of leased whole farms is posted on http://www.zwnews.com/dongo list.xls and an explanation is on http://www.zwnews.com/dongolist.cfm.

Floyd, Barry. "Changing Patterns of African Land Use in Southern Rhodesia." PhD thesis, Syracuse University, 1959; Lusaka, Zambia: Rhodes-Livingstone Institute.

Gundu, Veronica. "The Impact of Land Reform on Natural Resources: A Case Study of Land Use Changes in Mazowe District." MA diss., Department of Geography and Environmental Science, University of Zimbabwe, Harare.

Karumbidza, John Blessing. "A Fragile and Unsustained Miracle: Analysing the Development Potential of Zimbabwe's Resettlement Schemes, 1980–2000." PhD thesis, University of KwaZulu-Natal, 2009.

Manjengwa, Jeanette. "Local Environmental Action Planning in Zimbabwe: An Analysis of Its Contribution to Sustainable Development." PhD thesis, Institute for Development Policy and Management, University of Manchester, 2004.

Marongwe, Nelson. "Environmental Concerns in Fast Track Schemes in Mash-
    onaland Central: Mazowe District," draft document, Harare, Zimbabwe,
    2005.
————. "Interrogating Zimbabwe's Fast Track Land Reform and Resettlement
    Programme: A Focus on Beneficiary Selection." PhD thesis, Institute for
    Poverty, Land and Agrarian Studies (PLAAS), University of the Western
    Cape, 2008 [Marongwe, "Interrogating"].
Masst, Mette. "The Harvest of Independence: Commodity Boom and Socio-
    economic Differentiation Among Peasants in Zimbabwe." PhD thesis,
    Roskilde University, 1996 [Masst, "Harvest"].
Matondi, Prosper. "Mazowe District Report—Findings on Land Reform, Vol.
    II." Harare, Zimbabwe, 2005 [Matondi, "Mazowe"].
————. "Fast Tracking Land Reforms in Mazowe District in Zimbabwe." Ha-
    rare, Zimbabwe, 2011 [Matondi, "Fast Tracking"].
————. "Juggling Land Ownership Rights in Uncertain Times in Fast Track
    Farms in Mazowe District." Harare, Zimbabwe, 2011.
Moyo, Sam. "Changing Agrarian Relations After Redistributive Land Reform
    in Zimbabwe," draft, April 27, 2011, Harare, Zimbabwe.
Palmer, Robin. "Challenges in Asserting Women's Land Rights in Southern
    Africa." Presentation at Decentralising Land, Dispossessing Women? Re-
    covering Gender Voices and Experiences of Decentralised Land Reform in
    Africa, Maputo, Mozambique, May 2009.
Rifkind, Malcolm. "The Politics of Land in Rhodesia." MSc thesis, Edinburgh
    University, 1968, http://www.mct.open.ac.uk/zimbabwe.
Selby, Angus. "Commercial Farmers and the State: Interest Group Politics and
    Land Reform in Zimbabwe." PhD thesis, University of Oxford, 2006.
Tapfumaneyi, Asher Walter. "A Comparative Study of Forces Demobilisation:
    Southern Rhodesia 1945–1947 and Zimbabwe 1980–85." BA honors diss.,
    University of Zimbabwe, 1996.
Taruwinga, Kelman. "Remote Sensing and GIS Based Spatial and Temporal
    Change of Woodland Canopy Cover and Tree Density in Miombo Wood-
    land, Mazowe District, Zimbabwe." MSc thesis, Department of Geogra-
    phy and Environmental Science, University of Zimbabwe, Harare, 2011.
Women and Land Lobby Group. "Consultative Planning Workshop Report."
    Report of June 1998 workshop, Bronte Hotel, Harare, Zimbabwe.

Official Reports

"Agreement Between the Zimbabwe African National Union-Patriotic Front
    (ZANU-PF) and the Two Movement for Democratic Change (MDC)
    Formations, on Resolving the Challenges Facing Zimbabwe." Harare,

Zimbabwe, September 15, 2008 [known as the Global Political Agreement, GPA], available at http://www.info.gov.za/issues/zimbabwe/zzimbabwe_global_agreement_20080915.pdf.

Biti, Tendai. *The 2011 Mid-year Fiscal Policy Review,* July 26, 2011. Harare, Zimbabwe: Ministry of Finance, Government of Zimbabwe.

Central African Statistical Office. *Official Year Book of Southern Rhodesia, With Statistics Mainly up to 1950–No. 4–1952.* Salisbury, Southern Rhodesia: Rhodesian Printing and Publishing Company, 1952.

Council of the European Union. "Council Decision 2011/101/CFSP of 15 February 2011 Concerning Restrictive Measures Against Zimbabwe." *Official Journal of the European Union,* February 16, 2011.

Electoral Institute of Southern Africa. "Election Observer Mission Report: The Zimbabwe Harmonised Elections of 29 March 2008." Election Observer Mission Report, No 28. Pretoria, South Africa: Author, 2008.

European Parliament. "Account of the Mission to Observe the Parliamentary Elections in Zimbabwe 24–25 June 2000," July 6, 2000.

Government of Zimbabwe (GoZ). *Report of the Commission of Inquiry into Incomes, Prices and Conditions of Service,* 1981, chaired by Roger Riddell [known as the Riddell Commission report].

———. *Report of the Commission of Inquiry into the Agriculture Industry,* 1982, chaired by G. L. Chavunduka.

———. *Transitional National Development Plan 1982/83–84/85,* Vol. 1. Harare, Zimbabwe, 1982.

———. Technical Committee of the Inter-Ministerial Committee on Resettlement and Rural Development and National Economic Consultative Forum Land Reform Task Force. *Inception Phase Framework Plan 1999 to 2000. An Implementation Plan of the Land Reform and Resettlement Programme–Phase II.* Harare, Zimbabwe, n.d. (but surely 1998).

———. Ministry of Lands, Agriculture and Rural Resettlement. "Application for Land Under the Commercial Farm Settlement Scheme." Harare, Zimbabwe, 2000.

———. *Report of the Presidential Land Review Committee on the Implementation of the Fast Track Land Reform Programme, 2000–2002,* chaired by Charles M. B. Utete. Harare, Zimbabwe 2003, vols. I and II, available at http://www.sarpn.org/documents/d0001932/Utete_PLRC_Vol-I_2003.pdf and http://www.sarpn.org/documents/d0000746/Utete_Report_intro.pdf.

———. Ministry of Public Service, Labour and Social Welfare. *Zimbabwe: 2003 Poverty Assessment Study Survey, Main Report.* Harare, Zimbabwe, 2006.

———. Ministry of Lands, Land Reform and Resettlement & Informatics Institute, *A2 Land Audit Report,* Harare, Zimbabwe, 2006 (eight volumes, one for each province, issued at different times during 2006) [*A2 Land Audit Report*].

————. *Zimbabwe 2003 Poverty Assessment Study Survey Summary Report.* Harare, Zimbabwe: Ministry of Public Service, Labour and Social Welfare, 2006.

————. Ministry of Environment and Natural Resources Management. *Zimbabwe's Fourth National Report to the Convention on Biological Diversity.* Harare, Zimbabwe, 2010.

International Labour Organization (ILO). "Truth, Reconciliation and Justice in Zimbabwe. Report of the Commission of Inquiry Appointed Under Article 26 of the Constitution of the International Labour Organization . . ." Geneva, Switzerland: International Labour Office, 2009.

Southern Rhodesia Order in Council, 1898, Ordered at the Court at Balmoral by The Queen's Most Excellent Majesty, October 20, 1898.

"Southern Rhodesia. Report of the Constitutional Conference, Lancaster House, London, September–December 1979." Cmnd. 7802. London, UK: HMSO, 1980.

United Nations. *Zimbabwe: Towards a New Order.* 2 vols. New York: Author, 1980.

UN Development Program. "Zimbabwe: Land Reform and Resettlement: Assessment and Suggested Framework for the Future." Interim Mission Report. New York: UNDP, 2002.

UN Food and Agriculture Organization (FAO). "Gender, Property Rights and Livelihoods in the Era of AIDS." Proceedings Report of FAO Technical Consultation, Rome, November 28–30, 2007.

US Embassy in Harare, list of sanctioned individuals and companies, available at http://harare.usembassy.gov/uploads/GA/r_/GAr_mydP5GsiV8xOy-zfcQ/SDN_List1.pdf.

US Treasury. Sanctions legislation website: http://www.treasury.gov/resource-center/sanctions/Programs/Pages/zimb.aspx.

Vincent, V., and R. G. Thomas. *An Agricultural Survey of Southern Rhodesia.* Salisbury, Southern Rhodesia: Government Printer, 1960.

World Bank. "Agriculture Sector Study." Washington, DC: Author, 1983.

————. *Gender in Agriculture Sourcebook.* Washington, DC: Author, 2008.

World Bank Independent Evaluation Group. "Structural Adjustment and Zimbabwe's Poor." Washington, DC: World Bank, 1995.

Website

Some documents have been posted on a Zimbabwe Land website, www.mct.open.ac.uk/zimbabwe.

About the Authors

Dr. Joseph Hanlon is a visiting senior fellow at the London School of Economics and an honorary research fellow at the University of Manchester.

Dr. Jeanette Manjengwa is deputy director of the Institute for Environmental Studies at the University of Zimbabwe, and is also a resettlement farmer.

Teresa Smart is a visiting fellow at the Institute of Education, University of London.

Index

Also available from Kumarian Press

Just Give Money to the Poor
Joseph Hanlon, Armando Barrientos, and David Hulme

"The simplest of ideas can still hold much value. The collaborative work of Joseph Hanlon, Armando Barrientos, and David Hulme, *Just Give Money to the Poor: The Development Revolution From the Global South* discusses this revolutionary concept and how some developing countries are simply granting the poor money and watching how they use that money wisely, for education and for businesses to sustain the money they are given. Debating the problems and values of such a simple plan, *Just Give Money to the Poor* is a scholarly and thoughtful read that shouldn't be missed." —*Midwest Book Review*

Culture, Development, and Public Administration in Africa
Ogwo Jombo Umeh and Greg Andranovich

"Offers the reader an overview of the continent, with a particular focus on the countries of the Southern African Development Coordinating Conference. Succinctly, they provide us with a list of the critical issues confronting the administration of those countries, with a particular focus on the range of skills required for the major tasks at hand, constraints, and opportunities. The stress on methodology is particularly well placed in a critical study of culture and a book that wants to avoid dependence on Western models."
—*Public Administration Review,* March/April 2006

Beating Hunger: The Chivi Experience
Helen Wedgwood, Cathy Watson, Everjoice J. Win,
Clare Tawney, and Kuda Murwira

People's participation in development has been promoted for over 20 years, yet it is still commonplace for projects to be predesigned, without more than a token consultation with those farmers for whom they are intended. This book describes a project among small-scale farmers in the drought-prone and arid communal lands of Zimbabwe that, within the broad remit of promoting food security, helped the farmers identify their problems and choose their own solutions to them. The aim of the project was participatory technology development: to extend the range of soil and water-conserving farming techniques available to men and women, and to help them evaluate and disseminate these and their own traditional techniques so as to improve the returns from their land.

Visit Kumarian Press at **www.kpbooks.com** or call **toll-free 800.232.0223** for a complete catalog.

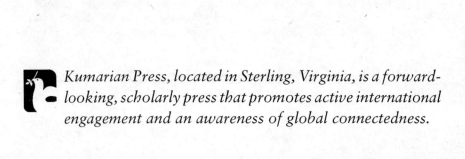

Kumarian Press, located in Sterling, Virginia, is a forward-looking, scholarly press that promotes active international engagement and an awareness of global connectedness.